The Century of Women

How Women Have Transformed the World since 1900

Maria Bucur
Indiana University–Bloomington

ROWMAN & LITTLEFIELD
Lanham • Boulder • New York • London

Executive Editor: Susan McEachern
Editorial Assistant: Katelyn Turner
Senior Marketing Manager: Kim Lyons

Published by Rowman & Littlefield
An imprint of The Rowman & Littlefield Publishing Group, Inc.
4501 Forbes Boulevard, Suite 200, Lanham, Maryland 20706
https://rowman.com

Unit A, Whitacre Mews, 26-34 Stannary Street, London SE11 4AB,
United Kingdom

British Library Cataloguing in Publication Information Available

The Library of Congress Cataloging-in-Publication Data Available

ISBN 978-1-4422-5738-2 (hardcover : alk. paper)
ISBN 978-1-4422-5739-9 (paperback : alk. paper)
ISBN 978-1-4422-5740-5 (ebook)

♾ ™ The paper used in this publication meets the minimum requirements of American
National Standard for Information Sciences Permanence of Paper for Printed Library
Materials, ANSI/NISO Z39.48-1992.

Printed in the United States of America

To all the foremothers on whose shoulders I stand taller and see farther toward the dawn of post-patriarchy

Contents

Acknowledgments

This book had been inside me for a long time before I realized it. It emerged from both the immersion in historical research and repeated frustrations I experienced after "discovering" history as a living tradition and feminism as a core commitment in the mid-1980s. Since then, every conversation I've had with a historian, every book I've read, and every class I've attended or taught have been stepping-stones toward this project. I am grateful first and foremost to all the feminist historians who modeled for me a way to approach the past with analytical lenses that engage with gender norms. Standing on their broad shoulders, I can see farther than my predecessors. From Judith Tucker and Richard Stites to Sonya Michel and Karen Offen, who asked uncomfortable but necessary questions about the past, I have drawn intellectual and personal sustenance.

Among my peers, I built a community from scholars and friends who were like-minded in their aspirations, and their collegiality and robust intellectual fellowship have kept me going. Marissa Moorman, Jeff Isaac, Kristen Ghodsee, Krassimira Daskalova, Leah Drayton, Jeff Wasserstrom, Francisca de Haan, Beth Holmgren, Nancy Wingfield, Melissa Moreton, Katalin Fabian, Lucy Fischman, Rob Fischman, Mary Gray, Catherine Guthrie, Anna Krylova, Rochelle Ruthchild, and my soul sister Mihaela Miroiu have all, at one time or another, asked tough questions, encouraged me to keep going, challenged my assumptions, and read my work with a generous and open mind.

This book would not have been written if I did not spend most of my working hours teaching or preparing for the classroom. When I wake up in the morning, I know that dozens of eighteen- to twenty-five-year-olds wait for me to make the world at once more complicated and clearer through the craft of history and gender analysis. Thinking about the future and the world these young people will build with the knowledge they gain in college becomes a great impetus for writing with them as the primary audience. And so, generations of my own students have been a source of inspiration. Among them Jill Massino, Anna Muller, Ben Thorne, Mara Lazda, Morgan Mohr, Nathan Wood, and Alex Tipei shared their passion for history with me and have passed forward their commitment to understanding the past with a feminist approach at the center of their own practices. Their work inspires me to push on. In Romania, where I have spent many summers since I left the country in the mid-1980s, generations of younger feminists interested in history have been an important sounding board for my ideas; among these feminists are Oana Băluță, Rucsandra Pop, Eliza Theodora Văcărescu, Mia Jinga, Diana Neaga, and Fatma Yilmaz.

And, of course, financial support helped me take time to write the manuscript. I want to thank Indiana University for the New Frontiers Grant I received in 2016 and the Woodrow Wilson Center for the research fellowship I received for the spring of 2015. In addition, the staff at the Schlesinger Library, part of the Radcliffe Institute for Advanced Study at Harvard University, provided generous support and a welcoming environment for research. I would be remiss not to thank Susan McEachern for believing in this project and seeing it through with great attention and care, together with an equally outstanding editorial staff. I am also grateful for the anonymous readers' comments and critiques, which provided invaluable feedback for improving the manuscript.

Finally, I am not whole without my family. I was raised by a feisty grandmother who worked hard every day of her life to make it easier for me to be in the world. My parents let me pursue my dreams, even when those dreams had nothing to do with their own values and ideas of a profession. My life partner's love and unswerving loyalty teaches me every day how to be a better human being. I started to write this book primarily because I want to offer my two boys a different vision for the future, one that embraces a recent past with women present and significant in every area of human interaction. I hope they will find in this text inspiration for how to be thoughtful feminists as they build the world of tomorrow.

Abbreviations

ACLU	American Civil Liberties Union
AHA	American Historical Association
AIDS	acquired immunodeficiency syndrome
ANC	African National Congress
BBC	British Broadcasting Corporation
CEO	chief economic officer
EU	European Union
FRIDA	Flexibility, Resources, Inclusivity, Diversity, Action
GDP	gross domestic product
HIV	human immunodeficiency virus
IAS	International AIDS Society
IAW	International Alliance of Women
ICC	International Criminal Court
ICW	International Congress of Women
IFRWH	International Federation for Research in Women's History
ILO	International Labour Organization
IMF	International Monetary Fund
IPPF	International Planned Parenthood Federation
LGBTQ	lesbian, gay, bisexual, transgender, and queer
MoMA	Museum of Modern Art
MP	Member of Parliament
NAACP	National Association for the Advancement of Colored People
NIH	National Institutes of Health
NPP	National Peasant Party
NGO	nongovernmental organization

OECD	Organisation for Economic Co-operation and Development
S&P	Standard & Poor's
UK	United Kingdom
UN	United Nations
UNESCO	United Nations Educational, Scientific, and Cultural Organization
UNICEF	United Nations International Children's Emergency Fund
US	United States
USSR	Union of Soviet Socialist Republics
WIDF	Women's International Democratic Federation
WILPF	Women's International League for Peace and Freedom
WTO	World Trade Organization

ONE

Introduction

A Feminist History of the World since 1900

I grew up at a time and in a place where gender inequality problems were supposed to have been fully resolved and women had the same rights and obligations toward the state. In 1968, the year of my birth, the world exploded with manifestations of youthful protest against the old order and with celebrations of love, sex, and peace. And yet, growing up in Bucharest, Romania, I found none of these victories for women's empowerment represented in history narratives produced under the communist regime of that period. It wasn't just that feminism was supposed to be a bourgeois, retrograde attitude that the communist regime rejected. Despite claims about the need to research the past from below, historical research and writing was still framed around wars and political events that had very little to do with long-term developments at the granular societal level, where women dwelled. Whenever I opened a history book, I saw nothing there to give me hope for my own potential as a woman: not only were women almost entirely absent, but what counted as important questions and social values had nothing to do with the realities of my gendered life. The writings and ideas of male philosophers and other thinkers became the core materials for the history of ideas, and they continue to do so in the present.[1] It was later in life, after leaving Romania and starting college in the United States, that I discovered one could write history with women as important players and not just decorations or colorful exceptions. At Georgetown, my first history class was taught by Judith Tucker, whose world history survey included many readings and discussions about women in Indian, South African, and Ottoman history.[2] I started to understand that historical narratives could be legitimately presented from a gender-inclusive perspective, and my own historical imagination grew wings after that class.

Almost forty years later, women's history and gender studies have grown tremendously, enriching and complicating how we look at the past to try to imagine the future. And yet, when it comes to narrating *longue durée* histories, women tend to fall by the wayside and gender regimes are rarely explicitly analyzed. As full-fledged historical actors, women seldom appear, and gender is rarely represented as a core element of how societies function and change over time. The works of Eric Hobsbawm and Jared Diamond best exemplify these types of historical syntheses.[3] Both seek to understand the major historical forces that drive change over time within broad temporal and geographic frameworks. Both authors render long-term historical processes legible and gripping through a combination of microhistory, comparative analysis, and concern with current challenges for humanity. Equally important, they speak to audiences of both experts and nonspecialists with a rare blend of scholarly sophistication and clarity of expression.

Yet, for all their fine qualities, these and most other authors who write about broad historical processes over long periods of time do not ask fundamental questions about gender regimes: What justifies the preoccupation with military violence as a core building block for periodization? Why are political institutions defined and controlled by male elites the main focus of narratives about political change? Why is the so-called public sphere so neatly separated from the so-called private sphere, when in the lives of most people that separation makes no sense? In short, why are the organizational principles of writing about historical change since 1900 following the same masculinist epistemological assumptions today as they did fifty years ago? What justifies the continued lack of engagement with feminist deconstructionism? What would the global history of the recent past look like if we took these critiques to heart and attempted to build a different kind of epistemology, a humanist feminist one? A related question is, what is to be gained and what is to be lost (and for whom) with such a shift?

Having come of age as a scholar during the years of post-structuralist hegemony in historical research, cultural studies, philosophy, and gender studies, I took that approach as a necessary first step for critiquing the insufficiencies I observed in methodology, theory, and the epistemological foundations of history.[4] By critiquing the notion that knowledge making could be separated from its sociocultural and political contexts, post-structuralist philosophers and historians beckoned new generations of scholars to question the idea that neutral or original truths anchored analyses of the past.[5] The language, verbal or visual, of historical artifacts was itself embedded in historical context and therefore ideological. The imbrication of historical evidence with the networks of power that produced it generated naturalized narratives that obscured core systems of thought and social organization, such as gender and class norms, as much as they revealed the past. Post-structuralist scholars called on historians to become more self-reflexive about the ideological underpinnings and power relations of their craft. I will have more to say about this subject in the chapter on knowledge.

Though the call for self-reflexivity spoke to me and still does, a quarter of a century later I find myself dissatisfied with the post-structuralist approach to historical analysis. Digging away at ideological assumptions, exposing and critiquing power relations, and deconstructing previous historical narratives has done little to avert the fragmentation of our intellectual landscape. I am well aware of the critiques cultural historians have leveled against metanarratives and overgeneralization.[6] But I want to move toward taking greater risks in writing about the world as a whole, rather than fragmented, as I see the deconstructivist ethos of my generation leading toward segmentation or even the inability of historical writing to assist us in making sense of the paradoxes and conflicts of our time. I also want to bring more hope and model optimism, even as I approach historical sources critically. There is less optimism in the scholarly discourse today than two generations ago, and I believe the humanities need to play a more constructive role in academia than they have in the past three decades.[7]

The Century of Women aims to blend judicious critique with audacious hope in radically altering the framework we use to make sense of the past, in this case the twentieth and early twenty-first centuries. Imagine a clean canvas on which an enormous diversity of colors and shapes can be painted; this is how I want to start. The first and most important question is, how do we determine that a historical fact is primary rather than secondary? Another way of thinking about this is to ask what changes have had the most significant long-term impact on humanity. Finally, and especially significant for the recent past, we must identify the most unprecedented shifts since approximately 1900 that have impacted societies across the world at large.

These questions allow me to lay bare our assumptions about what kinds of actions and people are considered relevant by historians. Since Herodotus, historians have taken it for granted that the stories about people holding political and military power (men) are the basic framework for understanding the past. Other events in the past were rendered meaningful in relation to these foundational events. But change is brought about first and foremost by life, rather than death, and by caretaking rather than by limiting access. And women are responsible for most of the activities in both of these areas—bringing life into the world and taking care of those around them. Why should we not have these forms of bringing about change over time become our building blocks for understanding the past?

By starting from these assumptions, rather than giving in to the established frame of reference based primarily on political and military power, I want to articulate a very different set of arguments about what the most important developments for humanity have been since the 1900s, as well as what these developments mean for my children and the students I teach. My argument for defining "the century of women" is simply that the most remarkable and unprecedented changes around the world between roughly 1900 and today can be fully grasped only by analyzing how women have been both the subject and object of these major shifts, from an unprecedented set of new rights to new cultural norms, and overall greater agency as a category of humans. Women have become the largest group of newly politically enfranchised people. Their ability to receive an education has vastly reshaped every discipline and area of human action into which they have ventured as learners and knowledge makers. Women's legal rights and protection against discrimination have increased over the twentieth century, greatly altering marital, parenting, and other familial practices. Women's greater choices over birth control and marriage have drastically reshaped the demographic outlook, and thus global politics and economic processes, in every country around the world.

Women's ability to enter the workforce and become economically self-sufficient has helped refashion the workplace, waged labor, the profits reaped by corporations, and the banking sector. Women's participation in the global markets as autonomous producers and consumers has helped reshape what services and goods are made and sold, as well as where and how they become available. As important as these shifts have been for all women and the rest of humanity, they have also helped usher in new forms of inequality among women of different cultural, political, religious, and ethnoracial backgrounds. In a more strongly interconnected service economy, women have often climbed the political, professional, social, and economic ladder on the shoulders of other women. The economic diversification and polarization of women in the twentieth century make up an important aspect of how I define "the century of women."

These changes can be observed across states widely different in terms of ideology, citizen rights, economic development, and sociocultural norms. This suggests that there is more to these shifts than the sum of their parts. Their unprecedented and in many instances irreversible impact across the world and beyond women's own lives suggests that we need to consider them not as side effects of other forces but rather as prime movers with explanatory power for other changes around the globe, both nationally and transnationally.

My project does not aim to replace one fantasy of comprehensiveness (e.g., the age of extremes) with another. There isn't one theme, force, or other linear explanatory thread running through this book to tie together all the stories and themes I discuss. There is, instead, an analytical angle that underlines it—gender analysis. By insisting that gender norms are socially constructed and therefore historical in nature, I look at the ways in which women have questioned existing discourses or how they sought to appropriate them for their own interests. These processes are extremely varied in time and in different parts of the world, but overall, the dynamic has been to move from appropriation of existing roles to questioning the assumptions that undergird them and seeking to redefine how gender roles operate and what they mean.

My goal is to provide a framework for thinking about the recent past that focuses on changes that can give us hope into the future without eschewing the controversies, destruction, and struggles that accompanied them. Ultimately, I want to come clean about the moral implications of how we teach critical thinking through these frameworks of interpretation and to offer my own narrative as one that privileges a focus on humanity's potential, accomplishments, and failures less on the battlefield and more in the places and communities that are common to most average people—from homes to schools and the workplace. Women have been central movers and shakers in these processes, with consequences we need to fully historicize as a way to better appreciate the potentialities and challenges of the world we inhabit today.

A MAP TO THE BOOK

The Century of Women describes and synthesizes major changes that have taken place over the twentieth and early twenty-first centuries in different parts of the world in terms of women's legal status, social standing, and advances in areas such as education and economic empowerment, together with backlashes against these developments. I do not aim to develop an encyclopedia of women since 1900 but rather weave the most important components of this century-long process into a narrative about how humanity has been transformed through women's historical agency. The types of developments I highlight include both broad long-term quantitative changes—birth rates, mortality, life-span, economic power, participation in politics, divorce rates, urbanization, access to education—as well as qualitative changes, such as the development of different types of ideologies, literature, civic activism, specific roles in politics, and relations in the family—in short, a shift in power relations in every aspect of human interaction. Many developments I focus on have been the subject of narrower historical analysis; therefore much of my discussion highlights their significance from a broader and *longue durée* comparative perspective.

But, while broadly comparative, my approach is grounded in my own intellectual expertise and preferences. I take a feminist approach to exploring historical agency, which means that I measure actions and impact in relation to the preexisting social and discursive practices that anchor gender roles rather than in relation to some abstract notion of "meaningful" or "impactful." To compare the actions of a systematically long-term marginalized category of people—women—with the actions of a privileged one—men—without taking into account their different positions of power in any society, is to be a poor analyst of humanity.[8]

My understanding of the past is broadly framed by a secular Western humanism that takes cultural differences across the globe, including religious ones, as important points of comparison. Yet I do not subscribe to the relativist perspective that such differences cannot be evaluated from a position that embraces specific moral and ethical values, nor to the inability of using these values to frame that comparison.[9] My feminist humanist secular values include respect for personal autonomy and for choices an individual makes unconstrained. However, in understanding processes that include any form of violence against this fundamental principle of personal autonomy, I do not defer to cultural traditions simply because they might diverge from my feminist humanist views. I evaluate such developments through my own specific perspective, the only one I can stand by in the last analysis.

I have chosen a thematic rather than chronological approach for a variety of reasons. First, a global timeline of significant changes in every area of human interaction and the periodization of these developments would render the book heavily focused on the global North. Additionally, I am primarily interested in what sorts of major changes can be seen across regimes and more traditional periodizations (e.g., pre– and post–World War I, World War II, the fall of Communism), as we examine the past 120 years as a whole. Finally, with similar issues developing at a different pace in different places, comparisons among them in a chronological narrative would be impossibly cumbersome.

Instead, the thematic approach allows me to focus on changes with the broadest and longest lasting consequences, while underscoring power differences among women. Along the way, I combine quantitative and qualitative approaches, as well as highlight important developments through microhistories of various women. My choice of specific biographies was guided by a desire to highlight extraordinary accomplishments seen from the perspective of the types of opportunities and obstacles these women faced in their societies. If some of the best-known women of the twentieth century, such as Eleanor Roosevelt, are discussed in lesser detail than lesser-known figures, like Chiquinha Gonzaga, it is because I also wanted to make known to readers individuals whose accomplishments deserve greater attention than they have received so far. These stories are sometimes braided through several chapters, reinforcing the importance of reading these thematic chapters as intertwined, even if they each tell somewhat separate stories. Chapters are divided by focus on specific areas of social interaction, rather than periods of time. Yet each chapter respects chronological order as much as possible.

I start by addressing politics (chapter 2) because I am focusing on a period of time when the institutions of the state have become much more expansive than at any other point in the past. How women understood politics and participated in reshaping institutions, laws, and citizenly practices became foundational for many other changes in education, economic empowerment, culture, knowledge making, and kinship, all of which I discuss subsequently in the book. The chapter first addresses how the suffrage movement developed and with what impact in different parts of the world. Focusing on both successes and failures, I move on to highlighting the ways in which international women's networks dedicated to suffrage rights morphed into networks advocating for peace, for indigenous people's rights, and for women's labor protection. Women's activism ultimately led to framing the goals and many programs of the most important international organization since the second half of the twentieth century, the United Nations (UN), through the Declaration of Universal Human Rights and the Commission on the Status of Women. Just as importantly, women's participation in politics played a central role in shaping the welfare state over the second half of the twentieth century.

In chapter 3 I tackle the most remarkable global change since 1900: the huge upsurge in population growth over the twentieth century with its differential leveling off in various parts of the world over the last half century. The focus in this chapter is on understanding both how this change came about as well as what it suggests moving forward. Like many other scholars of the past three decades, I regard the alarmist perspective of demographers and economic planners of the 1960s and '70s with critical distance. Instead, my analysis focuses on women as agents of change and on their ability to control their fertility as a phenomenon that needs to be understood in a complex web of political, cultural, and economic factors. Since 1900 the gradual acceptance of women's sexuality as an area of research, discussion, and policy making, and the subsequent development of safe technologies for birth control, have changed how women understand and act upon their fertility. Education has been the most important tool in this regard, and my chapter shows the important ways in which women have pushed for significant change in this area in every place on the planet, often against the wishes of the male political and economic elites. My analysis focuses also on the important legacies of European colonialism for how women's sexuality and women's education have manifested themselves in Africa, the Middle East, and Asia.

In chapter 4 I examine how women's increased participation in all areas of economic activity, from paid work to property ownership and from entrepreneurial leadership to consumption, has reshaped the global economy. In this area women introduced many unprecedented changes, among them the elimination of legal barriers against women's property ownership and their pursuit of any professional field. Yet full equality between men and women still eludes us, most prominently in the area of continuing wage disparities despite legal sanctions against such practices. In the last decade, with a significant rise of women in positions of economic and political authority, we are seeing greater pressures for eliminating these disparities by paying attention to all the attendant elements of economic gender inequality, such as educational and investment opportunities and work-life balance policies. Recent discussions about sexual violence in the workplace are helping to bring into focus some of these fundamental underlying forms of gender inequality. But it remains to be seen how successful these challenges will become in the following decades.

There are also important new differences between women in their abilities to seek economic empowerment: women's significant participation in global migration and the absence of effective work-life balance policies in most countries have generated new forms of abusive behavior on the part of employers, many of them women, in the caretaking service economy. These trends continue today and will likely shape women's access to jobs and thus economic power into the future. If women do not take charge of these issues to address the global inequalities developing today, it is unlikely that we will arrive at a better balance between the aspirations women have in the economic realm and the caretaking needs of their families.

Having examined women's impact on economic processes in the twentieth century, I turn to knowledge making (chapter 5). This chapter documents the unleashing of women's creative potential in helping solve problems big and small and imagining a better future for humanity. More than in any other area of human activity, we can see here the unprecedented boon brought about by the doubling of the number of people who can pursue education at every level and can work in any area of scholarly inquiry. In particular, feminist thinkers have provided provocative critiques of the basic building blocks of knowledge making. By exposing the masculinist assumptions behind categories of analysis, research methods, values, and meaning, these scholars have enabled us to better understand the foundations of patriarchy. Moving from critique to developing new analytical insights, these and many other women scholars have greatly enhanced our understanding of humanity as well as our ability to deal more effectively with problems. Not all of the women featured in this chapter self-identified as feminist. Still, their ability to pursue knowledge without the barriers women had faced in the past is in itself one of the unique features of the scholarly landscape since 1900.

It is no coincidence that this chapter is focused heavily on the achievements of women from the developed and developing world. Having the aim to focus on deep long-term changes pushed me to look at sites of knowledge making where women have secured the most stable institutional positions. Those locations happen to be primarily in Europe and North America, with some very notable Asian exceptions, for reasons rendered clear by the previous chapters on politics and economics. This chapter draws attention to the weaknesses that have resulted from these institutional inequalities, many of them the result of generations of colonial rule. In areas such as ecological sustainability, women from the global North have often been at odds with women from indigenous societies in the global South.

By contrast, examining how women shaped culture (chapter 6) is a more globally encompassing phenomenon since this is an area in which they have always played an important role everywhere, within the arts, music, and literature. This chapter discusses important changes in the world of established aesthetic genres, as well as women's contributions to the development of new ones, such as film, photography, and stand-up comedy.

In chapter 7 I turn to recent changes in how kinship has been significantly reshaped as a concept and social practice, especially in the latter part of the twentieth century and onward into the future. Many of these changes came about because of transformations described in the previous chapters, hence the narrower chronological span. I consider them the most profound alterations of how humanity acts today by comparison to 1900. These changes are especially important for trying to understand the future of human relations and interactions. From the rise of female-headed and double-earner families to the decline of marriage as the most prevalent institution undergirding kinship, how women and men decide to relate to older generations and create their own familial communities has changed tremendously, especially since the 1960s. These appear to be permanent shifts, and they challenge many of the assumptions politicians, economists, and scholars of all stripes have about how and why people act and what makes our societies function stably. These new realities behoove us to start imagining the world before us as an unfolding human experiment with new variables and priorities. Without women participating directly in making sense of it, the world of tomorrow will be impoverished and unable to function well. At the same time, women need to understand themselves as primary and responsible historical agents in shaping this future, ready to assume the burdens of the empowerment and challenges that the past hundred years have opened up for us.

The epilogue offers overarching conclusions about women's contributions to reshaping the last 120 years. It argues that the point of focusing on women has been to provide better thinking about the current "culture wars." In the face of continued reifications of "identity politics," my narrative highlights the diverse contributions and disagreements among women as historical agents. Ultimately, my point is that gender continues to be an important category of analysis but without suggesting universal transhistorical qualities among all women, other than their exclusion from access to most forms of power at the hands of masculinist regimes.

The book ends with a bibliographic essay describing the historiographic tradition that inspired this study. It is both a critique and a tribute to the scholars on whose shoulders I stand gratefully. For readers interested in further exploring themes in the book, I have also created additional teaching and research tools, which can be easily located online. The *Century of Women* blog at http://midlifewonderer.tumblr.com offers a growing number of mini biographies of the women discussed in this book, with the goal of reaching one thousand biographies by 2020. The website http://centuryofwomen.com provides access to relevant primary-source collections and databases. The website presents brief descriptions of these materials, connecting them to themes and individuals highlighted in the book. It features, for instance, interviews with musicians Nina Simone and Mary Lou Williams, both of whom are discussed in chapter 6. Other links enable viewers to explore digital exhibits of artists described in the book, such as Cindy Sherman. The website will continue to add new materials after the publication of the book.

NOTES

1. For a recent example of the stubborn dismissal of gender considerations in the history of historical writing, see John Burrow, *A History of Histories: Epics, Chronicles, Romances and Inquiries from Herodotus and Thucydides to the Twentieth Century* (New York: Vintage Books, 2009).
2. Judith Tucker's work includes prominent studies on the history of Islamic law and gender roles, such as *Women in Nineteenth-Century Egypt* (Cambridge: Cambridge University Press, 1985) and *Women, Family, and Gender in Islamic Law* (Cambridge: Cambridge University Press, 2008).
3. Eric Hobsbawm, *The Age of Extremes: A History of the World, 1914–1991* (New York: Vintage Books, 1996); Jared Diamond, *Guns, Germs, and Steel: The Fates of Human Societies* (New York: W. W. Norton, 1996).
4. Mark Poster, "In Place of a Conclusion: History as Knowledge," in *Cultural History and Postmodernity: Disciplinary Readings and Challenges* (New York: Columbia University Press, 1997), 153–58; Willie Thompson, *Postmodernism and History* (Basingstoke, UK: Palgrave Macmillan, 2004).
5. Jean-François Lyotard, *The Postmodern Condition: A Report on Knowledge* (Minneapolis: University of Minnesota Press, 1984); Donna Haraway, "Situated Knowledges: The Science Question in Feminism and the Privilege of Partial Perspective," *Feminist Studies* 14, no. 3 (Autumn 1988): 575–99; Sandra Harding, "Standpoint Theories: Productively Controversial," *Hypatia: A Journal of Feminist Philosophy* 24, no. 4 (2009): 192–200.
6. Lyotard, *Postmodern Condition*.
7. A recent volume by Jo Guldi and David Armitage, *The History Manifesto* (Cambridge: Cambridge University Press, 2015), makes a similar point with a focus on the rise of what they identify as "short-termism" in the past several decades.
8. I am fully aware of exceptions to these generalizations, in terms of both exceptional women's privilege and the lack of privilege that many subcategories of men,

such as those born into racial, ethnic, and religious minority status, experience systematically.

9. For a feminist critique of such relativist perspectives, see Sandra Harding, "Rethinking Standpoint Epistemology: What Is 'Strong Objectivity?'" *Centennial Review* 36, no. 3 (Fall 1992): 437–70.

TWO

Politics

If you insist upon fighting to protect me, or "our" country, let it be understood soberly and rationally between us that you are fighting to gratify a sex instinct which I cannot share; to procure benefits where I have not shared and probably will not share; but not to gratify my instincts, or to protect myself or my country.

—Virginia Woolf[1]

At the dawn of the twentieth century, as systems of government throughout the world were moving toward parliamentary regimes, women were excluded from voting and standing for political office in all but a handful of states. By 1945 there were twenty-six parliamentary regimes around the world, with women counting as less than 3 percent of those elected to serve as members of parliament (MPs).[2] By 2017 women could exercise some voting rights in every country.[3] The number of women elected to serve has increased fourfold, with women representing 23.4 percent of MPs worldwide.[4] The regional averages range greatly—from 41.7 percent in Scandinavia to 15 percent in the Pacific. The rest of the world hovers at a closer range of 28.2 percent in the Americas to 19.7 percent in Asia and 18.9 percent in Arab states. In some parts of the world we are approaching gender parity in parliamentary representation, while in other places we are still a very long way from there. Though by no means an equitable gender breakdown, this spectacular rise in women's participation in parliamentary politics represents a momentous historical shift driven by women themselves, whose century-long struggles to reshape citizenship, state institutions, and political practices have had wide and unprecedented implications for every human being.

A similar arc from absence to almost parity in parts of the world describes women's participation in governance. In 2006 a handful of governments around the world were approaching gender parity (40+ percent) in places like Scandinavia, as well as in Spain, Chile, and South Africa.[5] In 2015 the newly elected prime minister of Canada, Justin Trudeau (b. 1971), formed a cabinet with an equal gender balance. In 2017 the newly elected president of France, Emmanuel Macron (b. 1977), appointed an equal number of women as men in his cabinet. On the opposite end of the spectrum, many more countries have fewer than 10 percent women serving at the top level of the executive, among them Portugal, India, Israel, Turkey, and Mexico.[6] The map of gender representation has become highly varied and defies any easy regional, ideological, or cultural generalization. Yet these figures tell a story of hope above frustration. Gender has become a core consideration in how political parties function, how political movements are organized, and the types of issues they push into the public arena. Women have been central in shaping this process everywhere.

Long before the twentieth century, women helped shape politics. Elite women like Empress Catherine the Great of Russia (1729–1796) and Empress Zetian Wu of China (624–705) participated in building state institutions and expanding the political and military power of the dynasties over which they ruled.[7] Marginalized women such as Harriet Tubman (1822–1913) and Ida B. Wells (1862–1931) sought to change regimes of oppression through their entwined struggle against racism and misogyny in the nineteenth century in the United States. There are many other examples of the brilliant and often tragic lives of women, most of them poorly documented and even lesser known, who pushed against the boundaries of the established patriarchal order of their times. There are also examples of women whose brutality paralleled and in fact emulated the same vicious patriarchal order and who mastered and manipulated gender norms to extricate themselves from the subordinate condition of their lives.[8]

However, women globally became a category of humans with full rights and obligations as individual members of the polis only in the twentieth century, and this truly unprecedented change thoroughly reshaped politics, from ideology to participation in making, implementing, and using political rights. As the world has moved from considering only half of the population—men—as worthy of having a public voice in politics to including all people as members of the polis, this radical expansion has fundamentally altered political ideas and practices in parliamentary democracies, monarchies, theocratic autocracies, and communist regimes alike. This chapter focuses on the most important global changes that have occurred through the participation of women in politics.

EARLY STRUGGLES FOR POLITICAL PARTICIPATION

In a few parts of the world, by the late nineteenth century, the repeated denial of women's voting rights, even as men's expanded, became a vocal issue in political debates. In North America and parts of the UK and British Commonwealth (New Zealand, Australia), subcategories of women (primarily Anglo-Saxon whites) gained some voting rights by the 1890s, though full political equality with men would not come until the twentieth century. In the rest of the world, feminist voices and women's suffrage movements developed more vigorously after 1900, partly emulating or responding to the developments in the United States and Great Britain and partly reacting to the patriarchal political institutions and practices in their own states.[9] For many of these women, especially those living in imperial and colonial settings, the struggle for political rights combined nationalism and feminism, and it developed a critique of xenophobia or racism with a critique of misogyny. The first successful case was Finland, where in 1906 women began to exercise the right to vote and stand for elections under Russian imperial rule as part of a larger Finnish home-rule movement.

At the forefront of these struggles were two categories of women, who sometimes joined forces but often worked separately or even antagonistically. One was made up of women from the ruling elites and middle classes, who became disenchanted with the gilded cage they inhabited and used their privilege to advance both their own interests and wider feminist agendas.[10] Due to their social privileges and wealth, these women benefited from better educational opportunities than others did. The German socialist leader Clara Zetkin (1857–1933) was the daughter of a schoolmaster and of a highly educated middle-class mother. Huda Sha'arawi (1879–1947), the founder of the Egyptian Feminist Union, came from a wealthy family, with a father who served as the first president of the Egyptian Representative Council.

Women who came from a working-class background or whose families had already been involved in labor rights activism in the late nineteenth century made up another strong current of political activism that tended to be connected to egalitarianism and focused more on labor rights and protection than on other social and moral issues.[11] Puerto Rican anarchist activist Luisa Capetillo (1879–1922) came from such a background, as did the better-known Emma Goldman (1869–1940). The daughter of immigrants from Europe, Capetillo was raised by her domestic servant mother and laborer father in the spirit of love of education and concern with social justice. She became a union leader in Puerto Rico and lent her feminist voice to shaping anarcho-socialist movements in Puerto Rico and other North American locations, including Cuba and the United States.

Many of these activists, especially in the early years of the century, worked alongside and sometimes through political institutions that had been established and were led by men, such as socialist labor unions and nationalist parties. In other cases, women established their own institutions, overwhelmingly driven to separatism by the lack of support for their voices and interests among the established male-dominated political institutions. In the United States, the Women's Peace Party, led by the formidable Jane Addams (1860–1935), was an early case of taking a separate path. All of these activities expanded the political playing field in terms of ideological platforms, programs, followers, organizers, and public opinion. In doing so, they challenged and transformed the meaning of what political ideology, movement, party, program, or governing strategy meant. It would be unthinkable to imagine the unequivocal demands for gender parity in politics at the beginning of the twenty-first century in places as historically different as Romania and Kenya without these transformations.[12]

The ideological orientation of advocates for women's political rights varied greatly, from pro-communist to strictly nationalist and even racist. Among those who joined and helped reshape communism, Alexandra Kollontai (1872–1952) was an early leader. A woman of the Russian aristocracy by both birth and marriage, Kollontai made a conscious choice early in her years as a wife and mother to reject the patriarchal institutions of privilege and control—marriage, private property, and capitalist forms of ownership and production—as means to redress the profound social injustices she experienced and observed. The beneficiary of economic privilege and education from her family, Kollontai became familiar early on with the writings of Karl Marx (1818–1883) and was especially impressed by the writings of both August Bebel (1840–1913) and Friedrich Engels (1820–1895) that linked marriage and patriarchy as intertwined forms of oppression.[13] For Kollontai, political and economic power were closely connected; women's enfranchisement would only gain value as part of a larger struggle for economic injustice, which she perceived as inextricably tied to the gendered oppression of all women through capitalism. Kollontai took the analysis offered by these early socialist writers and turned them into a much sharper and more radical critique of patriarchy. She placed gender regimes at the core of capitalist exploitation and injustice, and projected into the future revolutionary ideas about gender relations free from the constraints of marriage.

More than any other communist revolutionary in imperial Russia, Kollontai developed an original analysis of gender inequality and proposed the ideology of free love—doing away with the institutions of marriage and parenting as they had been solidified through law and practice, to pave the way for a new form of equality and new types of communal loyalties.[14] Her radicalism consisted of searching further than either Bebel or Engels probed into the private realm of familial relations to connect women's oppression at home to the power men had arrogated themselves through political and economic exclusive rights. Kollontai called for freeing women from the norms of marriage and motherhood and turning household and parenting obligations into communal, social, and therefore public issues.[15] She envisioned a world in which any person could grow up to the full potential of her or his abilities, so that all would be ready to dedicate themselves to the common good without unequal burdens placed on their shoulders by virtue of their gender. In Kollontai's notion of rights, voting was only a small element of how politics and citizenship became translated into everyday practice, both in public and in private. These ideas put Kollontai at odds with many other contemporary feminists, who insisted on focusing on voting rights above other goals for political empowerment. In fact, she spoke repeatedly against many feminists of her day, whom she viewed as beholden to the capitalist system that ensured their subordination to men. Yet her free-love ideology also found many sympathizers, among them contemporary anarchists Goldman and Capetillo and, starting in the 1960s, radical feminists.

Kollontai's reimagining of gender roles as part of the communist struggle against capitalism became translated into policies from the very start of Bolshevik rule. Though she had established herself as an independent thinker rather than loyalist follower, Vladimir I. Lenin (1870–1924) asked her to join him in the unfolding revolution and return to Russia during World War I.[16] After participating in the successful Bolshevik takeover in October 1917, Kollontai became the first woman in the world appointed to a high government position, and not by virtue of birth or marriage: Commissar of Social Welfare. Thus, the policies of the first and longest lasting communist regime in the world were shaped from the beginning by the revolutionary ideas of Kollontai in areas such as public health, labor conditions, parental leave, childcare, and retirement.

Kollontai was among a group of remarkable women who had joined the Bolsheviks and competed for leadership positions in the party, among them Inessa Armand (1874–1920) and Nadezhda Krupskaya (1869–1939). But none had the audaciousness of her vision in terms of upending gender norms. In 1920 the female leadership of the party brought into being the Zhenotdel, the government department assigned to oversee women's issues. Shortly thereafter, Kollontai assumed the leadership of this institution to oversee the quest for eliminating gender inequality from working conditions, wages, education, and familial duties. With her predictable boldness and uncompromising attitude, she ended up alienating many among the leadership and rank-and-file alike, including other female Bolshevik leaders. Unbending in her ideas about social justice, equality, and freedom, Kollontai rubbed Lenin and Nikolai Bukharin (1888–1938) the wrong way and ended up being removed from the Zhenotdel's leadership by 1922.[17]

Throughout the 1920s, nevertheless, the Zhenotdel remained an important institution for imagining new gender identities and crafting unprecedented social experiments in liberating women from their traditional household chores and supporting their aspirations in the professional and political public spheres. The Zhenotdel developed an extensive network of new state institutions and workplace practices with resources devoted exclusively to women's needs as workers, homemakers, and mothers, decades before any such efforts would become mainstream in democratic states in the West.

Joseph Stalin (1878–1953) disbanded the Zhenotdel in 1930. Its revolutionary potential was tamed into a much more institutionally driven, top-down set of programs, eliminating the grassroots activism that Kollontai and other early leaders had encouraged.[18] In the early days of the Zhenotdel, social assistance programs such as canteens and childcare had freed up women from caretaking burdens to take up paid employment and political activism. As funding diminished and the regime moved away from a commitment to easing women's caretaking responsibilities at home, the double burden became prevalent. With less time on their hands, political activism became a luxury for women. In the meantime, men enjoyed the privilege of having time to participate in politics while also pursuing a professional career.

This fundamental failure of the communist regime to tend to the double burden was replicated in Eastern Europe after 1945 and eventually in China, North Korea, Cuba, and Angola. In all of these regimes, one could observe a relatively higher percentage of women elected to the National Assemblies, which were bodies with little power in these one-party states. In more politically powerful bodies, such as the central committee of the communist party, regional party leadership positions, or even municipal committees, all time-demanding positions, women tended to be greatly underrepresented in relation to their percentage of the total constituency. Overall, women's membership in officially sanctioned parties did not make up more than a third of the total. The long-term legacies of this lower level of participation in party politics on the part of women living under communist regimes can be observed today. In the early decades of postcommunist rule in Eastern Europe and Russia, the percentage of women running for and, especially, elected to any political seat has plummeted to under 10 percent in many places.[19]

However, ideas and policies developed by the Zhenotdel and promoted internationally by Kollontai and other Bolshevik women leaders reverberated widely throughout the world and impacted thinking about women's role in political life and the role of the state in welfare matters, in places as far-flung as China and the United States. Florence Luscomb (1887–1985) was an American feminist leader with socialist leanings who embraced pacifism during World War I and antiracism into the 1920s. In the summer of 1935 she made a trip to the Soviet Union, visiting the thriving metropolis of Moscow and smaller cities like Batumi. Her travel journal and notes include comparisons of metrics about industrialization, education, healthcare, and economic power for women in the Soviet Union with the United States. These documents show how much the experience influenced Luscomb's own ideas about the role of the state in developing institutions and policies necessary for bridging the gap between her home country and the Soviet Union in terms of women's well-being.[20] Luscomb saw Soviet gender policies worth emulating back home, such as the socialized medicine practices that made it affordable and easily accessible for all people to have healthcare, and the modernizing and secularizing shifts in gender policies that brought women into the workplace and city council. She spent the rest of her life dedicated to enacting such changes at home through repeated unsuccessful attempts at running for elected office and activism in organizations such as the NAACP, ACLU, and later anti–Vietnam War networks. A long-term member of the Women's International League for Peace and Freedom (WILPF), Luscomb closely emulated Kollontai's ideas in her personal life, choosing a collective home with other single women over matrimony.[21]

In the United States, Great Britain, and parts of the British Commonwealth (Australia and New Zealand) women gained political rights through relentless efforts in the form of petitions, marches, and other types of public pressure and civil disobedience. In each country, women's movements varied in their degrees of radicalness and inclusion of lower-class and especially nonwhite women. Among these early generations of feminists, activists often excluded—often implicitly and sometimes explicitly—Aborigines in Australia and African Americans in the United States from their considerations of what discrimination meant and how to eliminate it.[22] Yet even during the early decades of the twentieth century, feminists were among the most vocal advocates of full political equality regardless of gender, race, religion, or class. In fact, the most important contribution women activists made in these countries after gaining voting rights was to push for their expansion to categories of other marginalized populations.

In the United States, Luscomb and many like her became involved in working with the NAACP and ACLU to eliminate institutional racism and sexism from local, regional, and national state programs and legislation.[23] In Australia, where all white women gained the vote in 1902 and the first female MP was elected in 1920, feminists like Constance Cooke (1882–1967) and Mary Bennett (1881–1961) arrogated to themselves the role of spokeswomen for Aboriginal people, whose rights were being eroded even as white women were gaining more. Cooke and others like her have been critiqued as insufficiently open in their propositions, selfish in their goals for publicity and leadership, and ultimately racist.[24] There is no question that many of these women, like their counterparts in India, Romania, or Egypt, in many ways reflected the racist/ethnocentric cultural and social mores of their times even as they showed openness toward substantial change in women's education and political participation. By the same token, feminists like Bennett and Cooke spoke out at international conferences against their government's policies and sometimes against explicit demands by their male colleagues, producing vocal public indictments of the official treatment of Aborigines. These feminists insisted on treating the Aboriginal "race" as a population deserving of respect for their traditions and familial ties and especially of individual protection as a fundamental aspect of their humanity. In a period when it was mainstream to discuss nonwhites as insufficiently civilized or racially inferior and undeserving of full consideration as citizens, these feminists kept pressure on the male-dominated political establishment and eventually helped bring about more progressive policies.[25] For these women, their racial privilege signified both a sense of civilizational superiority vis-à-vis Aborigines, but also a sense of responsibility, however tinged with paternalism, toward protecting especially the more vulnerable among them—children and women. Before the 1960s, it was primarily these feminist activists who challenged the policies of the male political establishment.

During the decade following World War I, North American feminists became an inspiration for activists in Latin America. A number of international networks were established at that time, which provided a platform for white women of European descent, like Bertha Lutz (1894–1976) of Brazil, to garner recognition and direct support from overseas for their own quest to gain political rights.[26] Lutz became one of the leading figures in the Pan-American networks that, intent first and foremost on extending full voting rights and equal access to education to all women, developed in the following two decades. By 1945 six Central and Latin American states had granted women the vote. These feminist movements, as Ellen DuBois stated, "eventually displaced the Europeans and [North] Americans as leaders in global suffragism."[27] At the founding of the United Nations, Lutz was one of the four female signatories of the Charter, having been sent there as a delegate with the express goal of ensuring explicit gender equality in the founding act.

In many imperial and colonial settings around the world, early-twentieth-century advocates for women's enfranchisement rallied their passion for political action behind contemporaneous national liberation movements. In Egypt, nationalism developed starting in the mid-nineteenth century as a response to both Ottoman (initially) and British (subsequently) abuses of power in their relations with the local elites. Entering the 1900s, questions about gender norms became publicly present through the efforts of a generation of women who, like the men of the social elites, had gained access to feminist and nationalist international networks by virtue of their education, travel opportunities, and interactions with European women of feminist leanings.

Out of these various sources, Huda Sha'arawi and her contemporaries crafted a feminism that sought to entwine empowerment for all Egyptian women, elite and poor, Muslim and Christian, as a component of the flourishing Egyptian nationalism. Historian Margot Badran identifies Sha'arawi as one of the feminist leaders who "generated a construct of nationalism in which women's liberation was embedded and fought concurrently as feminists and nationalists," a contribution rarely noted by historians of nationalism.[28] These feminists insisted on defining rights and duties as citizens with gender as an explicit component alongside race, religion, or class.

Raised in the gender-segregated tradition of the Muslim elites, Sha'arawi benefited from early homeschooling but was married at thirteen and was expected to perform the usual duties of a respectable aristocratic wife to her politically active spouse. Yet Sha'arawi would not conform to the expectations of her family and shortly after discovering that her husband had a concubine with whom he also had children, she separated from him for seven years. During this period she turned toward enhancing her education through the study of French, Arabic, the Quran, and European secular ideas. She remained primarily surrounded by women, and her feminism was shaped by the experiences of frustration and marginalization that this segregated environment brought about. Sha'arawi later reconciled with her spouse for the sake of a beloved brother, who would not accept getting married until Huda herself returned to her husband; but by then she was no longer content to live the life of isolated privilege typical for her social standing.

Soon thereafter Sha'arawi joined the nationalist anti-British movement and became a force to reckon with. She developed extensive links with other aristocratic, educated women in Cairo through a number of educational and philanthropic organizations in which she was active.[29] In March 1919, through this growing network of like-minded feminist nationalists, she helped organize a major event that brought an unprecedented sight before Egyptian society: hundreds of women, veiled and walking together or riding in carriages, took to the streets of Cairo to challenge British rule in Egypt, in solidarity with the Waft nationalist movement. This was a shocking view, for women of the upper classes had never appeared in public in such fashion before. The protest brought a great deal of attention to the nationalist cause from the Egyptian and British press alike.[30] The male nationalist leaders were pleased with these unprecedented demonstrations of visible support as a symbol of where all Egyptian women stood in relation to the struggle for independence from Britain.

But even as they placed their energies, time, social status, and even honor in the service of the national liberation movement, Egyptian feminists were subsequently sidelined. In 1923, when the new Constitution was debated, the male leaders of the successful nationalist party denied women political rights. It took three more decades for the issue to be seriously considered again, after a new generation of women activists turned these disappointments into new goals for political action. Egyptian feminism became more complex and divided over this issue in the coming decades, among groups as diverse as ultraconservative Islamists and secular liberals. An all-women's political organization, the Egyptian Feminist Union, came into being as a result of this process of ideological diversification.

After independence, the landscape of Egyptian politics became significantly more fragmented and gained more radical tendencies on the part of both unabashed feminists like Doria Shafik (1908–1975) as well as Islamist traditionalists. Shafik and other secular feminists continued to press the question of women's suffrage, an unfulfilled promise. Others were content to focus on social aspects of citizenship, such as state funding for education. Even though feminists faced a tough uphill battle with the male political establishment, inclusive of imprisonment, they managed to retain a public presence and voice in the debates about civil, political, and economic rights. In the absence of women representatives in government, these activists developed their own NGOs to support women's education, employment opportunities, and access to healthcare, in the hope that access to full political rights would follow.

Shafik was a prominent leader during this period of partial success and renewed frustrations with Egypt's new nationalist regime, and she led the struggle for women's enfranchisement through relentless campaigns in the press and direct protest before Parliament.[31] After an unsuccessful feminist march on the Parliament in 1951 by around 1,500 participants who demanded the vote for all women, she resorted to other forms of political protest, including a hunger strike in 1954. This public stunt won Shafik global renown and invitations to speak about her feminist struggles to audiences around the world including in Pakistan, France, and the United States. She became a model for feminist nationalists in other postcolonial states.

In Egypt, Shafik's efforts resulted in granting women some voting rights, though not full political equality with men. Emboldened by this success and increasing international fame, Shafik continued her activism undeterred by the growing autocratic powers of Gamal Abdel Nasser (1918–1970). In 1957 she went on a second hunger strike to protest the president's dictatorial regime, for which Shafik was put under house arrest and forbidden to have a public voice. She lived in seclusion for the rest of her life. Shafik's choice to develop a separate path from other nationalist feminists led to both a greater boldness on behalf of women's rights as well as greater isolation from the mainstream of women's movements in Egypt, a complex lesson not lost on subsequent generations of women activists in the Middle East and North Africa up to today.[32]

Similar patterns of feminist nationalist activism with little support among male-dominated nationalist movements can be seen in many other countries. Romanian feminist leaders supported irredentist aspirations of enlarging the country after World War I under the condition of support for women's enfranchisement.[33] In the early years of the twentieth century, the Romanian feminist movement in Austria-Hungary had allied itself with the nationalist movement in a similar fashion as feminists in Egypt or India.[34] Yet after the country gained large territories at the peace conference following the Great War, the most prominent Romanian parties, such as the National Liberals, stood resolutely against women's enfranchisement during the debates about voting rights around the postwar Constitution.

The only allies Romanian feminists found in the subsequent decades were the Social Democrats, a weak party, and the growing National Peasant Party (NPP), which also supported a eugenicist, ethnonationalist, and at times racist radical reshaping of citizenship.[35] Feminists like Veturia Manuilă (1896–1986) had supported the nationalist movement in Transylvania and remained loyal to its leadership as it formed the NPP. Subsequently Manuilă found ways to promote participation in political life by emphasizing the unique and central role women played as mothers and wives through the eugenicist discourse about the health of the nation, which was popular at that time.[36] She was among many others who favored the idea that women had biological responsibilities toward their society to bring into life and raise the next generation of healthy citizens. This biodeterminism, supporters of eugenics believed, underscored the powerful role women played in generating progress and well-being, and many women found its focus on traditional aspects of motherhood a comforting element. They found effective ways to articulate claims for political rights within this racist ideology.

With the NPP extending voting rights in local elections in 1929 to a small category of women,[37] the loyalty of many feminists toward the eugenicist movement grew, especially since many leaders of that movement openly shunned negative measures like sterilization.[38] In making these choices, supporters of women's political rights placed concerns about racial, ethnic, or religious discrimination on a secondary plane to their own empowerment, not unlike other feminists in Europe and North America. Alliances between women's advocates and ethnonationalist eugenics movements created a synergy that poisoned parliamentary democracy not only in Romania but also in many other countries, such as Chile, Germany, and Italy.[39]

Women contributed actively to rendering this type of biopolitical discourse more broadly appealing. Upon traveling for postgraduate medical studies at Johns Hopkins in the mid-1920s, Manuilă became a fervent advocate of developing a professional school for women that would train future social assistance workers. In 1929 Romania, she opened the first

School for Social Assistance, whose curriculum and overall educational aspirations combined a desire to empower women economically and professionally with a squarely eugenicist outlook on how to define social problems and their solutions. This path limited women's potential roles in politics, the economy, and society overall to a biopolitically defined set of attributes. The consequences of such alliances between women activists and the established nationalist mainstream proved self-limiting at best, and tragic at worst, especially during World War II.

During the first four decades of the twentieth century, women across the world became more interested in political activism either through enfranchisement or as part of other agendas that questioned the established power relations in politics on behalf of those who were marginalized. Whether or not they were successful in their quests for empowerment, women managed to introduce broader, though not always progressive, lasting changes into the political landscape of their countries. The presence of women in established political parties changed the tone and shape of political platforms and policies, as we can see in the case of the Soviet Union in the 1920s. For parties that aimed to develop new regimes, especially among recently liberated colonial territories, women helped broaden their appeal and boast their legitimacy in representing the interests of the population at large. Even when they were unsuccessful in gaining voting rights, women's insistence on being heard, seen, and counted as part of the citizenry helped introduce new issues in policy making, from education to workplace safety, that altered the meaning of social responsibility and especially state responsibility toward its citizens. In short, before World War II, from Latin America to Eastern Europe, women altered the vocabulary and scope of politics.

This generation of activists was disproportionately made up of well-educated women, which often corresponded to a position of social and often ethnic or racial privilege. Even the most radical anti-Establishment activists tended to have benefited from exceptional opportunities at home or through their families to pursue educational or professional ambitions rarely available to women at that time. Because of this, it is common to see such activists act out their sense of privilege, often as self-described leaders and spokeswomen for others more vulnerable (e.g., poor women, ethnic minorities) rather than as partners and supporters of such categories of people. Recently, historians have heaped increasing criticism against such limitations, holding women to a higher standard of ethics and especially humility than the male establishment. But if we look at the historical record in its own immediate context, such limitations notwithstanding, women seldom used their voice in politics for the sole purpose of individual self-empowerment. More often they aimed to alter the larger landscape on behalf of others. This can be seen in the unprecedented international networks women established over the twentieth century, as will be shown more fully in a separate section of this chapter.

FROM ENFRANCHISEMENT TO IDENTITY POLITICS

As women gained voting rights especially after World War II, their con-tributions to politics amplified. Historians often describe the decades after women's victories in gaining political rights as a period of stagna-tion or retreat. Seen from the perspective of a whole century and in a worldwide comparative context, these developments can be better de-scribed as realignment and deepening.

In countries where they gained the vote in the 1920s and '30s, women became more intensely interested in political participation and pushed for a distinct gender perspective on questions of citizenship rights and the responsibility of the state, especially as these women lived in the same countries that were hit hard by the Great Depression. This is the period that saw a growth in state programs for the poor alongside new protections for war widows and orphans. In the United States, the New Deal under the presidency of Franklin Delano Roosevelt (1882–1945) gen-erated new forms of state investment in the welfare of the general popu-lation.[40] Whether building highways, dams, or trails, the government provided new pathways for employment, though only for men. Women became more divided along class and race in their response to policies based on the ideology of the male breadwinner. Some reconciled them-selves to the solution and focused more on managing their households efficiently as a way to combat poverty, while others, and especially wom-en of color, did not have the option not to work. Through the leadership of activists like Mary McLeod Bethune (1875–1955), the Roosevelt admin-istration addressed more directly problems faced by African Americans and women in particular. Her work on the president's informal Black Cabinet and as a leader in the National Youth Administration enabled Bethune to bring national attention to the racial and gender elements of the Depression with specific, targeted policies.[41] Though she worked tire-lessly to forge alliances across the racial line and gained the support of Eleanor Roosevelt (1884–1962), such partnerships were rare at that time.

During the same period, other women began to focus their postsuf-frage activism on maternalist arguments about protection for or empow-erment of women as moral leaders and the mothers of future genera-tions.[42] Some, like Margaret Sanger (1879–1966), also an American, of-fered passionate arguments for women's further empowerment and in-dependence.[43] Others used the appeal to tradition and religious values to suggest women would become strong allies of the established order, if only they were given a chance to play a more active role in politics.[44]

The devastation of World War II and post-1945 political realignment along the Cold War divide provided new ground for women's greater participation in politics. In the process of decolonization that followed, they tried to become and sometimes succeeded in becoming partners in nationalist anticolonial activism and gaining full political rights often at the same time as the male population in the newly formed states.[45] Not all postcolonial African and Asian states saw the same pattern of women's increased access to politics; there are no consistent differences in terms of religion, ethnicity, or colonial legacies. In places like Mozambique and South Africa, by the end of the 1990s, women's participation in legislative politics was around 30 percent, approaching averages common in Western Europe and greatly surpassing the United States' 13 percent. In other places it remained lower.[46]

Women political activists in Africa found a welcoming space among the ranks of socialist or communist parties/movements, sometimes through unions they could finally join. As liberation movements grew in places like Zambia and South Africa, many gravitated toward the language of class oppression and reclaiming of economic power by workers. With small entrepreneurial classes in these countries other than the occupying white Europeans, liberal ideologies about ownership rights had limited traction here. Movements that focused on the value of the individual through the work he or she contributed to the common good had greater resonance.

In South Africa, starting in the 1950s, national organizations mobilized the energies of women who aimed to gain full equality in politics and eliminate social and economic discrimination. The Federation of South African Women, launched in 1954, helped organize a series of protests and other events that represented publicly their concern with government policies to limit the freedom of movement of the black population.[47] The policy of issuing passes as the only legitimate proof for using public spaces, and hence working, attending school, and using other public institutions vital to one's life, increasingly constrained the ability of black women to make a living. The active alliance between this women's organization and the African National Congress (ANC) provided a solid foundation for opposition to the racist regime.

When the government cracked down on antipass protests in 1960 and banned the ANC, the landscape of political activism shifted radically, and women had to take on new political roles, often by default. The jailing of thousands of mostly male leaders and activists silenced their voices. In the aftermath, wives, daughters, sisters, lovers, and mothers of these political prisoners picked up the mantle of anti-apartheid activism through the existing women's political networks. The increasingly brutal policies of the regime sent many into exile, where these women became voices of the anticolonial liberation movement, sometimes through word and sometimes through song. The impact of Miriam Makeba (1932–2008), for instance, will be further discussed in chapter 6 ("Culture").

Still, local activism continued in South Africa, with the radicalized student Black Consciousness Movement playing the most prominent role. Women were active and some took leadership roles in that organization. The meeting of South African women activists with radical black power groups while abroad in the United States led to the founding of the Black Women's Federation in 1975. It remained active for two years, at which point it was also banned. Until the return of the ANC to power and the defeat of apartheid in 1992, South African women managed to be most impactful from overseas, as Makeba was, or by sustaining the spirit of resistance through underground forms of dissent. One of the lasting legacies of this activism has been the commitment to workers' rights and to the eradication of discrimination against women in the workplace. Another specific aspect of women's political activism in South Africa during these periods of extreme state violence was the strong alliance women from various ethnic groups, such as Indian and Zulu, forged in fighting apartheid.[48]

In some places where postcolonial independence came sooner, women became involved in governance early on, sometimes rising to top levels of government service. From the short list of women who served as prime minister or president of a country in the twentieth century, the number of heads of state in postcolonial regimes is remarkably high, including India, Bangladesh, Sri Lanka, the Central African Republic, Rwanda, and Indonesia. Indian prime minister Indira Gandhi (1917–1984) was the first woman to serve as elected leader of a major country and emerging democracy. She served for three terms (1966–1977 and 1980–1984), the longest-serving elected leader of that country to date. She remains a controversial figure because of her policies of centralization, nepotism, war with Pakistan (1971), and tough stance against Sikh extremists, among many issues. Yet Gandhi remained popular both in and out of office. She was eliminated from the political scene in 1984 in a gruesome assassination at the hands of her personal bodyguards. Not a self-described feminist, Gandhi nonetheless offered strong support for women as the largest group of impoverished people in India. Her understanding of India's social problems was explicitly gendered while also paternalist, reflecting her elite status and high caste upbringing. Over her long career, Gandhi oversaw the expansion of state policies in both public and private life, with a specific focus on enhancing women's lives: "If the home is inadequate . . . then that country cannot have harmony. . . . That is why women's education is almost more important than the education of boys and men. . . . [Y]ou will make your own contribution to creating peace and harmony, to bringing beauty in the lives of our people and our country. I think this is the special responsibility of the women of India."[49] At the same time, Gandhi also supported intrusive birth control policies aimed primarily at poor and rural women.

In 1999 a BBC poll declared Indira Gandhi to be the woman of the millennium, ahead of British personalities such as Emmeline Pankhurst (1858–1928), Queen Elizabeth I (1533–1603), and Margaret Thatcher (1925–2013). One Pakistani journalist said, "She was a true feminist to the core, a woman of substance who helped the country through a testing phase, possessed all the virtues of a woman and fought valiantly for women's rights in a man's world."[50] Gandhi remained a model for women aspiring to political activism in postcolonial regimes. According to one scholar, to date, 74 percent of the women who have held top government positions are in the developing world.[51]

Starting in the 1960s, feminism became increasingly radicalized, as part of the wave of protest that young generations rode to challenge the powers of the Establishment, from militarism to racism and heterosexism. The resurgence of antiwar movements in Europe and North America was mirrored by the radicalization of student movements in South America, Africa, and Asia.[52] As a fast-growing proportion of the student population, women pushed their male colleagues, often unsuccessfully, to embrace partnership in protest. When it proved impossible to work together, women abandoned that strategy more readily than before and formed radicalized, separate political movements. Known as the "second wave" in Western Europe, North America, and Australia, this generation of feminists sought to close the gender gap in wages, access to professional ranks, legalization of birth control, and other forms of gender discrimination still allowed by democratic and autocratic regimes.[53] Many combined their struggle for women's political rights with activism around questions of heteronormativity, racism, aboriginal rights, and environmental justice.[54]

This was the generation of Americans Gloria Steinem (b. 1934), Ti-Grace Atkinson (b. 1938), Shulamith Firestone (1945–2012), and Kate Millett (1934–2017); Brazilian Lélia Gonzalez (1935–1994); Australian Germaine Greer (b. 1939); Japanese Mitsu Tanaka (b. 1945); and (West) German Petra Kelly (1947–1992). They came from very different backgrounds yet arrived at similar understandings that every aspect of their gender role, from working to giving birth, had important political elements: it fell on their shoulders to expose sexist practices around them as a form of social justice. Their challenges to entrenched patriarchy, racism, and heteronormativity met with enthusiastic support on the part of many women and men.

Yet they also became the object of much criticism about the radicalism and purported "unnaturalness" of the gender roles they imagined. American Phyllis Schlafly (1924–2016) became a household name only because of her relentless and ultimately successful attempt to defeat the equal rights amendment that had been a primary focus of the second-wave feminist movement in the United States. Margaret Thatcher, the first woman prime minister of Great Britain, was also unsympathetic to the quests of second-wave feminists, refusing to identify any women's problems as part of systemic forms of gender inequality. Instead, like other conservative critics, she blamed women: "I hope we shall see more and more women combining marriage and a career. Prejudice against this dual role is not confined to men. Far too often, I regret to say, it comes from our own sex."[55]

The most impressive political transformation effected by this generation of feminists was to render women's issues more visible through new means of organizing and communicating, some violent and others peaceful. These feminists made persuasive connections between explicit forms of political sexism and implicit aspects of continued discrimination against women. By combining women's issues with other societal problems, these activists captured the attention of the male establishment in ways that helped push forward solutions to political and social injustice. For instance, in the late-1960s antiwar demonstrations, many women connected military and domestic violence. Other women focused on the government's relative lack of support for women's education and the eradication of gender discrimination at work, at a time when a growing part of the government budget was dedicated to military operations overseas. By linking military affairs, government funding, and gender justice as part of connected political processes, this generation of feminists hoped to hold politicians accountable to a higher standard of commitment to women's full citizenship. They wanted politicians to look beyond laws and formal rules into the ethos of the age.[56]

The shifts described above in the language and reach of feminist discourses in political life can be seen in liberal western democracies, most prominently the United States, Australia, Britain, and France. Similar shifts from a rights-based to a broader discourse about gender justice in politics took place in Latin America and parts of Africa. In Latin America, women swelled the ranks of the leftist movements that criticized the impact of US policies on the continent, which had generated growing economic disparities in these societies. Activists like Gonzalez became vocal as leaders of a new wave of criticism against the established political system: she focused on the specific racist elements of the electoral system, the government policies on education and economic development, and welfare measures that were not helping women of color, the most vulnerable population.[57]

Feminists of this generation provided visible role models and networks of solidarity for women whose activism rose out of tragic circumstances, rather than personal radical beliefs. The Mothers of the Plaza de Mayo became a force in Argentine politics in 1977 as a desperate response to the disappearance of numerous young people at the hands of the military junta dictatorship that had recently taken over. The *madres* were not self-styled radicals; they were distressed mothers looking for their children. Their political action consisted of peaceful rallies held at the centrally located Plaza de Mayo in Buenos Aires: the mothers walked around it with white scarves on their heads, inscribed with the names of the disappeared.[58] The ruthless response of the junta, which abducted several mothers, including the group's leader, Azucena Villaflor

(1924–1977), brought increased international pressure and sympathy for the movement. Maternalism and pious Catholicism could become the source of a human rights campaign that could help bring down the military junta and demand an end to autocratic rule. The movement inspired women activists around the world, giving rise to other "Women in Black" groups in states with military violence occurring daily, such as Israel (1988) and Serbia (1991).[59]

In the 1960s, feminist activists became pioneering leaders in environmental politics in many countries, as the antinuclear and peace movements of the 1960s morphed into a movement focused on the danger of the reckless depletion of the world's natural resources. The idea of generating political movements that focused on the relationship between humans and their environment was not new, but the impetus and people leading the movement were of a new kind. In industrialized countries, women as caretakers saw some of the most intimate results of unregulated pollution, and they stood up for their families in places like Niagara Falls, where the Love Canal landfill led to disastrous effects for the local inhabitants. In developing countries, women worked primarily in agriculture and observed their environment become depleted of its natural resources, even as the local communities remained poor. During this period, with increased access to education and international networks of support, indigenous women on every continent began to call attention to environmental problems.

Among these leaders, Wangari Maathai (1940–2011) best embodies the combined struggle for protecting environmental resources with empowering women as responsible guardians of these vulnerable assets.[60] In 1977, working as a grassroots activist through the National Council of Women of Kenya, Maathai created the Green Belt Movement, which has sought to prevent soil erosion and deforestation through intensive campaigns for planting trees. She later founded the first environmentalist party in Kenya (2003). Though she was the object of discrimination and intimidation by many in the political leadership in Kenya, Maathai managed these stormy waters with a steadfast dedication that won her great acclaim and long-lasting impact in environmental and women's rights activism internationally.[61] In 2004, after more than fifty million trees were planted through her efforts at the head of the Green Belt Movement, Maathai became the first African woman to receive the Nobel Peace Prize and the first person to be recognized thus for environmental activism.

WOMEN AND THE LAW: FROM OBJECTS TO FRAMERS

In the twentieth century, political institutions and policies have come to be more actively shaped not only by politicians, but also by lawyers and judges, especially as constitutional regimes came to power in various corners of the world.[62] During this period, women moved from being primarily objects of legal restrictions to becoming students of law, legal thinkers, and eventually practitioners alongside men. Their voices have helped reshape concepts of justice both in theory and in practice, especially with regard to gender discrimination. The world is far from equitable in terms of women making it to the top of this field, but it has been changed radically through the participation of women in the legal profession.[63]

At the beginning of the twentieth century, women were not allowed to sit for the bar exam in any country around the world, but they could attend law classes in some places, primarily in Europe and North America. Within two decades, professional organizations began to open up to women in a handful of countries on those same continents, and more women became interested in studying law and challenging the interdictions placed against their membership in the profession. By the middle of the twentieth century, however, women were studying for law degrees and entering the ranks of the legal profession on every continent. Obstacles remained in terms of legal restrictions against married women working (especially in the Middle East) and the existence of preferential treatment for men with regard to moving up the professional ladder in countries where women could practice law. Still, by the 1970s we begin to see women partners at top-notch firms, women working as federal judges, women hired as tenure-track professors in law schools, and women as part of the law-enforcement apparatus. These changes took place on every continent.

The political impact of women's entry into the legal profession depended a great deal on the local context in which they lived, and out of this great diversity I provide several evocative examples from different parts of the world. In the next section I discuss the impact of women in matters of international law and human rights, which has been long-lasting and has reached into every corner of the world. In this section I focus primarily on domestic changes brought about by women's participation in shaping the law.

In the United States, even before they were allowed to attend law schools and take the bar exam, women engaged in the study of law played an important role in transforming the practice of legal aid for the poor.[64] Starting during the Civil War and then over the next half century, organizations such as the Working Women's Protective Union and later the Chicago Legal Aid Society came together to provide information and eventually more substantive support for poor people in cases of abuse by spouses, employers, or other people. The vast majority of the cases involved poor women, often migrants and women of color, who sought solutions for their destitute situations, which often derived from abusive husbands who withheld financial support or employers who either did not pay their wages or fired them without proper cause.

Many of these organizations were founded and staffed primarily by women with some legal formal and informal education, including those who thought of themselves as social workers.[65] As legal aid societies began growing during the 1910s, and especially with the coming of the Great Depression, they also became differentiated by gender. Organizations dominated by male lawyers who had passed the bar became more specialized in the types of cases they took on and the sort of advice they provided, steering clear of empathetic, directive social aid work. Yet organizations in which women remained in leadership positions continued the intertwined work of legal and social aid. For instance, the Chicago Legal Aid Society provided legal advice about rights and strategies to secure a positive outcome for women who sought a divorce, while it also assisted the same clients in procuring food and other necessary basics.[66] What distinguished these approaches was their focus on finding solutions to the needs of the poor and seeking to eliminate forms of abuse system-wide into the future, rather than simply practicing law for a specific category of clients.

Such legal aid organizations established the foundations for future developments in legal training and criminal justice programs as well as for the rise of new social welfare programs, especially in the 1930s. Their impact on economic life, social relations, and culture will be discussed in greater detail in subsequent chapters. The impact of these developments in politics has to do with the pragmatic problem-solving attitude of many of these organizations as platforms for women reformers on behalf of poor women and, more broadly, impoverished populations. Women's marginal position in the law profession before the 1920s and their exclusion from full political rights provided a context of frustration and at the same time pushed many to become more creative in their quest to impact law practice and lawmaking.

As they gained voting rights and the ability to join the ranks of professional lawyers, women took these experiences with originality, creativity, and pragmatic problem-solving toward new areas of lawmaking and criminal justice. Domestic abuse became an important area of legal protection largely because of the work done by such women lawyers. Laws and policies that focused on identifying and later eliminating gender, race, and sexual discrimination in the workplace also grew out of these early efforts by women.

In terms of appointments as judges, the 1970s saw significant expansion in women's participation at higher levels of the court system across the world.[67] In 1970 Margarita Argúas (1902–1986) became the first woman appointed to the Supreme Court of Argentina, more than a decade before Sandra Day O'Connor (b. 1930) became the first female appointee to the US Supreme Court. By 2010 women constituted 28 percent of the judiciary appointments in Sub-Saharan Africa, 30 percent of the federal appointments in the United States, and more than 40 percent of the judges in the former Soviet bloc and Soviet central Asia. Legal scholars still disagree over the exact impact of these rising numbers in reshaping the quality and direction of how laws are applied in countries around the world.[68] But there is greater agreement that women judges are perceived as less corruptible than their male counterparts. From Ghana to Romania, this has led to the appointment of women judges to important positions tied to curbing political corruption.[69] There is also growing consensus that women's presence in the judiciary has enhanced access to the court system and to legal protection for vulnerable populations (e.g., women, children, ethnic and religious minorities).[70] Many scholars also agree that women jurists "apply a more interdisciplinary approach to researching a decision, not only relying on their professional techniques, but integrating to a greater extent social workers and other family experts in their work."[71] In Muslim countries, the growing presence of women judges has provided greater equity in communities where secular and religious courts coexist.[72] Women often prefer to be represented by female lawyers and come before a female judge as a means to curb the position taken by Islamic courts, especially on matters of divorce and property. In addition, from Europe to Latin America, cases involving sexual harassment, domestic violence, and other forms of gender discrimination have become the focus of increasing activity by the highest courts. Issues that used to be relegated to the private sphere have become part of the public, and especially legal, discourse and policy making. Women experts in the law have encouraged and enabled the state to become more present and gain greater powers in interpersonal relations.

WOMEN AND INTERNATIONAL POLITICAL ACTIVITIES

Looking back over the twentieth century to understand the impact of women's international activism, we can start with one statistic: 15.5 percent of the Nobel Peace Prize laureates are women, the most balanced gender ratio among all Nobel Prize recipients. It is also the most ethnically and regionally diverse set of winners among all categories of the prize. The female laureates have seldom held political office (Maathai was one of the few elected women politicians to do so) by contrast with their male counterparts, most of whom have been individuals in positions of high political power. Seen through this perspective, the percentage of women awarded the Nobel Peace Prize becomes more impressive. It suggests that women have managed to impact the quest for peace in international relations regardless of their ability to close the political gender gap inside their own countries.

Behind these metrics are transnational networks of cooperation among women's organizations that started to develop at the beginning of the twentieth century.[73] It is impossible to understand the global impact of women's political activism in the twentieth century without looking into the transnational networks that brought women together, helped them understand local conditions in a larger international context, enabled them to gain leverage internally, and sometimes led to women reshaping international relations very directly. Women were pioneers in building networks for peace and international stability as a counterbalance to the warmongering that embroiled much of the world before 1950. Over the twentieth century they became central architects in introducing human rights as an important area of international policy making, and have brought questions of social justice to the attention of diplomats and state leaders. Overall, women's transnational networks were central to introducing peace as a lasting goal for humanity into international institutions such as the League of Nations and later the United Nations.

The best known of these networks are the International Congress of Women (ICW), established in the United States by Susan B. Anthony (1820–1906) and Elizabeth Cady Stanton (1815–1902) in 1888; the International Alliance of Women (IAW; initially named International Woman Suffrage Alliance), an ICW breakaway network established in 1899 by two German feminists to bring together women interested strictly in suffrage rights; the Women's International League for Peace and Freedom (WILPF), started during World War I (1915) at the initiative of Dutch feminist Aletta Jacobs (1854–1929) to focus on ending the war through peaceful means; and the Women's International Democratic Federation (WIDF), established in 1945 in Paris at the end of World War II to focus on promoting women's rights and peace.[74] Many other regionally or culturally defined (by religion, for instance) transnational networks developed alongside or in response to these groups, such as the Pan-Pacific and Southeast Asia Women's Association, the International Congress of Working Women, and B'nai B'rith Women.

Initially, these networks were dominated by European, North American, and British Commonwealth women of the same elite and educated background as the pioneering feminists discussed earlier in this chapter. The ICW attracted less radical activists than the other networks, which also tended to have a more diverse regional makeup, inclusive of feminists from Asia, Latin America, and Africa. While they occasionally cooperated, these organizations also developed rivalries connected to ideology, class, and imperialism, especially during the increasingly polarized environment of the Cold War.[75] Overall, these divisions are a sign of the complexity, vigor, and lasting impact of women's international activism.

Before the League of Nations became a subject of discussion among the leading politicians in the warring countries, under Jane Addams's leadership (as of 1915) the ICW adopted a resolution that called for the establishment of a Society of Nations, an international body to oversee the peaceful resolution of all international conflicts. Publicized during an

ICW congress held at The Hague in 1915, the document repeatedly connected women's suffrage to building a lasting peace. It defined women's full political rights as a condition sine qua non for international peace: "in the interests of lasting peace and civilization the Conference which shall frame the Peace settlement after the war should pass a resolution affirming the need in all countries of extending the parliamentary franchise to women."[76] Finally, the resolutions adopted at this historic congress included a definition of self-determination that connected sovereignty inextricably to universal suffrage.

At Versailles, Addams reiterated these principles on behalf of the ICW with all the participants she was able to meet, including Woodrow Wilson.[77] As the Covenant of the League of Nations was being negotiated, questions about a community's right to self-determination in terms of joining another state or forming its own came to the fore. Women activists pressed the negotiators for the participation of women, regardless of their suffrage rights at that time, in deciding the fate of all the territories under discussion. And, indeed, women were empowered to vote in all the plebiscites held in the aftermath of World War I, helping determine the future of their homelands in terms of sovereignty, from Lithuania to Peru.[78] As it turned out, women international activists did not articulate a separate vision from the male political establishment about the future of European colonies in Africa, Asia, and the Middle East.[79]

When the League of Nations was created in 1920, women's international organizations had already formulated a series of proposals for the need to use it to bring attention to women's and children's rights. There wasn't unanimity as to what the priorities would be. But the presence of women from across the world in these discussions succeeded in giving rise to a number of League sections that included women and provided a permanent platform for continuing to address questions of gender inequality in the global context. On bodies such as the Women's Consultative Committee on Nationality and the Advisory Committee on the Traffic in Women and Children, women were present both as policy makers as well as objects of international policy on matters of citizenship rights, travel restrictions, labor, and other political issues.

The wide impact of such activities can be gleaned from the negotiations they engendered among member states. As international law began to take shape, questions about the treatment of individual citizens across borders came to be regulated through the League. The Women's Consultative Committee on Nationality focused on the status of women as citizens when they married a man with a different citizenship from theirs. Such marriages were not new to the twentieth century. However, the notion that women's position needed to be discussed both at the international level and through an organization that hoped to bind all sovereign states to a common standard was in fact unprecedented. Equally unprecedented was the participation of women themselves in developing such policies, even when internal laws did not allow them to participate directly in developing national policies due to their lack of voting rights.

Furthermore, the Advisory Committee on the Traffic in Women and Children opened up a series of other important strands of international policy making that were essentially bound to gendered assumptions about the rights of individuals; the freedom to travel across borders; and the responsibilities of the state toward individual citizens. Women had been trafficked throughout history, but starting in the late nineteenth century, a variety of temperance and other women's movements, especially in North America and Great Britain, had advocated relentlessly for special legislation and law enforcement measures to protect women from abuse by sexual entrepreneurs.[80] What counted as abuse, what counted as consent, and who the sexual entrepreneurs (as opposed to the victims) were in these networks was a matter of great debate among social reformers and politicians.

The League's Advisory Committee on the Traffic in Women and Children shifted these debates to a greater level of visibility both internally and internationally, and helped define an international set of standards and policies that subsequently shaped internal policies and international cooperation among member states in terms of catching and punishing abusers. Some pressure to establish such policies came from racist fears of contamination, which were publicized aggressively by eugenicists (men and occasionally women) in the United States and European states. But other members of the Advisory Committee, like Alma Sundquist (1872–1940) of Sweden, were more interested in protecting women themselves and disseminating better knowledge about the spread of venereal disease. In addition, Sundquist's work for the League of Nations linked concerns regarding human trafficking to questions about women's rights and protection as workers. As an officer of the International Congress of Working Women, she advocated with the International Labour Organization (ILO) on behalf of working women's rights, such as better wages and working conditions, pushing a more overtly gendered consideration in labor protection.

After the founding of the League of Nations, the ICW, IAW, and WILPF became particularly important in providing support for feminists across the world, especially those who entwined their struggle for female suffrage with anti-imperial or anticolonial nationalism. Women like the Romanian nationalist feminist Alexandrina Cantacuzino (1876–1944) used their international connections and prominence in the League and the ICW, where Cantacuzino acted as a vice president from 1925 to 1936, to promote their vision of rights for women both internationally and at home. The Romanian press was more willing to comment favorably on Cantacuzino's struggle for female enfranchisement when her activities involved speaking before the League of Nations on behalf of women's issues or when she participated in international ICW conferences. In turn, she used this publicity to press the political elites to consider women as potential prominent allies in maintaining regional stability, through the establishment in 1923 of the Little Entente of Women, which aimed to promote support for and good relations among feminists in Eastern Europe.[81]

Women's international activism continued to flourish and diversify throughout the 1920s and into the 1930s, even as women's organizations were internally reevaluating their goals and strategies, especially as more countries granted women the vote. It was also clear that increasing nationalism and militarism pushed questions about women's rights as citizens in a different direction, even as the Great Depression brought into renewed focus poverty and unemployment in connection to familial welfare. But in the longer run, social welfare as a matter of both internal policy making and a concern of inter-state relations became a permanent feature of international relations, and it expanded significantly especially in the second half of the century, with the establishment of the United Nations.[82]

Preventing a repeat of the atrocities of World War II became a question of intense international negotiation starting in 1945; it led to creating an institution that would provide stronger limitations against international violence as well as better standards and greater incentives for international cooperation than the League of Nations. While the ability of the United Nations to live up to these high hopes has come under criticism everywhere in the world,[83] the UN has had a lasting and profound impact on bringing attention to gendered forms of abuse and has helped define human rights and related policies across the world.

The work of women through the UN to reduce gendered forms of injustice was crucial especially in the area of human rights, and it started with the Universal Declaration of Human Rights.[84] Although Eleanor Roosevelt chaired the Human Rights Commission, she was not a proponent of explicitly including references to women in the Declaration. She "personally understood 'all men' to include everyone, male or female."[85] Roosevelt had the difficult role of reconciling the vastly different outlooks of the other members of the commission, whose preoccupations ranged from representing the Soviet version of protection for workers to protection for religious difference as expressed in Islamic law and custom. Equally difficult, though ultimately not insurmountable, was the pressure Roosevelt felt in terms of representing the huge diversity of women's interests through the framing of this document: "I knew that as the only woman on the delegation I was not very welcome. Moreover, if I failed to be a useful member, it would not be considered merely that I as an individual had failed, but that all women had failed, and there would be little chance for others to serve in the near future."[86]

In the end, the explicit references to women in the Declaration adopted in 1948, together with equally explicit references to gender equality in terms of marriage and divorce, were a result of pressures coming from the Indian feminist Hansa Mehta (1897–1995), who warned her colleagues on the Commission that "the words *all men* would be construed literally in some countries so as to exclude women."[87] In addition, the Soviet observers on the Commission also pushed strenuously for the explicit reference "to women's equality with men."[88] The Declaration brought gender inequality to global visibility and defined it as a fundamental distinction in both how individuals come to act and how they need to be protected by sovereign states. The Charter and the international order profoundly changed the way in which all subsequent debates about women's rights have proceeded until today. And since the Declaration developed new language and standards for why human rights should be a core concern of international relations, this document became a founding text in the international arena, from international law to bilateral state relations and nongovernmental international activism.

The role of the UN in maintaining useful data, advocating for new forms of protection for women, and overall bringing in gender considerations in all areas of international policy making cannot be overestimated. While countries have not often agreed on specific recommendations, the UN has managed to at least bring attention to and put pressure on policy makers to address gender injustice. One powerful example will serve to show the long-term impact of the UN on rendering gender central to international conflict resolution. During the unfolding of the Yugoslav Wars of the 1990s, the UN created an International Criminal Court (ICC) that investigated war crimes and crimes against humanity perpetrated by various warring factions. As the ICC looked into rapes and other forms of sexual violence that came into evidence, the court helped reshape the meaning of crimes against humanity to include such actions. Subsequently, the UN Security Council passed Resolution 1820 (2008), which provides new standards in this regard: "rape and other forms of sexual violence can constitute a war crime, a crime against humanity, or a constitutive act with respect to genocide."[89] The resolution has not had the power to change the gendered aspects of military aggression by itself. However, it enabled activists and political representatives of member states to introduce these new norms in how they attempt to eliminate sexual violence, from Rwanda to Guantanamo.

By the beginning of the twenty-first century, those who aim to win political contests in parliamentary systems know they need to think about gender disparities with regard to support for military action. In the United States, there is more than a twelve-point spread between women's (46.8 percent) and men's (59 percent) support for international state-sponsored violence.[90] The scholarship on gender and international security has shown that historically women have tended to disapprove of military action: "when we moved from the abstract to the concrete—from hypothetical wars to the Gulf War—the distance separating women and men grew, and on every measure, women reacted more negatively."[91] The notable exceptions to this attitude are cases of humanitarian intervention, a new category of militarism introduced through the auspices of the United Nations and the Universal Declaration of Human Rights.[92] In the case of atrocities among civilians, women have been more sympathetic toward military interventions.

WHAT DIFFERENCE DOES GENDER MAKE?

It is impossible to provide a precise quantitative answer to this question at present, primarily because there is no consensus over what to measure exactly and how to measure it. And yet there is ample evidence for stating that politics today, both internally and internationally, looks and acts significantly different than it did in 1900 greatly because of the challenges posed by women since then. This is not to say that men have not played important roles during this same period. They have also reframed what both "politics" and "gender in politics" mean, but more consistently as a response to the unprecedented participation of women in politics. Adolf Hitler, Lenin, Mao Zedong, Nelson Mandela, and countless other male political leaders built their ideas, movements, and actions partly in response to the entry of women into the political imagination of the time. This is also an unprecedented development in the political history of the twentieth century, viewed in the context of all the wars fought and genocidal actions of various political regimes during this period.

* * *

This chapter has highlighted the innovations and long-term changes that women helped introduce in politics across the world since 1900. In addition to the obvious and essential issue of doubling the size of the enfranchised citizenry, women's voices as citizens and politicians have brought greater variety in the themes, language, style, and scope of political action. Most important among these changes are the development of social welfare institutions and practices as core components of state responsibility. Alongside them are the feminist challenges against gender inequality, and the insistence that the state include gender among the forms of identity protected against discrimination, alongside race, ethnicity, and religion. The politicization of motherhood as "maternalism" has also been an important outcome of women's participation in politics, with sometimes self-limiting results, as with eugenics, and other times greater political outcomes, as with the Mothers of the Plaza de Mayo. In addition, women played foundational and leading roles in both minority/aboriginal rights movements and environmental activism, both political creations of the twentieth century that have become increasingly important in the present. Finally, the peace and antimilitarist movements in the twentieth century cannot be understood without women's participation in them from the movements' beginnings up to the present.

NOTES

1. Virginia Woolf, *Three Guineas* (New York: Harbinger, 1963), 108.
2. I take participation in parliamentary regime as a fundamental form of political activity, regardless of the ideological orientation of that regime or the ability of the individual voter or politician to effectively shape policy. This is not to discount critiques of suffragism as shortsighted in terms of eliminating gender inequalities. Rather, it is a baseline, especially since by the end of World War I universal male suffrage was a reality in most territories that did not live under direct colonial/imperial rule.
3. Full electoral equality around the globe still eludes us, as women can only vote in certain elections—for instance, only in local contests in Saudi Arabia—while men have the right to vote in all elections. In 2016 women were still unable to pass their citizenship to their children in twenty-seven countries around the world, most of them predominantly or exclusively Muslim. See UN High Commissioner for Refugees, "Background Note on Gender Equality, Nationality Laws and Statelessness 2016," accessed August 17, 2017, http://www.refworld.org/docid/56de83ca4.html.
4. See statistics by the Inter-Parliamentary Union, accessed August 17, 2017, http://www.ipu.org/wmn-e/world.htm. I quote the regional averages for the single house or lower house, higher than those in the upper house or senate. In the following sentences I describe regions as defined in this document.
5. Janine Mossuz-Lavau, "Les femmes et le pouvoir exécutif depuis 1981: La France au regard du monde," *Histoire@Politique* 1, no. 1 (2007), http://www.cairn.info/revue-histoire-politique-2007-1-page-5.htm.
6. Ibid.; see also World Bank, "Proportion of Seats Held by Women in National Parliaments," accessed September 29, 2017, http://data.worldbank.org/indicator/SG.GEN.PARL.ZS. I offer this list to suggest the phenomenon is present on every continent, in both the developed and developing worlds, as well as in states with very different religious and ideological electoral traditions.
7. On Zetian Wu, see Christopher Beckwith, *Empires of the Silk Road: A History of Central Eurasia from the Bronze Age to the Present* (Princeton, NJ: Princeton University Press, 2009); on Catherine the Great, see John T. Alexander, *Catherine the Great: Life and Legend* (New York: Oxford University Press, 1988). Although in some languages (most relevant for this book are Mandarin, Japanese, Korean, and Hungarian) the family name is traditionally placed before that person's individual name, I have opted for the first name then surname order.
8. Elizabeth Bathory (1560–1614), the Hungarian noblewoman with a penchant for torture, captured the attention of many writers across time as a symbol of cruelty. Isabella of Castile (1451–1504) has also been described as a partner in cruelty to her husband, Philip, in their relentless pursuit of "purifying" the country of non-Catholics, especially Jews, with the help of the Catholic Inquisition.
9. Karen Offen, ed., *Globalizing Feminisms, 1789–1945* (New York: Routledge, 2010).
10. Seth Koven and Sonya Michel, "Womanly Duties: Maternalist Politics and the Origins of Welfare States in France, Germany, Great Britain, and the United States, 1880–1920," *American Historical Review* 95, no. 4 (October 1990): 1076–1108; Maroula Joannou and June Purvis, eds., *The Women's Suffrage Movement: New Feminist Perspectives* (Manchester: Manchester University Press, 1998).
11. Eileen Boris and A. Orleck, "Feminism and the Labor Movement: A Century of Collaboration and Conflict," *New Labor Forum* 20 (Winter 2011): 33–41; Paul Avrich and Karen Avrich, *Sasha and Emma: The Anarchist Odyssey of Alexander Berkman and*

Emma Goldman (Cambridge: Belknap, 2012); Sheila Rowbotham, *Women in Movement: Feminism and Social Action* (London: Routledge, 1992).

12. For Kenya, see Winnie Kabintie, "Women in Politics in Kenya: Hurdles and 'Gender Parity,'" accessed August 17, 2017, http://www.kenyaforum.net/2012/10/26/women-in-politics-in-kenya-hurdles-and-%E2%80%98gender-parity%E2%80%99, and Aili Mari Tripp et al., eds., *African Women's Movements: Transforming Political Landscapes* (New York: Cambridge University Press, 2009); for Romania, see Mihaela Miroiu, "On Women, Feminism, and Democracy," in *Post-Communist Romania at Twenty-Five: Linking Past, Present, and Future*, ed. Lavinia Stan and Diane Vancea (Lanham, MD: Lexington Books, 2015), 87–110.

13. August Bebel, *Woman and Socialism* (1879; repr. New York: Socialist Literature, 1910); Friedrich Engels, *The Origin of the Family, Private Property and the State* (Chicago: Charles H. Kerr, 1902).

14. Scholars have alternately identified Kollontai as either a socialist or a communist. Based on her own writings (*The Autobiography of a Sexually Emancipated Communist Woman*) and her official positions as part of a communist government, I identify Kollontai as a communist.

15. Elizabeth A. Wood, *The Baba and the Comrade: Gender and Politics in Revolutionary Russia* (Bloomington: Indiana University Press, 1997).

16. Barbara Clements, "Bolshevik Women and the Utopianism of the Zhenotdel," *Slavic Review* 51, no. 3 (Autumn 1992): 485–96.

17. Ibid.

18. Wood, *Baba and the Comrade*.

19. Maria Bucur and Mihaela Miroiu, *Birth of Democratic Citizenship: Women in Modern Romania* (Bloomington: Indiana University Press, 2018).

20. See the Florence Luscomb papers at the Schlesinger Library, Radcliffe Institute, Harvard University. I want to thank the archivists at the Schlesinger Library for their generous help with my research.

21. Sharon Hartman Strom, *Political Woman: Florence Luscomb and the Legacy of Radical Reform* (Philadelphia: Temple University Press, 2001).

22. Sheila Rowbotham, *A Century of Women: The History of Women in Britain and the United States in the Twentieth Century* (New York: Verso, 2012).

23. Strom, *Political Woman*.

24. Jane Carey and Claire McLisky, eds., *Creating White Australia* (Sydney: Sydney University Press, 2009).

25. Fiona Paisley, "'Unnecessary Crimes and Tragedies': Race, Gender and Sexuality in Australian Policies of Aboriginal Child Removal," in *Gender, Sexuality and Colonial Modernities*, ed. Antoinette Burton (New York: Routledge, 2005), 135–48.

26. Katherine M. Marino, "Transnational Pan-American Feminism: The Friendship of Bertha Lutz and Mary Wilhelmine Williams, 1926–1944," *Journal of Women's History* 26, no. 2 (2014): 63–87.

27. Ellen DuBois, "Woman Suffrage: The View from the Pacific," *Pacific Historical Review* 69, no. 4 (November 2000): 539–51.

28. Margot Badran, "Dual Liberation: Feminism and Nationalism in Egypt, 1870s–1925," *Feminist Issues* 8, no. 1 (1988): 16.

29. Ibid.

30. Ibid.

31. Cynthia Nelson, *Doria Shafik, Egyptian Feminist: A Woman Apart* (Cairo: American University in Cairo Press, 2015).

32. Ibid.

33. On the issue of women's participation in referendums about irredenta after World War I, see also the section on "Women and International Political Activities" in this chapter.

34. Oana Sînziana Păltineanu, "Converging Suffrage Politics: The Romanian Women's Movement in Hungary and Its Allies before World War I," *Aspasia* 9 (2015): 44–64.

35. Maria Bucur, "Gender and Fascism in Interwar Romania," in *Women, Gender and the Extreme Right in Europe*, ed. Kevin Passmore (Manchester: Manchester University Press, 2003), 58–79.

36. On Manuilă's thoughts on women's vote, see Veturia Manuilă, "Din drumul de o sută de ani spre emanciparea femeii române," accessed August 17, 2017, http://www.alternativaonline.ca/VeturiaManuila.html. On her links with the eugenicist movement, see Maria Bucur, *Eugenics and Modernization in Interwar Romania* (Pittsburgh: Pittsburgh University Press, 2002).

37. Women who had a high school education, were older than thirty, and were married were able to vote in local elections after 1929. The percentage of women who qualified under these rules in a country where the rate of illiteracy for women was still more than 50 percent can only be assumed to be tiny. More importantly, there were no educational and marital restrictions placed on men, who could start participating in elections and vote at the age of twenty-one.

38. Bucur, *Eugenics and Modernization*; Maria Bucur, "In Praise of Wellborn Mothers: On Eugenics and Gender Roles in Interwar Romania," *East European Politics and Societies* 9, no. 1 (Winter 1995): 123–42.

39. Susanne Klausen and Alison Bashford, "Fertility Control: Eugenics, Neo-Malthusianism, and Feminism," in *The Oxford Handbook of the History of Eugenics*, ed. Alison Bashford and Philippa Levine (Oxford: Oxford University Press, 2010), 98–115.

40. Susan Ware, *Beyond Suffrage: Women in the New Deal* (Cambridge, MA: Harvard University Press, 1987).

41. Joyce A. Hanson, *Mary McLeod Bethune and Black Women's Political Activism* (Columbia: University of Missouri Press, 2003).

42. Koven and Michel, "Womanly Duties."

43. Jean H. Baker, *Margaret Sanger: A Life of Passion* (New York: Hill and Wang, 2011).

44. Klausen and Bashford, "Fertility Control"; Maria Bucur, "Remapping the Historiography of Modernization and State-Building in Southeastern Europe through Hygiene, Health and Eugenics," in *Health, Hygiene and Eugenics in Southeastern Europe to 1945*, ed. Marius Turda et al. (Budapest: Central European University Press, 2011), 427–46.

45. Tripp et al., eds., *African Women's Movements*.

46. "Proportion of Seats Held by Women in National Parliaments," accessed August 17, 2017, http://data.worldbank.org/indicator/SG.GEN.PARL.ZS?page=3.

47. Shireen Hassim, *Women's Organizations and Democracy in South Africa: Contesting Authority* (Madison: University of Wisconsin Press, 2005).

48. Ibid.

49. Indira Gandhi, "What Educated Women Can Do," speech delivered at the Golden Jubilee Celebrations of the Indraprastha College for Women, New Delhi, November 23, 1974, accessed August 17, 2017, http://www.edchange.org/multicultural/speeches/indira_gandhi_educated.html.

50. "Indira Gandhi 'Greatest Woman,'" BBC, December 1, 1999, accessed August 17, 2017, http://news.bbc.co.uk/2/hi/543743.stm, quote by Pakistani journalist Khalil Ahmed.

51. Karen O'Connor, ed., *Gender and Women's Leadership: A Reference Handbook* (New York: Sage, 2010), 1:324.

52. George N. Katsiaficas, *The Imagination of the New Left: A Global Analysis of 1968* (Boston: South End Press, 1999).

53. I use the term "second wave" sparingly, since the metaphor of the first, second, and third waves has been closely connected to the North American context where it emerged. From a global perspective, feminism has seen many more waves, each with its own periodization and particularities connected more closely to the immediate or regional context than to the ideologies of the various waves of feminism in North America. For a longer critique of the terminology, see Nancy A. Hewitt, *No Permanent Waves: Recasting Histories of U.S. Feminism* (New Brunswick, NJ: Rutgers University

Press, 2010); Kathleen A. Laughlin et al., "Is It Time to Jump Ship? Historians Rethink the Waves Metaphor," *Feminist Formations* 22, no. 1 (Spring 2010): 76–135.

54. Stephanie Gilmore, ed., *Feminist Coalitions: Historical Perspectives on Second-Wave Feminism in the United States* (Urbana: University of Illinois Press, 2008).

55. Margaret Thatcher, "Wake Up, Women!" *Sunday Graphic*, February 17, 1952, accessed August 17, 2017, http://www.margaretthatcher.org/document/100936.

56. Harriet Hyman Alonso, *Peace as a Women's Issue: A History of the U.S. Movement for World Peace and Women's Rights* (Syracuse, NY: Syracuse University Press, 1993).

57. Lélia Gonzalez, *Women Organizing for Change: Confronting Crisis in Latin America* (Rome: Isis International, 1988).

58. Jane Slaughter and Melissa K. Bokovoy, *Sharing the Stage: Biography and Gender in Western Civilization* (Belmont, CA: Wadsworth Publishing, 2008), vol. 2, chapter 14; Antonius Robben, *The Ethnography of Political Violence: Political Violence and Trauma in Argentina* (Philadelphia: University of Pennsylvania Press, 2007), chapter 13.

59. "Women in Black," accessed August 17, 2017, http://womeninblack.org.

60. Nanjala Nyabola, "Wangari Maathai Was Not a Good Woman. Kenya Needs More of Them," *African Arguments*, October 6, 2015, accessed August 17, 2017, http://africanarguments.org/2015/10/06/wangari-maathai-was-not-a-good-woman-kenya-needs-many-more-of-them. The punchy title evokes the line made famous by the US historian Laurel Thatcher Ulrich, "well-behaved women seldom make history," in "Vertuous Women Found: New England Ministerial Literature, 1668–1735," *American Quarterly* 28, No. 1 (Spring 1976): 20.

61. Wangari Maathai, *Unbowed: A Memoir* (New York: Random House, 2006).

62. Though in essence a professional field, the law is an area so closely tied to the exercise of political power that I include the discussion in this section. Many of the insights provided here are parts of the story about knowledge making, which I develop in a separate chapter.

63. Hannah Brenner, "Expanding the Pathways to Gender Equality in the Legal Profession," *Legal Ethics* 17, no. 261 (2014): 261–80.

64. Felice Batlan, "Legal Aid, Women Lay Lawyers, and the Rewriting of History, 1863–1930," in *Feminist Legal History: Essays on Women and Law*, ed. Tracy Thomas and Tracey Boisseau (New York: New York University Press, 2011), 173–88.

65. Ibid., 185.

66. Ibid.

67. Gretchen Bauer and Josephine Dawuni, eds., *Gender and the Judiciary in Africa: From Obscurity to Parity?* (New York: Routledge, 2016), 7.

68. "Gender and Judging," special issue, *International Journal of the Legal Profession* 15, nos. 1–2 (March–July 2008).

69. For Ghana, see Bauer and Dawuni, eds., *Gender and the Judiciary in Africa*; for Romania, see Christopher Condon and George Parker, "Justice Minister's Corruption Crusade Puts Romania Back on Road to EU," *Financial Times*, May 15, 2006, accessed August 17, 2017, http://www.ft.com/intl/cms/s/0/5a05653a-e3af-11da-a015-0000779e2340.html#axzz3xipVz63X (site discontinued).

70. Ethan Michelson, "Women in the Legal Profession, 1970–2010: A Study of the Global Supply of Lawyers," *Indiana Journal of Global Legal Studies* 20, no. 2 (2013), 1103–4.

71. Ulrike Schultz and Gisela Shaw, "Editorial: Gender and Judging," *International Journal of the Legal Profession* 15, nos. 1–2 (March–July 2008): 6.

72. Margot Badran, ed., *Gender and Islam in Africa: Rights, Sexuality, and Law* (Washington, DC: Woodrow Wilson Center Press; Stanford, CA: Stanford University Press, 2011).

73. Leila Rupp, *Worlds of Women: The Making of an International Women's Movement* (Princeton, NJ: Princeton University Press, 1997).

74. Ibid.

75. Ibid.

76. "Resolutions Adopted at The Hague Congress," in *Women at The Hague: The International Congress of Women and Its Results*, ed. Jane Addams, Emily Greene Balch, and Alice Hamilton (New York: Macmillan, 1915), 150–59.

77. Jane Addams, *Peace and Bread in Time of War* (New York: Macmillan, 1922).

78. Karen C. Knop, *Diversity and Self-Determination in International Law* (New York: Cambridge University Press, 2002), 297.

79. After World War II, international women's networks such as the WIDF and WILPF became much more active in speaking on behalf of women's struggles for empowerment in Africa, Asia, and the Middle East. See Iris Berger, *Decolonizing Women's Activism: Africa in the Transformation of International Women's Movements* (Alexandria, VA: Alexander Street, 2012), accessed December 22, 2017, https://search. alexanderstreet.com/view/work/bibliographic_entity%7Cbibliographic_ details%7C2476917.

80. Ian Tyrrell, *Woman's World/Woman's Empire: The Woman's Christian Temperance Union in International Perspective, 1880–1930* (Chapel Hill: University of North Carolina Press, 1991).

81. Roxana Cheşchebec, "Feminist Ideologies and Activism in Romania (Approx. 1890s 1940s): Nationalism and Internationalism in Romanian Projects for Women's Emancipation" (PhD diss., Central European University, 2005).

82. Michael Mann, *The Sources of Social Power*, vol. 4, *Globalizations, 1945–2011* (New York: Cambridge University Press, 2013).

83. See, for instance, the statements of UN Secretary-General Kofi Annan, in "Annan Says UN Has Often Failed to Deliver on Protecting and Promoting Human Rights," accessed August 17, 2017, http://www.un.org/apps/news/story.asp?NewsID= 20911#.WiR0NEqnGM9.

84. Mary Ann Glendon, *World Made New: Eleanor Roosevelt and the Universal Declaration of Human Rights* (New York: Random House, 2001).

85. Ibid., 90.

86. Eleanor Roosevelt, *On My Own* (New York: Harper, 1958), 47.

87. Glendon, *World Made New*, 90; italics in the original.

88. Torild Skard, "Getting Our History Right: How Were the Equal Rights of Women and Men Included in the Charter of the United Nations?" *Forum for Development Studies*, no. 1 (June 2008): 37–60.

89. UN Security Council, "Resolution 1829 (2008)," accessed August 17, 2017, http:// www.securitycouncilreport.org/atf/cf/%7B65BFCF9B-6D27-4E9C-8CD3- CF6E4FF96FF9%7D/CAC%20S%20RES%201820.pdf.

90. Richard C. Eichenberg, "Gender Differences in Public Attitudes toward the Use of Force by the United States, 1990–2003," *International Security* 28, no. 1 (Summer 2003): 110–41.

91. Virginia Sapiro and Pamela Johnston Conover, "Gender, Feminist Consciousness, and War," *American Journal of Political Science* 37, no. 4 (November 1993): 1095.

92. Eichenberg, "Gender Differences."

THREE

Population

No woman can call herself free unless she can choose consciously whether she will or will not be a mother.

—Margaret Sanger[1]

An often overlooked major historical change in the twentieth century is the unprecedented steep growth of the world's population after 1900, followed by an equally abrupt slowing down starting in the 1970s. If, in the early nineteenth century, around one billion people lived in the world, that total doubled over the next 123 years (1927). After that milestone in the first half of the twentieth century, the world population doubled again in forty-seven years (1974), showing an unprecedented growth rate, and is likely to double again to eight billion by 2024, marking a relative slowdown of the rate of growth, from forty-one to fifty years.[2] Though much of that growth happened in the developing world, especially Asia and Sub-Saharan Africa, these statistics are part of an overall global shift.

How many of us share the planet today and how we are using its resources are closely connected to this challenge, which has more to do with shifts in women's behavior than with any other element, such as technology, medical care, or legal restrictions. The complex factors connected to this change deserve close attention: sexuality (as identity and, especially, behavior), birth control, marriage and divorce, education, and migration have all contributed to how fast the population has grown.[3] In all these matters both men and women have played essential roles. Yet the specific changes that have driven the growth and then slowdown of the world's population especially after 1900 align more closely with how women have taken on different roles in both their intimate lives and in society, while the change in male behavior has been less dramatic.

45

This chapter follows the main paths women took over the twentieth century to arrive at the growth we are seeing today. My analysis also examines continuing differences among women living in different regions of the world, which highlight important variances in gender norms and specifically in how women's sexuality is viewed. The changes I describe here in women's health, education, and overall well-being as a collective driving force toward more autonomous choices regarding reproduction and longer and healthier lives can become important lessons for the future. Additionally, the variances I bring into the discussion suggest that more focused and locally nuanced approaches will be needed if the goal of policy makers and social reformers is to support the improvement of the most vulnerable female populations in the world: those living in the global South and in states with a Muslim majority.

SEXUALITY AND REPRODUCTION

Birthing and raising children have always been used to define women's role in the family and society. Assumptions about women's unique caretaking role in early childhood have anchored kinship relations and the nature of the family, and they became translated into religious dogma and eventually secular law. It is not a great revelation to say this is one of the means by which men articulated their own ability to protect women and women's need of protection, thereby generating the sexist hierarchy in the family that became thoroughly entrenched long before the modern period. Economic and cultural aspects of this process will be revisited in subsequent chapters; here I want to focus on how women challenged related assumptions about sexuality and reproduction in the twentieth century.

For a long time before the modern period, sexuality was not a matter of explicit political discourse or policy.[4] Instead, religious and other types of sociocultural institutions circumscribed sexual norms and practices, confining them to the familial/kinship realm. In some societies, such as Christian Europe and China, pornography, cloaked in secrecy and guilt, became a substitute for honest talk. In others, such as the Ottoman Empire, diversity in sexual practices was allowed or even encouraged but still as a precursor to the establishment of heterosexual couples and marriage with the goal of reproduction. Even in secularizing countries in Western Europe, in the late nineteenth century both male elites and women reformers criticized discussions of sexuality as immoral, filthy, and beyond the pale, even as sexual behavior and the rise of sexually transmitted diseases suggested that talk would not stop action.[5] In countries where secularization was just beginning in legal and cultural practice, discussions of sexuality were even more of a taboo, reserved to the pulpit or minaret and on occasion the courthouse, rather than other public arenas like the press and educational institutions.[6]

Enter Marie Stopes (1880–1958) and Margaret Sanger, two sex reformers who did more to advance the notion of active sexuality as a normal behavior in women than anyone else until the publication of the famous Alfred C. Kinsey (1894–1956) study *Sexual Behavior in the Human Female* (1953).[7] Sanger operated in the United States, while Stopes worked in Great Britain, and as contemporaries the two had the opportunity to collaborate but chose to pursue separate paths.[8] Stopes was trained as a bioscientist and in 1902 she became the youngest person to receive a PhD in paleobotany in the UK. She began her activism as she came to realize the inadequacies of her own sexual intimacy with her husband. Stopes used her own experience as a case study for resolving what she saw as a universal problem: men assumed wrongly that women's sexuality was not like theirs and were unwilling to think of erotic love as a partnership that needed to be mutually nurtured. She stopped short of suggesting that all erotic relations deserved this sort of treatment, focusing instead on married couples' intimacy. But she insisted that a healthy and happy marriage depended on acknowledging the sexual needs of both partners and taking pleasure in satisfying those needs. Few women, and even fewer men, were willing to stand up and state these thoughts.

The result of her wrestling with rethinking female sexuality as both normal and necessary was the book *Married Love* (1918). *Married Love* appears both conservative and revolutionary, depending on the perspective of the reader.[9] In many ways, Stopes was a woman of her time. She opposed abortion and articulated her views of birth control through fashionable "race hygiene"; that is, the eugenicist discourse of the day.[10] She was openly anti-Semitic. She was an advocate of marriage and respectability rather than of free love. And she was very clear about the book being aimed at "normal" couples, meaning heterosexual married ones.

But she also wrote in unprecedented ways about the importance of treating marriage as a partnership between two autonomous individuals. In the introduction to the book, she clarified what profound misperceptions of female sexuality she was writing against: "The amazing statement of a distinguished American gynecologist, who said, 'I do not believe mutual pleasure in the sexual act has any particular bearing on the happiness of life.'"[11] This doctor did not deny that men's sexual desires were normal; it was the question of the *mutual*—read: women's pleasure—that he found irrelevant for a couple's happiness and women's in particular; this is what Stopes railed against.

One needs to understand the contribution of *Married Love* against the distance the author was traveling with that book, from established gender norms and especially women's sexuality toward new ideas and practices. That the book was not published for years after it was completed because it was deemed obscene or risqué tells us a great deal about what was considered acceptable at that time, especially for a woman author. The scandal about Stopes's book revolved around not only what it said but also who said it. For a woman to speak about her own sexuality nonchalantly as a scientific fact was jarring to most social critics, both men and women.

Still, *Married Love* became an instant megasuccess, selling out five editions in Europe just in 1918. By 1931 the book had sold more than 750,000 copies, and it could not even be purchased in the United States until after that year, when the charge of obscenity initially leveled against it was finally lifted.[12] Within four years, a survey of American academics listed *Married Love* among the twenty-five most influential books published in the previous fifty years, ahead of Freud's *Interpretation of Dreams*, among other notable titles.[13]

The most important contributions of the book in terms of upending sexual norms had to do with the clear language and unapologetic style of the text; it was meant to become a manual for both men and women rather than a scientific treatise. If men's sexuality and erotic desires had been the subject of many ruminations—scientific or artistic—for a long time, presenting women as subjects of erotic desires, and their needs as sexual partners, as deserving the attention of public discussion and intimate action was completely new. The distance from taboo to open discussion rendered this book revolutionary in terms of legitimating women's agency as autonomous sexual beings. *Married Love* offered a vocabulary for the desires, fears, and frustrations women had felt but could not articulate before. And its delayed publication might have been a blessing, for by 1918 many more women in Europe and North America were looking for such a vocabulary, having become more economically self-sufficient and overall culturally daring over the years of World War I.

Both *Married Love* and Stopes's subsequent work advocated for women's access to birth control, though not abortion, which she never approved of. In particular, she opened at least five birth control clinics in the UK, partly inspired by Margaret Sanger's activities in the same area.[14] She also researched and helped popularize a number of birth control techniques, primarily coitus interruptus, and products, such as the sponge. Her clinics were open to any married women, regardless of class, ethnicity, or race, and offered services free of charge. The subsequent legalization of birth control and the enhancement of control over their sexuality for millions of women in the UK and many other places in Europe can be traced back to these pioneering efforts.

During the same period Margaret Sanger, less trained in formal education but equally dedicated to providing women with the necessary tools to control their sexuality, pursued the goal of developing safe birth control techniques and making them available in the United States to every woman who needed them. Her philosophy was simple: "No woman can call herself free unless she can choose consciously whether she will or will not be a mother."[15] This was the sentiment that until the 1960s animated Sanger's work to open birth control clinics all over the country and beyond. It eventually gave rise to Planned Parenthood, the largest and most important institution for family planning and prevention of sexually transmitted diseases in the United States to date, and the largest such nongovernmental organization in the world.

Sanger's work was animated by her feminism and strong connections with the socialist and anarchist movements, especially starting in the 1910s.[16] She wrote sex advice columns for women, a novelty at that time, and she pursued door-to-door advocacy for birth control especially with migrant and working-class women. As a nurse, she saw many tragic outcomes of the lack of access to birth control, especially for poor women. In 1914 she launched *The Woman Rebel*, a newsletter aimed at educating women about various techniques for birth control, for which she was indicted on charges of obscenity.

This is also when she traveled to England and observed the birth control devices, especially sponges, available there. Upon her return to the United States, she decided to open birth control clinics for working-class women. In 1917 she was tried for distributing contraceptives, with the judge deciding that women were not entitled to "the right to copulate with a feeling of security that there will be no resulting conception," in short, reaffirming the legal standing of the sexual double standard.[17] By contrast, during the same period, the military establishment began to issue condoms to soldiers fighting in the war as an important health precaution against sexually transmitted diseases.

Sanger's ideas eventually prevailed, especially because many more physicians began to support her views and started to prescribe contraceptives more liberally. By 1937 the American Medical Association changed its policy on teaching about and prescribing contraceptives, and began to include birth control as a core component of medical training. Sanger's struggles on paper, in the street, and in the courtroom, and her willingness to serve repeated jail sentences for this cause were a primary reason for this important change in how we think about female sexuality today.

Initially, birth control as a concept and practice did not gain as much acceptance in the rest of the world as in North America and Western Europe. But Sanger's efforts were global and found important partners in places like India and China.[18] Though she visited China only briefly in 1922, Sanger's work became very influential there, where many women were active in the medical profession and searched for better birth control options for women. The first birth control clinic opened in Beijing soon after Sanger's visit and used some of her materials to educate poor women.[19]

Sanger's work was even more influential in India, where she traveled on several occasions. In the 1930s she developed a complicated relationship with Mohandas Gandhi (1869–1948) and Rabindranath Tagore (1861–1941), two of the most prominent Indian personalities at that time.[20] Tagore was more sympathetic to Sanger's idea of providing birth control to women as a matter of principle, while Gandhi's more traditional views of women translated into his support only for abstinence as a form of female birth control.

More importantly, both the All India Women's Conference and many physicians in India supported Sanger's call to enhance education about and access to inexpensive birth control to the poorest women in India. In 1952 she returned to independent India to help launch the International Planned Parenthood Federation (IPPF) together with the organization's first president, Lady Dhanvanthi Rama Rau (1893–1987). These efforts had mixed results, which suggests that important inadequacies remained in women's access to birth control. Recent scholarship shows that semicoercive sterilization programs sponsored by the Indian government and international organizations to reduce population growth, including the IPPF, especially targeted people of lower castes and the rural poor.[21] Criticism of these programs has become vocal and is generating more nuanced and locally based avenues for access to birth control as an individual choice rather than by government mandate.

Today the IPPF has 164 member associations and serves more than five million people in 172 countries, with an explicit agenda of advocating for rights-based approaches to birth control rather than top-down coercive methods. It runs sixty-five thousand service points worldwide. In 2016 those facilities delivered 182.5 million sexual and reproductive health services, of which 1.2 million were abortions.[22] In short, today it would be impossible to think of reproductive rights and services across the world without the pioneering and lifelong dedication of Sanger and many other activists like her. Women are still not fully free to choose how they manage their reproductive capabilities, but their choices generally increased over the second half of the twentieth century. Those choices have had a direct impact on slowing down the growth of the world's population.

ABORTION

Abortion was the predominant method of limiting natural fertility before contraceptive methods were developed and perfected in the twentieth century. Religious institutions and writings provided various limitations against this practice in the premodern period. A recent study ties the criminalization of abortion in the West to a combination of religious dogma and courts, common law practices, and the development of medical expertise.[23] By the end of the nineteenth century, abortion, though practiced widely, had become criminalized in most European states, including their colonial possessions, although it was unevenly prosecuted.

The first state to legalize abortion on demand was the Soviet Union. Though later limiting it in both law and practice, in the early 1920s the Soviet regime allowed women to make their own choices about reproduction. Since most contraceptive methods remained unavailable, save for the rhythm method, until today women in Russia have used abortion as the primary means for controlling their fertility. Most other communist regimes (Romania is an exception) decriminalized abortion and made access to it a regular component of their public health services.[24] In Romania, decriminalization in the early 1950s was followed by recriminalization in 1966, which for a couple of years led to a spike in births, after which the rate went down significantly, primarily due to the high number of illegal and unsafe abortions performed.[25] Another important deviation from these practices is China, where initially the communist regime encouraged workers to reproduce for the future well-being of the proletariat, but eventually shifted its policy to pressuring women to have only one child out of fear of overpopulation.[26]

In Western Europe and North America, the development of safe and effective contraceptives provided more options for women seeking to limit their fertility, especially starting in the 1960s. But for the poor (and, by extension, ethnic/racial minorities), abortion remained a much more affordable and familiar method. Feminist activism on behalf of abortion rights eventually led to the decriminalization of this birth control method in most of Europe, with the exception of several predominantly Catholic countries such as Ireland and Spain. By the beginning of the twenty-first century, abortion became a "last resort" form of fertility control in the developed world. The number of abortions in this region has decreased to twenty-seven per one thousand women, down 42 percent from the early 1990s.[27]

In other parts of the world abortion remains a more important means, whether legal or not, for women to control their fertility. In Latin America and the Caribbean, 97 percent of women of childbearing age live in countries where abortion is restricted or banned.[28] Still, the abortion rate has gone up from forty per one thousand women in the early 1990s to forty-four per one thousand in the 2010s. Thirty-two percent of pregnancies ended in abortions during the 2010–2014 period. In most of the developing world, abortion has remained relatively constant as a means of limiting fertility, with 24 percent of pregnancies ending in abortion. According to recent studies, the legal status of the procedure seems to play no role in how often women choose to terminate a pregnancy. Education about and access to contraceptives is a far more important factor. It is estimated that 225 million women in the developing world are faced with unwanted pregnancies.[29] That only 56 million abortions per year occurred in the world in 2010–2014 in a population of more than 1.7 billion women of childbearing age (15–49) suggests abortion is a procedure that women use as a last resort rather than casually.[30]

GENITAL CUTTING AND WOMEN'S SEXUALITY

The shift toward viewing women's sexuality as an autonomous component of their lives has not proceeded in the same way everywhere around the world. Female genital cutting continues as a common practice in more than thirty countries, primarily in Africa, the Middle East, and Asia, but to a lesser extent also in Europe, North America, and Australia, especially with the growth of transcontinental migration.[31] In 2016 more than two hundred million women around the world had undergone the procedure, primarily at the hands of other women. This is a very old practice that was also reintroduced in Europe in the nineteenth century by male doctors as a way to control "unruly" female sexuality, such as masturbation.

As feminist reformers ramped up critiques against such practices, genital cutting was terminated in the early twentieth century in some places, especially Europe and North America. In other regions, especially where the practice was connected to much older grassroots traditions about gender roles, female genital mutilation continued without much change in attitude of the primarily female practitioners for much of the twentieth century. In some colonial African states, the practice became a form of gendered resistance to European occupation. Young women even took the step to self-circumcise as a way to mark their authentic local roots against evangelical missionaries' attempts to stamp out such "godless" practices.[32]

Since the second half of the twentieth century the UN has played an important role in turning informal pressure to end genital cutting into a very public indictment, linking female genital mutilation to the violation of women's basic human rights as defined by the UN Universal Declaration of Human Rights.[33] Scientists began doing research on genital mutilation and provided evidence of its associated recurring pain, diminishing sex drive, and medical complications, such as difficulty with birthing and higher risk of HIV transmission.[34] Many states where the practice was common subsequently passed legislation making various forms of female genital mutilation illegal. But the shift away from this practice has been much slower than the enactment of official policies outlawing it. Practitioners, a majority of them women, continue to identify it as an important rite of passage that brings girls into the community of womanhood and reaffirms elderly women's own social authority in the group. They claim that eliminating it would break up that female bond and render uncircumcised girls outcasts in their society.

As recently as 2016, women in Indonesia, a country where around 50 percent of young women still undergo the procedure, praised it as non-harmful and a point of pride for young women.[35] The main controversy that continues to surround female genital cutting has to do with how we understand cultural difference and women's agency in performing the circumcision. Mutilating the clitoris or vagina through cutting has earned much criticism from Western secular observers. Yet many Western women choose to pierce and insert a variety of objects in their bodies, inclusive of nipples and the clitoris, and to dramatically alter their appearance through plastic surgery without having to suffer the ire of the medical establishment. If significant groups of women refuse to consider themselves as victims of the practice, regardless of the research that points toward a number of possible or even frequent long-term deleterious medical effects of genital mutilation, the argument about violating their human rights assumes connotations of racist universalism.[36]

According to UNICEF, men in countries where genital mutilation is a common practice seem more favorably disposed toward ending it than women do: In Guinea 41 percent of young men ages fifteen to nineteen favor ending genital cutting, while only 27 percent of young women in the same age range, who most likely would have recently witnessed or experienced the procedure, do. In Sierra Leone, the disparity is even larger—36 percent among men to 13 percent among women.[37] This practice and especially ongoing debates about its meaning suggest that there are limits to gender self-identification across other (ethnic, religious, kinship) divides, and that our ability to understand women's sexuality in the context of many political and cultural changes over the twentieth century cannot discount such persisting differences as any kind of lag in development. The challenge for the twenty-first century is to develop a more self-consciously diverse understanding of these practices and the norms they embody. We need to begin a conversation about sexuality and reproduction that can engage women in different societies with greater respect toward these differences and greater humility toward what some consider "normal" but others don't.

NEW FORMS OF CONTROLLING FERTILITY

The opening of the discourse and eventually clinics for birth control in the first half of the twentieth century helped usher in more research on birth control techniques, such as coitus interruptus, and technologies, such as the Pill. Condoms had been in use for hundreds of years but became more common with the study of sexually transmitted diseases at the end of the nineteenth century. By World War I, for instance, British soldiers were issued condoms as part of their regulation supplies. But condoms rendered women dependent on men in timing pregnancies.

It took Margaret Sanger's unabated focus on empowering every woman to control her sexuality to develop the hormonal contraceptive pill that is so commonly used all over the world today. But it also took a lot of funding to pursue this project in which male-dominated research programs in medicine were uninterested.[38] The single most important individual who helped turn Sanger's dream into a safe product was Katharine Dexter McCormick (1875–1967), a biologist who spent her life working with Sanger on birth control advocacy. Born into a prominent lawyer's family in Chicago, she later moved to Boston and attended MIT around the same time as Florence Luscomb (see chapter 2, "Politics"), with whom she marched on many occasions to advocate for women's suffrage. After graduating with a BS in biology—the second woman to graduate from that university—McCormick aspired to a career as a scientist but instead married Stanley, the heir to the McCormick fortune.

Within a few years, Stanley was diagnosed with schizophrenia and placed in a mental institution, and Katharine assumed legal and financial authority over his well-being and much of the McCormick fortune. She spent the rest of her life dedicating her energy and wealth to supporting science research, initially in the area of mental illness and specifically schizophrenia and subsequently in oral contraception in the form of a pill for women. In 1951 she identified Gregory Pincus (1903–1967), a scientist who had been working on such a pill, as the right partner whose work she would fund. Pincus was subsequently joined by John Rock (1890–1984), and the two worked for the next few years to develop a formula for preventing ovulation. By 1957 the Pill had been approved in the United States, and by 1960 doctors started to prescribe it to women as oral contraception.[39]

The Pill happened to arrive on the market around the same time that a number of other forces were converging to produce what scholars have identified as the "sexual revolution" of the 1960s. The availability of oral contraceptives certainly upended how men and women controlled their sexuality and in particular who would be responsible for birth control. With women presumably able to control their own risk of pregnancy with the Pill, men's expectations about women's availability as sexual partners also changed. There seems to be a clear correlation between the availability of the Pill and the age at which women begin to be sexually active.

Starting in the 1960s, with safer birth control available, women especially in Western Europe and North America started to have sex much earlier than had been the case since the nineteenth century. By 1980 the average age when a Swedish woman had her first sexual encounter was fifteen, almost the same as for men. But for almost half of the women, this first encounter was nonconsensual. The proportion of women from other regions who share this experience ranges from 24 percent in the United

States to 30 percent in South Africa and around 50 percent in the Caribbean.[40]

The impact of the Pill was initially much less in countries where religious constrictions (e.g., Catholicism) or state ideology (e.g., natalism) made it illegal or practically impossible to secure access to oral contraceptives.[41] Though Sanger had imagined the Pill being available at a low cost, economic barriers also limited access to such contraceptives for the poorest and especially nonwhite women in countries like the United States. In other countries, especially in the developing world, access to contraceptives became part of top-down international campaigns to control high birth rates, by tying it to access by governments of these countries to other international resources, like loans and new technologies.[42] In India the UN introduced IUDs and, later, vasectomies as preferred forms of birth control, which women and then men were pressured to adopt on the basis of false promises of financial and other rewards. In Nigeria, international funding organizations similarly pressured the government into introducing birth control policies and educational programs that would lead to a decrease in the birth rate, as a condition for continued financial support.[43]

Historians like Matthew Connelly have suggested that the "population bomb" agenda of the 1960s was undergirded by racist considerations about *where* overpopulation was a problem and sexist views about *who* would be best equipped to decide how to control reproduction.[44] High birth rates among Catholics in Europe were not considered a problem for the international community. High birth rates among women in South Asian, African, and Latin American states that received international aid were construed as a problem for the international community. Experts, at that time predominantly men, were called to provide solutions generally without consulting women, the objects of most of these policies.

Other technological advancements in the second half of the twentieth century led to further severing biology from destiny as far as women's fertility was concerned. Sterilization as a reversible procedure in both women and men had already been tried as a coercive procedure in a number of countries, most notably the United States and Germany.[45] Selective breeding, including sterilization, was already a common practice with other species, but new legislation was introduced in many countries, dictating both positive measures (who would be allowed to reproduce and what support the state might provide for those couples) and negative ones (how the state would intervene to stop the reproduction of "unhealthy" populations).[46] With a few exceptions, such as India, these policies were almost exclusively directed at controlling women.

One should clarify that, although some women, especially supporters of eugenics, favored such legislation, sterilization and natalist measures were introduced and passed almost exclusively by male legislatures and dictatorships. Indira Gandhi's regime was the only female-led one to advocate for a top-down coercive policy of controlling women's and men's reproductive capacities. What most maternalist and eugenicist women activists (e.g., Sanger) advocated for was increasing women's ability to control their fertility rather than increasing the state's ability to control women's fertility. [47]

One important technological development in divorcing fertility from biology has been the successful perfection of in vitro fertilization. Initially pioneered by two British doctors, Patrick Steptoe (1913–1988) and Robert Edwards (1925–2013), between 1976 and 1978, the technique was further improved by two US doctors, the wife-husband team of Georgeanna (1912–2005) and Howard Jones (1910–2015). In vitro fertilization has remained, however, an expensive procedure and thus available primarily to women from countries where socialized medicine covers such procedures. Elsewhere, from the developing world to the United States, this option remains restricted to wealthy women.

In vitro fertilization subsequently gave rise to a further redefinition of parenting and the family, impacting fertility among women in ever more diversifying ways. For heterosexual couples with medical conditions that prevented successful fertilization, the option of a surrogate pregnancy became a reality. For same-sex couples, in vitro fertilization opened up the possibility of having biological children without any heterosexual intercourse, empowering those couples to make very different choices about being a couple and becoming parents. Finally, in vitro fertilization made it possible for women who want to choose biological single parenting, to do so.

Another more recent practice to remove sex from pregnancy and parenting has been the rise of surrogate pregnancy since the 1990s. As wealthy couples from the developed world work around limitations such as the inability to conceive naturally or undergo the labor of pregnancy, the medical profession and government policies have opened up the use of in vitro fertilization for the benefit not of the carrier, but of the sperm and egg "owners." The practice of "womb outsourcing" or "pregnancy surrogacy" has grown significantly in the past two decades and has moved from the developed world to encompass countries in the global South.

India, in particular, has emerged as a preferred marketplace for surrogacy services for a variety of reasons. In some countries, such as France, Italy, Germany, Japan, and China, surrogacy is illegal. In other countries, especially in the developed world, it may be legal, but it is also heavily regulated and extremely expensive. In the United States, one recent study places the costs at between $50,000 and $250,000 per procedure. [48] In India, the same services are advertised at a total cost of $19,000 for a guaranteed vaginal delivery. [49] By 2012 Indian fertility clinics were bringing in more than $400 million per year in revenue, thus representing a veritable cottage industry.

However, studies by nursing experts and women activists point toward the gross exploitation of many surrogate mothers: often women are promised conditions of work and delivery that are not followed in practice; and they do not control the income garnered from the work they have performed, as the funds are transferred directly to the control of their husbands. With more research published on these forms of abuse, women with the financial means to afford surrogacy need to make better-informed choices: regardless of the promises of shiny brochures, does an inexpensive surrogacy deliver services where both laborer and "owner" are treated fairly and with basic dignity?

Overall, in all of these articulations of fertility and parenting, women fundamentally control the choice of pursuing any of the options mentioned above. Although not everywhere to the same extent, women have gained the ability to make so many more choices than ever in the past. Legislation, financial restraints, and religious constrictions still play important roles in how women sort out their choice whether, when, and how to reproduce. Yet the power of those factors has become less hegemonic than it used to be a hundred years ago.

MARRIAGE AND REPRODUCTION

Why, when, who, for how long, and with what assumptions about "the family" people marry is vastly different today from the beginning of the twentieth century. Many factors, especially changing legal definitions of spousal roles and rights in the family, together with the specific economic implications of these rights, have played a role in this shift. They will be discussed further in chapter 7 ("Kinship"). But the change in how women have come to understand and control their sexuality is as important as those factors and is ultimately the most significant element in the global surge and eventual slowdown of the world population.

In the nineteenth century most Western countries defined a woman's role in marriage as subordinate to the husband in terms of control over the couple's wealth, inheritance, and, especially relevant for this discussion, parenting responsibilities.[50] Men's sexual transgressions were openly acknowledged and accepted in the law. Only demonstrable and extended physical estrangement from the wife (e.g., moving out of the family home and living with another woman in a way that was publicly observable) would count as adultery for men. For women, sexual purity before marriage was the norm in both law and practice, and any form of adulterous behavior was unacceptable.[51] These sexual norms in marriage became extended to the rest of the world in the late nineteenth century as European empires grew their colonial possessions and introduced new law codes at the expense of local traditions.[52] In many other countries, the European sexual norms in marriage became a symbol of civilization toward which the emerging local male elites aspired.[53]

For as long as marriage was a cultural norm and women's position in society legally and economically dependent on being married, women who were not independently wealthy had very few choices (taking the veil in Christian societies, for instance) in resisting the patriarchal structure of marriage.[54] And with a lack of viable birth control options, women remained limited by their physiological ability to give birth, with little agency in the process.

As women began to gain voting rights into the twentieth century, the legal definition of their rights in marriage also changed. This was not a "natural" and inevitable shift. Without women being able to become lawyers and defend the principle of gender equality in marriage, these ideas made little headway.[55] But eventually, as both political rights and the legal profession came to represent more robustly the interests and needs of women, the needle began to move toward greater equality.

As women's second-class legal status in marriage started to become undone, they started to make different choices about when to enter and exit marriage and with whom, and whether to have children. In the first half of the twentieth century, women continued to get married at an early age. After 1950, however, they started to get married later, with the trend continuing into the present. By 2000 the average age of marriage for women was in the midtwenties or higher for most of the world, save for countries in Sub-Saharan Africa and South Asia. The lowest averages are in Niger and Mali—around 17.6 and 17.8, respectively—and India, where the average is just above 20.[56] In 2016 39 percent of girls in Sub-Saharan Africa and 42 percent in West and Central Africa were married before the age of eighteen.[57] And since women tend to have their children after getting married, this factor alone helps explain in part the decline of population growth rates across the world.[58] Given more choices in marriage rights and birth control, women have opted to use them to space out their pregnancies differently than before the twentieth century, starting five to ten years later than previously, even though sexual activity starts much earlier.

Divorce has also seen significant changes over the twentieth century, correlated primarily with women's changing legal, educational, and economic opportunities.[59] With the equalization of chances to retain financial independence and custody of children, women have been more willing to pursue divorce and cohabitation. The most recent research on nuptiality patterns shows an inverted U-shaped pattern in divorce rates, with a spike in the 1970s, together with a decrease in marriage overall and a parallel rise in cohabitation patterns.[60] Also rising is the tendency among many women, especially those with higher education, to remarry after divorce. Overall, one can see that women have started to make more diverse choices about when to marry—later than they used to in the nineteenth century; whether to marry, with cohabitation growing steadily since 1970 among economically and educationally diverse populations; whom to marry, with same-sex marriage becoming socially and legally approved in many countries around the world; and whether to stay in a marriage.

This trend has not continued unchallenged, and in fact the declining birth rates have prompted some politicians and religious leaders to criticize women's freedoms as destructive to society. These critiques tend to come from both men and women who see secularization, access to birth control, and other related matters, such as women's education, as constituting a closely related set of problems that need to be fixed.[61] Such critiques have sometimes led to new forms of violence against women, from forced marriage and impregnation to killings. The recent abduction of hundreds of girls by the fundamentalist Islamic terrorist group Boko Haram in Nigeria is one example of such reactions.[62] Attacks by fundamentalist evangelicals at birth control clinics in the United States are another example of this rise in violence against women.[63] Same-sex marriage has also yet to see broad approval in countries where religious strictures still weigh heavily on secular laws about marriage, such as Iran and Russia. Yet there is no mistaking the global trend in the direction of marriage at a later age and with fewer births, whenever women have those choices.

BEYOND HETERONORMATIVITY

Though not necessarily intended by feminist activists, the normalization of openly discussing women's sexuality laid the groundwork for questioning heteronormativity. Evidence of same-sex eroticism abounds among many species and in various historical periods and places, yet heterosexuality became an undisputed norm in the West by the modern period. By the end of the nineteenth century heteronormativity was becoming a hegemonically globalized, colonially driven force that challenged homoerotic traditions around the world.[64] Yet Western scientists and artists began to challenge these norms around 1900 in a new, modernist vein, and brought about what we have come to identify more recently as the gay rights movement.[65] Challenges to heteronormativity can be seen in artistic modernist circles in other parts of the world, such as China, Mexico, Australia, or Japan, often as a response to developments taking place in Europe.[66]

Initially speaking primarily as individuals, artists like Oscar Wilde (1854–1900) and writers like Gertrude Stein (1874–1946) performed homosexuality as a matter of personal choice, which came at a steep personal cost, as sodomy was defined as a criminal act in many places around the world.[67] Lesbians were also publicly shunned and punished for such behavior, but their so-called offenses were more often identified in terms of other moral crimes, such as prostitution, vagrancy, or sexual assault.[68] At the same time, biologists and other scientists had become more interested in human sexuality, as illustrated by Stopes and Sanger above.[69] The discipline of sexology developed new clinical discourses about normal and "deviant" sexuality, much of it based on small samples and anecdotal observations.[70]

Among these growing communities of sexologists, Magnus Hirschfeld (1868–1935), a German, developed a new template for understanding sexuality on a spectrum between homo- and heteroeroticism, in contrast to the prevailing binary theories (e.g., normal versus abnormal).[71] His interest and research focused primarily on male homosexuality, and he is considered the father of the modern gay rights movement, because his work ranged from clinical studies to political activism.[72] To his credit, and unlike many other prominent figures in the gay world at that time, Hirschfeld was not averse to working with women interested in normalizing various sexual practices among women beyond the accepted heteronormativity of the day. He supported the efforts of Helene Stöcker (1869–1943) to decriminalize abortion in Germany at the beginning of the twentieth century. He also joined Stöcker in making sure lesbian sexuality would not become criminalized when the German Parliament made an effort in that direction in 1909.[73] Their efforts were later undermined by the Nazi regime, though the work they did came back into research and activist focus starting in the 1960s.

Overall, the criminalization of various definitions of homosexuality continued over the twentieth century without much reform until the 1960s, when LGBT activism saw new forms of engagement. A violent encounter between patrons and police in 1969 at the Stonewall Inn gay bar in New York became a spark for widespread protests in the United States and eventually Western Europe.[74] Having hidden for generations in the shadows of respectability and sexual suppression, the gay population joined the growing street protests against the heteronormative establishment. The tide of repression started to turn in the 1970s, especially in Western Europe and North America.

The move toward greater tolerance for and eventually complete normalization of same-sex relations has been uneven across the world. Legalization of same-sex marriage started in 2000, and by 2018 twenty-six countries in Europe and North and South America, as well as Australia, New Zealand, South Africa, and Taiwan, had passed such laws. While South Africa passed a law legalizing same-sex marriage in 2006, the United States did so only in 2015, and parts of the European Union (EU), such as Italy and Poland, have yet to consider it.[75]

Whether legal or not, same-sex relations and families have become more common in the past thirty years and have broadened the diversity of approaches to nuptiality for individuals and couples. In the absence of

LGBTQ-friendly laws regarding adoption and with the introduction of in-vitro fertilization, same-sex couples with financial means have started to avail themselves of various forms of surrogate birthing. Given the relatively small percentage of self-identified gay people, though, such changes have not had a large impact on the global rate of fertility. The cultural impact of these changes will be explored in greater depth in chapter 7.

LITERACY AND FERTILITY

When attempting to understand the profound shifts in population growth over the twentieth century, sociologists and demographers have tried to identify what other broad, transnational developments show strong correlations with this shift. Many have explored to what extent those changes can be called causes or effects of the spike and subsequent slowdown in population growth. Debates around these questions continue to abound, though there is growing consensus around one specific issue: education.[76] In a recent overview of the debates and ongoing research on this matter, Wolfgang Lutz and Qiang Ren state unequivocally that "in almost all regressions for the fertility rate, female literacy seems to be the single most important factor," leading the authors to conclude that "the relationship of female literacy to the total fertility rate is more pronounced than that to the growth rates across all points in time."[77]

Taking this correlation as a starting point, we might ask what the historical factors have been that brought about better education opportunities for women in the twentieth century. Such factors can help us better understand how women's attitudes toward their own fertility have changed in the last hundred years. Much of the literature on this topic focuses on the state and political factors, a top-down and masculinist approach to understanding change.[78] My approach focuses more directly on the kind of activism and informal pressure women applied in their communities as members of an ethnic group or religion or as individual citizens to ensure that educational opportunities open to boys would also extend to girls. Women had many partners among male reformers and even politicians situated within the policy-making establishment. Yet, without pressure from below specifically on the part of women, changes that paved the way toward universal literacy around the world would not have happened.

Universal literacy is still a goal, rather than a reality. However, with 83 percent of the world's population having achieved functional literacy by 2010 from an average of 20 percent in 1900, the goal is in sight.[79] To understand women's role in this process we need to start by acknowledging the absence of women's educational opportunities and abysmal level of literacy among women in the late nineteenth and early twentieth centuries. This was a period when men's literacy levels and participation in all levels of education were growing substantially in many parts of the world, such as Europe, the Americas, and parts of Asia.

In parts of the world where women's education was more universally recognized as a social norm rather than an aspiration, such as the United States and parts of Western Europe (the Scandinavian countries, Great Britain, France, and Germany), women's rates of illiteracy were significantly lower than in the rest of the world and already correlated strongly with a slower birth-rate growth.[80] At the beginning of the twentieth century the overall rate of illiteracy among women in the rest of the world was significantly higher than among men, reaching into 80 to 90 percent in parts of Europe, Asia, and especially Africa.[81] Reasons for this gender imbalance range from cultural to political—from the basic lack of valuing women's intellectual skills in society to the lack of available institutions and resources, state or private, to accommodate interest in education among women.

The beginnings of investing heavily in women's primary schooling happened first in parts of Western Europe (Britain, France, Scandinavia, Germany), North America (United States and Canada), and Australia in the last quarter of the nineteenth century. Educational opportunities were initially tied to religious institutions' initiatives and were sometimes gender-segregated. In societies where gender segregation was a norm, if not the law (e.g., Islamic states), girls' access to education was compounded by the lack of available, well-trained female teachers, who could not themselves be trained in male institutions. In less restrictive environments, women interested in becoming teachers could sometimes gain access to male-dominated institutions, but more as an exception than as accepted practice. In the nineteenth century, the gender disparity in access to various levels of education and to training future generations of women teachers led to the creation of women's colleges in the United States.[82]

In the rest of the world, girls' access to education was even more haphazard and limited to women of the elite. If any institutions existed, they were generally established by religious foundations or patrician philanthropists whose goals were not to eradicate illiteracy or unleash the creativity of young girls. Instead, education was to serve the goals of the elites and the religious establishment, disciplining the young women into adults who would act according to the prevailing gender norms. There were exceptions to this in families where parents or other close relatives took a special interest in a particularly bright girl and offered her opportunities to study content generally not made available to women, such as philosophical treatises, theology, and legal critical studies.[83]

It was especially from the crop of women who were either being educated informally by enlightened parents or who were frustrated by the few formal educational opportunities open to women that strong activism on behalf of women's education developed in the late nineteenth century and notably into the twentieth century. The generation that matured around 1900 faced a diversifying transnational context. Exchanges of ideas and educational practices were growing across borders, greatly spurred by the nationalist sentiments that were starting to animate more men of the political establishment, especially in imperial or colonial settings in Asia, Australia, Africa, and Europe. The trend initially focused on boys' education in both basic disciplines (reading and arithmetic) as well as new areas of technological advancement, such as engineering and medicine. By the 1900s the imperial gaze of educated women in Europe and North America became more fixated on educational activities for women in the colonies. In a growing number of states attempting to emulate Western modernity, girls' education became an emblem of civilization and empowerment.

These openings became opportunities women sought to mold according to their own aspirations, which initially were modest, focusing on basic literacy and the opportunity to attend gymnasia and universities without a particular focus on any specific disciplines except for teacher-training programs. In the increasingly popular nationalist tropes of liberation and empowerment through educational enlightenment, women eked out arguments about the importance of training future mothers to be good patriots and role models for their sons and sometimes daughters.[84] These arguments were hard to reject, and they helped turn some nationalist male politicians into allies of women's educational reform.

The development of Turkish nationalism under Mustafa Kemal Atatürk (1881–1938) is a good example of such an alliance. A great deal of scholarly and political attention has focused on Atatürk's role in modernizing women's education and reshaping gender norms (e.g., regarding veiling) in this Islamic society after World War I.[85] Atatürk's ideas were themselves shaped by women reformers of his generation with whom he found common ground.[86] Among them are Halide Edib (1884–1964) and Şükufe Nihal (1896–1973). Edib's role in Turkish politics is linked to her steadfast support for women's rights—especially education—as well as her vocal nationalism. She was also a firm believer in the importance of developing reform by not abandoning the tenets of Islam.

In 1908 Edib began writing activist articles that stressed the importance and benefits of enhancing women's access to education. As a result, in the 1910s, while the Young Turk government pursued sweeping reforms in social and political life, Edib became a special consultant to the ministry of education on reforming girls' education; as such, she was the first woman to be appointed to such a high government post in the Ottoman Empire.[87] World War I caught these reforms in midstream, but they recommenced in the early 1920s, after the Greek-Turkish war. By then Edib had become embroiled in nationalist politics and was eventually forced into exile. But the reforms she initiated before the war were the seeds that germinated under Atatürk's regime.

Nihal, a more secularizing feminist than Edib, began working as an activist with the Society for the Defense of Women's Rights in the decade before World War I, with the goal of empowering women to become more independent politically, economically, and socially. She was less concerned with upholding Islamic traditions than tearing down barriers against women's full access to and support for education on an equal footing as men. She wrote many journal articles on behalf of this cause and organized numerous conferences and other events as a way to mobilize other women reformers and raise funds for women's education. During the war and after Atatürk became the leader of the new nationalist government, Nihal wrote passionately about the goals supported by this government to provide women with greater access to education.[88] For her, as for many of her fellow feminist activists, women's education was the most important measure of any society's level of civilization and progress in the modern world. Atatürk agreed, and these ideas were turned into law and received government financial support. As women's literacy in Turkey grew over the twentieth century, their fertility declined substantially. In 1950 Turkish women had an average of seven births per woman. By 2005 the fertility rate declined by more than 71 percent to two births per woman, below replacement level.[89]

The narrative of women's role in advancing the cause of women's education in the first half of the twentieth century is similar in many other places around the world, such as China, Iran, Egypt, and Brazil.[90] Feminist activists often took up the twin struggle for political and education empowerment. In places where the male establishment was not amenable to full voting rights for women, such as the Middle East and Eastern Europe, activists were more successful in their quest for enhancing women's educational opportunities by securing the support of the political establishment as a matter of "patriotism" or "civilization." Even then, there was often insufficient government funding for women's education and access to economic opportunities opened up by their newly gained skills. In many cases women themselves stepped up to provide personal funds, raise money on behalf of schools, or develop professional tracks, such as teacher training and social welfare programs, which would open up new opportunities for women.

Yet not all such efforts by women on behalf of other women were designed to simply enlighten and empower future generations. In many colonial settings, especially in Africa, as well as in states where European conqueror populations had displaced the native populations, such as the United States, Australia, Canada, or Brazil, the educational opportunities of indigenous populations were closely monitored to prevent unruly outcomes. Well into the twentieth century, the philosophy of most of these regimes was that the culture of these native populations was inferior to the Europeans and in need of help according to the racist civilizing ideologies of the late nineteenth and early twentieth centuries. Women participated in these activities both as followers as well as leaders in the colonizing mission.[91]

In the United States, schools that aimed to "tame" and "civilize" young members of Native American tribes have become well-known examples of oppression through education. Starting in the late nineteenth century, white women reformers went into Native communities to establish religious, secular, and later government-funded schools for girls as part of their progressive agenda for women's rights.[92] But their efforts were framed within a racist view of the identity and potential of these girls: the language, traditions, and even names of the young pupils were to be discarded like shameful shells rather than valuable elements of these young women's identities. The curriculum of these schools predominantly focused on vocational, lower-end skills, such as sewing, cooking, and other domestic work, denying the pupils aspirations toward higher education, a greater variety of professional careers, and overall the possibility of both seeing themselves as and acting like the equals of their white contemporaries.[93]

But Native American women did not stand idly by (nor did Aboriginal women in Australia).[94] Zitkala-Ša[95] (1876–1938) was a Sioux woman who grew up on the Yankton Reservation in South Dakota. At eight she was recruited by Quaker missionaries and taken to a boarding school in Indiana, designed for "poor children, white, colored, and Indian," where she was to learn the skills of being an assimilated worker.[96] Instead, Zitkala-Ša took to the violin like a fish to water and became an accomplished musician. As her identity was being stripped away, music helped her escape into a universe of her own making. She later played at the prestigious New England Conservatory of Music, represented the Carlisle Indian Industrial School at the Paris World Expo in 1899, and wrote *The Sun Dance Opera* (1913).

As she carved out a voice for herself from painful experiences at the hands of white education reformers, Zitkala-Ša also sought to widen the horizons of opportunity for other young Native American women. In 1921 she helped establish the Indian Welfare Committee of the General Federation of Women's Clubs and wrote many articles and pamphlets critiquing the existing education opportunities for Native American youths. She also collected and published many traditional oral stories, helping familiarize a wide audience with the rich cultural heritage of her and other Native American tribes, while preserving these treasures.[97]

Over the second half of the twentieth century important disparities became more apparent in women's access to basic education around the world. In socialist regimes, illiteracy was eradicated within one generation, a goal closely linked to activating women as part of the proletariat. In Western Europe and the rest of the developed world, women's education largely caught up with men's, with important caveats related to the quality of such education among minority populations. In postcolonial states, female political leaders helped sustain educational efforts for girls in places like India, Zambia, and Pakistan. In many other places, where strong female voices were absent at the top of the political decision-making hierarchy, girls' education continued to lag significantly behind that of boys.

By 1990 UNESCO came together with a number of other transnational organizations, such as the World Bank and UNICEF, to tackle the problem of access to education for children in the poorest areas of the world. The background document stated clearly that "[t]he most urgent priority is to ensure access to, and improve the quality of, education for girls," who represented 60 percent of the more than seventy million children not participating in formal education.[98] The rate of illiteracy for women was significantly higher than for men in all fourteen countries with rates higher than 70 percent: it ranged from 78.7 percent to 96.9 percent for women, with rates 11 to 20 percent higher than men's.[99]

This problem continues to plague communities in Sub-Saharan Africa, parts of the Middle East, and South Asia. Yet progress has been made. From 1999 to 2009 the percentage of out-of-school children went down dramatically in all three regions, from 21 to 9 percent in South Asia, from 23 to 14 percent in the Middle East, and, most spectacularly, from 41 to 23 percent in Sub-Saharan Africa.[100] A lot of work still needs to be done to eradicate female illiteracy, but UNESCO and other UN-related international bodies have contributed a great deal to drawing attention and funds toward this problem.

HIGHER EDUCATION AND FERTILITY

If basic education has been positively correlated with women's significantly greater ability and willingness to regulate their reproductive capabilities, the correlation is even closer when it comes to access to higher education, a development that became a global target for women at the beginning of the twentieth century and a growing reality over the second half of the 1900s. Investment in girls' education beyond primary school was a much more difficult and expensive proposition to support in many parts around the world until then, for a variety of reasons.

To begin with, in most of Africa and many parts of Asia under colonial or imperial rule,[101] native women's education as a long-term investment was on the lowest rung of priorities for the colonial/imperial powers, like Great Britain, Germany, Portugal, Japan, and Russia. Although the status of native women in these societies became a political football for some colonial administrations and their critics in places like Kenya and Australia, little actual development came of it.[102] At most, private initiatives funded by religious establishments or rich philanthropists sought to fill in the huge gender gap in availability of higher education. But those initiatives were few and far between and insufficient for making more than a marginal difference. A conversation about and subsequently policies related to women's access to education beyond basic literacy started to take place only after the end of colonial or imperial rule—in other words, in some parts of the world after World War I, and in most other parts, especially Africa and Asia, only after World War II.

Even in the changing postcolonial or newly independent context, without women as part of the policy-making elites, many states continued to lag in articulating policies and investing funds in women's higher education. Nationalist parties of various ideological shades favored prevalent masculinist notions about gender roles in society, which placed emphasis on better educational opportunities for boys above education for girls. As a result, women's participation in postindependence politics was often focused as much on expanding women's educational opportunities and resources for women's education as on political rights. Using the same nationalist jargon of the pro-independence politicians, women highlighted the importance of women's participation in educating future generations of patriots and in upholding the traditions, culture, and values of their nation through education and knowledgeable dissemination of these national treasures.

But when it came to making a sustained effort on behalf of women's education, the male political establishment often resisted opening up new opportunities. The educational path of Wangari Maathai in Kenya, whose extraordinary contributions to environmentalist activism have already been discussed, is a good case study. A brilliant student, she received encouragement and resources not from the Kenyan state but from foreign sources, such as a US-funded scholarship to attend college in Kansas and later a German-funded fellowship to pursue doctoral studies in Europe. Throughout her academic career, Maathai encountered repeated challenges, such as a refusal on the part of the University of Nairobi to hire her as faculty based on nothing other than her gender. She found her first job there through the intervention of the same German researcher who helped her receive a fellowship to pursue her PhD.[103]

Maathai's life is illustrative of women's difficulty in gaining access to higher education and academic employment in postcolonial settings. It is also exemplary with regard to changes in women's fertility, as access to higher education improved. In her case, attendance first at a boarding high school and subsequently at higher education institutions in the United States and Germany delayed Maathai's entry into matrimony and having three children. She had her first in 1969 at the age of twenty-nine, which was significantly later than the average for the arrival of a first child in her part of the world. She had her second child after finishing her

PhD in 1971, and the third in 1974, after she had secured a position as a lecturer at the University of Nairobi.

Indeed, the trend toward fewer births and starting later (in their mid-twenties) increased in the 1960s and 1970s among women around the world who attended college. However, as research has shown more recently, although this trend initially meant that women with higher education gave birth to fewer children, by the end of the twentieth century birth rates among women with a college education bounced back to some extent. While these women marry at an older age or decide to enter long-term cohabitation and space children more according to their career path and available family leave policies, they are making the choice to have more children than the generation of the 1960s and '70s.[104]

Investment in women's higher education in parts of the world that came under communist rule is another distinct set of cases for the change in women's fertility in the twentieth century. State socialist regimes initially had similar aims and policies, but over time they became diverse in implementation. The Soviet Union was the first to enact sweeping reforms in women's education, equal rights in marriage and divorce, access to birth control, and women's employment. There, the birth rate went down significantly over the first decades of communist rule and continued to go down until it reached below-replacement levels (1.5) after 1991.[105]

The most spectacular reduction of fertility could be seen, however, among women who had lived in rural and traditional Islamic societies prior to communist rule. Uzbekistan is such an example. A number of studies over the past two decades have amply documented the radical shift in women's lives there after 1917.[106] From the basic eradication of female illiteracy, which had been higher than 90 percent, to the introduction of higher education and employment opportunities for women, within a decade of Soviet rule Uzbek women found themselves confronted with a dizzying array of new choices and limitations. Soviet officials frowned upon the traditional forms of girls' education available before 1917 and eliminated them shortly after the Bolshevik takeover. In the 1920s and '30s they pursued an aggressive two-pronged campaign of anti-veiling and enrolling girls in modern secular schools. The process was not without opposition on the part of both men and women steeped in Islamic traditions, and the officials sometimes used violent means to achieve their goals. By the end of the 1930s unveiling had become official policy and girls were attending mixed-gender schools, something that had been generally inconceivable before 1917.[107]

Changes in women's behavior vis-à-vis birth control and marriage were slower in this area than in other parts of the Soviet Union, but birth rates still went down significantly over the eighty years of Soviet rule, reaching 4.18 by 1990 and 2.2 by 2013, twelve years after the dissolution of the Soviet Union.[108] This continued decline suggests that Uzbek women have not chosen to have more children, despite the change in political orientation of the state and revival of Islamic culture and traditions. The near parity of gender in terms of completing secondary education helps explain these trends.

However, not all communist regimes chose to interpret the ideological commitment to gender equality in the same way. In Romania, for instance, the early commitment to providing women with the educational, employment, and birth control means to become equal partners to men in building the workers' state gave way to a very different set of policies in the late 1960s, when the regime realized that its ability to replenish the workforce at the rates desired would not be possible if women were left to their own devices to decide when to have children. [109] Though a number of women in the party leadership tried to counter the eugenicist-nationalist ideas of Nicolae Ceauşescu, the regime made most forms of birth control unavailable or illegal, giving rise to some of the highest rates in Europe of female death and sterility due to botched abortions. [110] The policy failed miserably and the decriminalization of abortion was one of the first changes made after the fall of communism.

* * *

The unprecedented population growth experienced over the twentieth century and subsequent decrease in fertility rates is a complex process that has engaged many political, technological, cultural, and economic factors. Increased life expectancy has helped influence this process. But by far the most important element has been women's control over their fertility. This chapter has shown how women themselves pushed for this change and to what extent they were successful.

These choices impacted not just individual women's lives or women's condition in specific communities. They impacted those communities and the men who lived in them. The change from patriarchy toward partnership in marriage, at school, in the workplace, and at the ballot box has been a two-way street. It would have been impossible for the women described in this chapter to break the boundaries they did without the support of fathers, teachers, husbands, sons, and friends. But none of these changes would have happened without women wishing them, willing them, sacrificing for them, and stubbornly pushing for them.

It is also equally true that the notion of universal sisterhood is more of a fantasy than reality in terms of women's specific choices on matters of fertility and how they have asserted these options. The differences between the most gender-equitable policies and practices, such as we see in the Scandinavian countries, and the most restrictive practices and policies, such as in parts of Sub-Saharan Africa, represent some of the widest gaps in how far we are from achieving global gender parity. And it is not clear that women everywhere wish to achieve gender parity on matters of fertility and sexuality. But as the interconnectedness of the world increases into the future, the choices women make about their fertility and sexuality anywhere in the world will continue to have a growing impact on the population and use of resources everywhere around the world.

NOTES

1. Margaret Sanger, *Woman and the New Race* (New York: Brentano's, 1920), 94.
2. UN Department of Economic and Social Affairs, Population Division, *World Population Prospects: The 2017 Revision* (New York: United Nations, 2017), https://esa.un.org/unpd/wpp/Publications/Files/WPP2017_KeyFindings.pdf.
3. In this chapter, I focus primarily on sexuality, birth control, marriage and divorce, and education. Migration will be addressed in chapter 4 ("Economics").
4. Robert M. Buffington, Eithne Luibhéid, and Donna J. Guy, eds., *A Global History of Sexuality: The Modern Era* (Hoboken, NJ: Wiley Blackwell, 2014).
5. Judith Walkowitz, *City of Dreadful Delight: Narratives of Sexual Danger in Late-Victorian London* (Chicago: University of Chicago Press, 1992).
6. Afsaneh Najmabadi, *Women with Mustaches and Men without Beards: Gender and Sexual Anxieties of Iranian Modernity* (Berkeley: University of California Press, 2005).
7. Alfred Kinsey et al., *Sexual Behavior in the Human Female* (Philadelphia: W. B. Saunders, 1953).
8. Baker, *Margaret Sanger*; see also the description of their encounters on the *Margaret Sanger Papers Project* website, accessed August 17, 2017, https://sangerpapers.wordpress.com/tag/marie-stopes.
9. Robert A Peel, ed., *Marie Stopes, Eugenics and the English Birth Control Movement* (London: Galton Institute, 1997).
10. Her support for eugenics extended to advocating for sterilization of the weak and feebleminded, which betrayed both racism and elitism in relation to working-class women.
11. Marie Carmichael Stopes, *Married Love or Love in Marriage* (New York: Critic and Guide, 1918).
12. Jesse Wolfe, *Bloomsbury, Modernism, and the Reinvention of Intimacy* (New York: Cambridge University Press, 2011), 8.
13. Patricia Anderson, *Passion Lost: Public Sex, Private Desire in the Twentieth Century* (Toronto: Thomas Allen Publishers, 2001), 40.
14. Stopes claimed to have been the first to open such a clinic and sparred publicly with Sanger over this issue, even though they shared a great deal in common and had become friends. Baker, *Margaret Sanger*, 171–72.
15. Sanger, *Woman and the New Race*, 94.
16. Baker, *Margaret Sanger*; Jill Lepore, *The Secret History of Wonder Woman* (New York: Random House, 2014).
17. Jill Lepore, "Birthright: What's Next for Planned Parenthood?" *New Yorker*, November 14, 2011, http://www.newyorker.com/magazine/2011/11/14/birthright-jill-lepore.
18. Julie Thomas, "International Intercourse: Establishing a Transnational Discourse on Birth Control in the Interwar Era" (PhD diss., Indiana University, 2004).
19. See the papers presented on the panel "Margaret Sanger in China: The Emergence and Trajectory of the Birth Control Movement in China, 1920–40s," at the American Historical Association's annual conference in New York, 2014, accessed August 17, 2017, https://aha.confex.com/aha/2014/webprogram/Session10461.html. A brief discussion of this new research can be found also on the *Margaret Sanger Papers Project* website, accessed August 17, 2017, https://sangerpapers.wordpress.com/2014/01/09/what-happened-next-a-look-at-birth-control-organizing-in-china-following-margaret-sangers-1922-visit.

20. Margaret Sanger, *An Autobiography* (New York: W. W. Norton, 1938), especially chapters 37–38; Thomas, "International Intercourse."

21. The focus on decreasing the birth rate in India became a complicated and controversial matter in the 1950s, when a number of approaches, from IUD insertions to vasectomies, were attempted and subsequently discarded. See Matthew Connelly, *Fatal Misconception: The Struggle to Control World Population* (Cambridge: Belknap Press, 2010); Sanjam Ahluwalia and Daksha Parmar, "From Gandhi to Gandhi: Contraceptive Technologies and Sexual Politics in Post-Colonial India, 1947–1977," in *Reproductive States: Global Perspectives on the Invention and Implementation of Population Policy*, ed. Rickie Solinger and Mie Nakachi (New York: Oxford University Press, 2016), 124–55.

22. The 1.2 million abortions included surgical and medical terminations, as well as treatments of incomplete abortions. See the IPPF *Annual Performance Report 2016*, accessed August 17, 2017, https://www.ippf.org/sites/default/files/2017-07/IPPF%20Annual%20Performance%20Report%202016.pdf.

23. Wolfgang P. Müller, *The Criminalization of Abortion in the West: Its Origins in Medieval Law* (Ithaca, NY: Cornell University Press, 2012).

24. Solinger and Nakachi, eds., *Reproductive States*.

25. Gail Kligman, *The Politics of Duplicity: Controlling Reproduction in Ceausescu's Romania* (Berkeley: University of California Press, 1998).

26. Solinger and Nakachi, eds., *Reproductive States*.

27. "Induced Abortion Worldwide," *Guttmacher Institute*, accessed August 17, 2017, https://www.guttmacher.org/fact-sheet/induced-abortion-worldwide.

28. "Abortion in Latin America and the Caribbean: Fact Sheet," accessed August 17, 2017, https://www.guttmacher.org/sites/default/files/factsheet/ib_aww-latin-america.pdf.

29. S. Singh, J. E. Darroch, and L. S. Ashford, *Adding It Up: The Costs and Benefits of Investing in Sexual and Reproductive Health 2014* (New York: Guttmacher Institute, 2014), accessed December 24, 2017, https://www.guttmacher.org/sites/default/files/report_pdf/addingitup2014.pdf.

30. UN Population Institute, "The State of World Population 2011," accessed August 17, 2017, http://ec.europa.eu/health//sites/health/files/eu_world/docs/ev_20111110_co01_en.pdf.

31. The different terminology used by various participants in debates about this practice denotes their assumptions about the violence or lack thereof in terms of women's bodies, normal sexual functions, and their human rights overall. The UN terminology is "female genital mutilation," while many commentators and especially practitioners use the more neutral terms "circumcision" or "cutting." Given the serious ongoing disagreements about the nature and impact of these practices for women, I will use both "mutilation" and "cutting."

32. Lynn M. Thomas, *Politics of the Womb: Women, Reproduction, and the State in Kenya* (Berkeley: University of California Press, 2003).

33. See UN Resolution 48/104, "Declaration on the Elimination of Violence against Women," December 20, 1993, accessed August 17, 2017, http://www.un.org/documents/ga/res/48/a48r104.htm.

34. E. Leye, K. Roelens, and M. Temmerman, "Medical Aspects of Female Genital Mutilation," in *Proceedings of the Expert Meeting on Female Genital Mutilation in Europe. Ghent. Belgium, 5–7 November 1998*, ed. E. Leye, M. De Bruyn, and S. Meuwese, International Center for Reproductive Health Publications, no. 8 (Lokeren, BE: The Consultory, 2003).

35. Pam Belluck and Joe Cochrane, "Unicef Report Finds Female Genital Cutting to Be Common in Indonesia," *New York Times*, February 4, 2016.

36. Thomas, *Politics of the Womb*.

37. Tara John, "Female Genital Mutilation More Widespread Than Previously Thought, UNICEF Says," *Time*, February 4, 2016, http://time.com/4207731/200-million-women-children-fgm-unicef.

38. More on the changes that took place in medicine as a result of women's efforts is in chapter 5 ("Knowledge").

39. The Pill has continued to receive criticism from a variety of opponents, some of them feminists concerned with the inadequate level of testing of the drug before it was approved, as well as with the side effects of the drug. Elaine Tyler May , *America and the Pill: A History of Promise, Peril, and Liberation* (New York: Basic Books, 2011).

40. Noah Feinstein and Becky Prentice, eds., *Gender and AIDS Almanac* (New York: UNAIDS, 2001); Robert Blum et al., "Adolescent Health in the Caribbean: Risk and Protective Factors," *American Journal of Public Health* 93, no. 3 (March 2003): 456–60.

41. Robert Jütte, *Contraception: A History* (Cambridge: Polity, 2008).

42. Connelly, *Fatal Misconception*.

43. Solinger and Nakachi, eds., *Reproductive States*.

44. Connelly, *Fatal Misconception*.

45. Rebecca M. Kluchin, *Fit to Be Tied: Sterilization and Reproductive Rights in America, 1950–1980* (New Brunswick, NJ: Rutgers University Press, 2009); Marius Turda, ed., *The History of East-Central European Eugenics, 1900–1945: Sources and Commentaries* (London: Bloomsbury Academic, 2015).

46. Solinger and Nakachi, eds., *Reproductive States*.

47. Marian van der Klein et al., eds., *Maternalism Reconsidered: Motherhood, Welfare and Social Policy in the Twentieth Century* (New York: Berghahn, 2012).

48. David Frankford, Linda Bennington, and Jane Ryan, "Womb Outsourcing: Commercial Surrogacy in India," *American Journal of Maternal Child Nursing* 40, no. 5 (September–October 2015): 284–90.

49. "Cost of Surrogacy in India," accessed August 17, 2017, http://ivfinindia.in/cost-of-surrogacy-in-india.

50. Eva Schandevyl, ed., *Women in Law and Lawmaking in Nineteenth- and Twentieth-Century Europe* (Burlington, VT: Ashgate, 2014). The book highlights both the unequal status and also exceptions to it.

51. For widows who remarried, the expectation of sexual purity was expressed through rules such as denial of permission to marry until a long period of time (more than one year) had passed since the husband had died. For men the expectation of a mourning period did not translate into interdictions against marrying again. The regulation existed to make sure the widow would not give birth to a child in that intervening time.

52. Emily Burrill, *States of Marriage: Gender, Justice, and Rights in Colonial Mali* (Athens: Ohio University Press, 2015).

53. Najmabadi, *Women with Mustaches and Men without Beards*.

54. The monastic option has few parallels in non-Christian societies. It was an option for Buddhists, but not Muslims and Jews, for instance.

55. Susan D. Carle, ed., *Lawyers' Ethics and the Pursuit of Social Justice: A Critical Reader* (New York: New York University Press, 2005).

56. *World Bank Gender Statistics*, accessed August 17, 2017, http://data.worldbank.org/data-catalog/gender-statistics.

57. "Child Marriage Is a Violation of Human Rights, But Is All Too Common," accessed August 17, 2017, https://data.unicef.org/topic/child-protection/child-marriage.

58. In 2004 around sixty births per one thousand women ages fifteen to nineteen were recorded on average worldwide. In Sub-Saharan Africa the average was more than twice as large, at around 138. See Celine Ferre, "Age at First Child: Does Education Delay Fertility Timing? The Case of Kenya," Policy Research Working Paper 4833 (Washington, DC: World Bank, 2009), accessed August 17, 2017, http://www-wds.worldbank.org/external/default/WDSContentServer/WDSP/IB/2009/02/10/000158349_20090210091332/Rendered/PDF/WPS4833.pdf.

59. Betsey Stevenson and Justin Wolfers, "Marriage and Divorce: Changes and Their Driving Forces," *Journal of Economic Perspectives* 21, no. 2 (2007): 27–52.

60. Adam Isen and Betsey Stevenson, "Women's Education and Family Behavior: Trends in Marriage, Divorce and Fertility," CESifo Working Paper 2940 (2010), accessed August 17, 2017, http://www.econstor.eu/handle/10419/30703.

61. Ruth Rosen, "The War against Contraception: 'Women Need to Be Liberated from Their Libidos,'" *openDemocracy. free thinking for the world*, February 14, 2014, accessed August 17, 2017, https://www.opendemocracy.net/5050/ruth-rosen/war-against-contraception-%E2%80%9Cwomen-need-to-be-liberated-from-their-libidos.

62. Virginia Comolli, *Boko Haram: Nigeria's Islamist Insurgency* (New York: Oxford University Press, 2015).

63. Mark Juergensmeyer, *Terror in the Mind of God: The Global Rise of Religious Violence*, 3rd rev. ed. (Berkeley: University of California Press, 2003).

64. Michel Foucault, *The History of Sexuality*, vol. I, *An Introduction* (New York: Pantheon Books, 1978); Marc Epprecht, *Heterosexual Africa? The History of an Idea from the Age of Exploration to the Age of AIDS* (Athens: Ohio University Press, 2008).

65. Robert Beachy, *Gay Berlin: Birthplace of a Modern Identity* (New York: Knopf, 2014); Maria Bucur, *Gendering Modernism: A Historical Reappraisal of the Canon* (London: Bloomsbury Academic, 2017).

66. Peter Di Sciascio, "Australian Lesbian Artists of the Early Twentieth Century," in *Out Here: Gay and Lesbian Perspectives VI*, ed. Yorick Smaal and Graham Willett (Melbourne: Monash University Press, 2011), 135–55; Shu-mei Shih, *The Lure of the Modern: Writing Modernism in Semicolonial China, 1917–1937* (Berkeley: University of California Press, 2001); Robert McKee Irwin, *Mexican Masculinities* (Minneapolis: University of Minnesota Press, 2003).

67. Wilde's case received much attention and helped shape public attitudes about homosexuality as far away as Mexico. See Irwin, *Mexican Masculinities*.

68. Ruthann Robson, "Crime and Criminology," in *Encyclopedia of Lesbian and Gay Histories and Cultures*, ed. George Haggerty and Bonnie Zimmerman (New York: Taylor and Francis, 2000), 206–209.

69. Paul Peppis, *Sciences of Modernism: Ethnography, Sexology, and Psychology* (New York: Cambridge University Press, 2014).

70. This is in stark contrast with the studies published by Alfred Kinsey half a century later, which were based on long-term observation, interviews, and other forms of clinical research of a considerably larger size. This rendered his work difficult to dismiss, as the work of many others previously had been, by the mainstream scientific community. See Kinsey et al., *Sexual Behavior in the Human Female*.

71. Peppis, *Sciences of Modernism*.

72. Beachy, *Gay Berlin*.

73. On Stöcker's activism, see Ann Taylor Allen, "Mothers of the New Generation: Adele Schreiber, Helene Stöcker, and the Evolution of a German Idea of Motherhood, 1900–1914," *Signs* 10, no. 3 (1985): 418–38.

74. David Carter, *Stonewall: The Riots That Sparked the Gay Revolution* (New York: St. Martin's Press, 2004).

75. For an up-to-date count of this evolving list, see "Gay Marriage Around the World," Pew Research Center, accessed August 17, 2017, http://www.pewforum.org/2015/06/26/gay-marriage-around-the-world-2013.

76. Wolfgang Lutz and Qiang Ren, "Determinants of Human Population Growth," *Philosophical Transactions of the Royal Society of London* 357 (2002): 1197–210; David M. Heer, "Economic Development and Fertility," *Demography* 3, no. 2 (1966): 423–44; D. R. Leet, "Interrelations of Population Density, Urbanization, Literacy, and Fertility," *Explorations in Economic History* 14, no. 4 (1977): 388–401; Karen Oppenheim Mason, "Explaining Fertility Transitions," *Demography* 34, no. 4 (1997): 443–54; Wolfgang Lutz, ed., *The Future Population of the World: What Can We Assume Today?* rev. ed. (London: Earthscan, 1996).

77. Lutz and Ren, "Determinants of Human Population Growth," 1206.

78. Wendy Brown, "Finding the Man in the State," *Feminist Studies* 18, no. 1 (Spring 1992): 7–34.

79. For data about the first half of the twentieth century, see UNESCO, *Progress of Literacy in Various Countries: A Preliminary Statistical Study of Available Census Data since 1900* (Paris: UNESCO, 1953); for data about more recent trends, see "Data for the Sustainable Development Goals," accessed August 17, 2017, http://www.uis.unesco.org/literacy/Pages/default.aspx.

80. It is important to note, however, that even in states like the United States and the British Commonwealth, significant differences between the dominant white or dominant ethnicity female population and females in ethnoracial minorities persisted for much of the twentieth century.

81. UNESCO, *World Illiteracy at Mid-Century: A Statistical Study* (Paris: UNESCO, 1957). The study doesn't provide overall numbers because of the great heterogeneity in measurements around the world, but instead provides country-by-country assessments, where women appear almost universally with higher levels of illiteracy.

82. For a brief overview of these complex developments before the twentieth century, see Jennifer C. Madigan, "The Education of Girls and Women in the United States: A Historical Perspective," *Advances in Gender and Education* 1 (2009): 11–13.

83. Natalie Zemon Davies provides three such portraits of women from early modern Europe in her *Women on the Margins: Three Seventeenth-Century Lives* (Cambridge: Belknap Press, 1995). We have more recent, excellent examples from autobiographical accounts of many more women growing up in the late nineteenth century in places like (1) Istanbul: Leyla (Saz) Hanimefendi, *The Imperial Harem of the Sultans: Daily Life at the Ciragan Palace during the 19th Century: Memoirs of Leyla (Saz) Hanimefendi* (Istanbul: Peva Publications, 1994); (2) Bucharest: Elena Văcărescu, *Mémorial sur le mode mineur* (Paris: Jeune Parque, 1946); and (3) Cairo: Huda Sha'arawi, *Harem Years: The Memoirs of an Egyptian Feminist* (New York: Feminist Press, 1987).

84. Cheris Kramarae and Dale Spender, eds., *Routledge International Encyclopedia of Women: Global Women's Issues and Knowledge*, vol. 1, *Ability–Education: Globalization* (New York: Routledge, 2000).

85. Emel Dogramaci, *Atatürk and the Turkish Woman Today* (Istanbul: Atatürk Kultur, Dil ve Tarih Yuksek Kurumu, Atatürk Arastirma Merkezi, 1991).

86. Yeşim Arat, "The Project of Modernity and Women in Turkey," in *Rethinking Modernity and National Identity in Turkey*, ed. Sibel Bozdoğan and Reşat Kasaba (Seattle: University of Washington Press, 1997), 95–112.

87. Ayşe Durakbaşa, "Halide Edib Adivar," in *A Biographical Dictionary of Women's Movements and Feminisms: Central, Eastern, and South Eastern Europe, 19th and 20th Centuries*, ed. Francisca de Haan, Krassimira Daskalova, and Anna Loutfi (Budapest: Central European University Press, 2006), 120–23.

88. Aynur Soydan Erdemir, "A Woman's Challenge: The Voice of Şükufe Nihal in the Modernisation of Turkey," in *Women, Education, and Agency, 1600–2000*, ed. Jean Spence, Sarah Aiston, and Maureen M. Meikle (New York: Routledge, 2010), 134.

89. United Nations, *World Population Prospects: The 2000 Revision* (New York: United Nations, 2001).

90. "Women and Education in the Third World," special issue, *Comparative Education Review* 24, no. 2 (June 1980).

91. Nathan Nunn, "Gender and Missionary Influence in Colonial Africa," in *Africa's Development in Historical Perspective*, ed. Emmanuel Akyeampong et al. (New York: Cambridge University Press, 2014), 489–512.

92. Paivi Hoikkala, "The Hearts of the Nations: American Indian Women in the Twentieth Century," in *Indians in American History: An Introduction*, ed. Fred E. Hoxie and Peter Iverson (Wheeling, IL: Wiley Publishers, 1998), 253–76.

93. Deirdre A. Almeida, "The Hidden Half: A History of Native American Women's Education," *Harvard Educational Review* 67, no. 4 (Winter 1997): 757–71.

94. On the history of Aboriginal women's education in Australia, see Gillian Weiss, ed., *Trying to Get It Back: Indigenous Women, Education and Culture* (Waterloo, ON: Wilfrid Laurier University Press, 2000).

95. She is also known as Gertrude Simmons Bonnin, the European name given to her by Quaker missionaries. Her Sioux name translates as "Red Bird."

96. P. Jane Hafen, "Introduction," in Zitkala-Ša, *Dreams and Thunder: Stories, Poems, and the Sun Dance Opera* (Lincoln: University of Nebraska Press, 2001), xiii–xxiv.

97. Zitkala-Ša, Charles H. Fabens, and Matthew K. Sniffen, *Oklahoma's Poor Rich Indians: An Orgy of Graft and Exploitation of the Five Civilized Tribes, Legalized Robbery* (Philadelphia: Office of the Indian Rights Association, 1924).

98. Wadi D. Haddad et al., *Meeting Basic Learning Needs: A Vision for the 1990s. Background Document. World Conference on Education for All, 5–9 March 1990, Jomtien, Thailand* (New York: Inter-Agency Commission, 1990), 33 and 30. Though the document acknowledges five authors on the team preparing the document, Margaret Sutton, a scholar who works on gender and education reform around the world, provided the research and most substantial analysis in the document, as recounted by Margaret Sutton through personal communication, February 22, 2016.

99. Ibid., 71.

100. Edward B. Fiske, *World Atlas of Gender Equality in Education* (Paris: Unesco, 2012), 42.

101. To clarify this distinction, I categorize the type of rule that the British and French established in parts of Africa and Asia as colonial. Other states, such as Russia in relation to parts of Europe (including Bessarabia) and parts of Asia (including Mongolia), pursued an imperial policy of direct incorporation into the state, while resisting serious investment in these marginalized areas in anything else other than government institutions such as the military and local administration. A comprehensive policy related to girls' education in these areas was absent. For Russia, see Ben Eklof, *Russian Peasant Schools: Officialdom, Village Culture, and Popular Pedagogy, 1861–1914* (Berkeley: University of California Press, 1986).

102. Nupur Chaudhuri and Margaret Strobel, eds., *Western Women and Imperialism: Complicity and Resistance* (Bloomington: Indiana University Press, 1992). On the critiques by Australian feminists, see chapter 2 ("Politics") in this book.

103. For more details about her repeated frustrations as a woman academic, see Maathai, *Unbowed*.

104. See Isen and Stevenson, "Women's Education and Family Behavior."

105. Sergei V. Zakharov and Elena I. Ivanova, "Fertility Decline and Recent Changes in Russia: On the Threshold of the Second Demographic Transition," in *Russia's Demographic "Crisis": Conference Proceedings*, ed. Julie DaVanzo and Gwen Farnsworth, accessed August 17, 2017, http://www.rand.org/pubs/conf_proceedings/CF124/CF124.chap2.html.

106. Nancy R. Rosenberger, *Seeking Food Rights: Nation, Inequality and Repression in Uzbekistan* (Belmont, CA: Wadsworth, 2012); Marianne Kamp, *The New Woman in Uzbekistan: Islam, Modernity, and Unveiling under Communism* (Seattle: University of Washington Press, 2008); Adeeb Khalid, *Making Uzbekistan: Nation, Empire, and Revolution in the Early USSR* (Ithaca, NY: Cornell University Press, 2015).

107. Some informal basic education had been mixed for young children, especially when the teacher was a woman who would provide informal lessons in private homes. Formal educational institutions had been strictly segregated by gender. Kamp, *The New Woman in Uzbekistan*.

108. "Gender Data Portal: Uzbekistan," *World Bank*, accessed August 17, 2017, http://datatopics.worldbank.org/gender/country/uzbekistan; the earliest year for which the World Bank site has data is 1960, at which point Uzbek women's fertility was 6.71, by contrast with the 2.52 average in the Soviet Union at that time.

109. Luciana Jinga, *Gen și reprezentare în România comunistă: 1944–1989* (Iași, Romania: Polirom, 2015); Corina Doboș, Luciana Jinga, and Florin Soare, eds., *Politica pronatalistă a regimului Ceaușescu*, vol. 1, *O perspectivă comparativă* (Iași, Romania: Polirom, 2010); Kligman, *The Politics of Duplicity*.

110. Raluca Maria Popa, "'We Opposed It': The National Council of Women and the Ban on Abortion in Romania (1966)," *Aspasia* 10 (2016): 152–60.

FOUR

Economics

Women are the most underutilized economic asset in the world's economy.

— Ángel Gurría, Secretary-General, Organisation of Economic Co-operation and Development, 2012[1]

By far the most persistent forms of systemic gender inequality in modern history have been in the area of economic power. The twentieth century, especially during the second half, has seen dramatic transformations toward reducing these trends. Still, all economic regimes, from capitalist to corporatist, communist, or socialist, have proved resistant to eliminating gender inequality even when professing to have that as a fundamental goal. Women's economic empowerment has gained ground only in parts of the world, while many more women, especially in the global South, continue to lag behind men in terms of access to better economic opportunities such as equal pay for equal work, access to capital, and positions of authority.[2] Today, these problems are receiving strong criticism from feminist activists and transnational economic organizations, such as the International Monetary Fund (IMF). Recently the IMF identified the gender gap in economic inequality as a crucial global problem that needs to be solved if policy makers, business leaders, and citizens of all nations want to promote long-term strategies for economic growth for all, in every state around the world.[3]

The one somewhat brighter spot in this mixed global picture is the increase in economic opportunities in the service sector. At the same time, the globalization of economic processes, especially in the service sector, has driven a hard wedge between women who have gained access to higher economic opportunities and those who have not. In areas such as domestic work, well-educated and professionally ambitious women are benefiting from and helping reinforce the lower wages of women from especially the developing world as a means of climbing the ladder of economic empowerment.

Whether they have become beneficiaries or are simply those on whose backs economic growth has taken place, women have become fuller participants in the money economy than at any previous point in history. They have added their talents and energies from the factory floor to the boardroom. And they have significantly altered consumption patterns around the world through their choices as buyers. Though some of these trends represent continuities from the nineteenth century in parts of the world, especially Western Europe and North America, on a global scale they are a twentieth-century phenomenon. This chapter explores the complex and somewhat contradictory shifts that women have helped bring about in the world of economic activity in the twentieth century.

PROPERTY

Women have always been as much a part of the workforce as men.[4] However, their ability to control the results of their labor and turn it into economically valued activity has long hinged on legal definitions of "work" and "property." The spectacular growth of capitalism and industrialization over the nineteenth century helped define these concepts in gender-specific ways that pushed women into positions of invisibility and powerlessness, while protecting male-dominated forms of earning and controlling income.[5] As the money economy and waged labor began to replace other forms of economic exchange, women, who worked primarily in the home or in agriculture, found their economic autonomy decrease. By contrast, men became favored as paid laborers in many of the growing industries, enjoyed greater mobility from the countryside, were largely identified as possessing the physical strength required for most industrial jobs, and were viewed as the main breadwinners by employers. This trend became globalized through the development of colonial capitalism everywhere from East Asia to Southern Africa.[6] In the twentieth century women have made tremendous efforts to address this structural inequality but have been only partially successful in reversing the trend, with consequences that impact economic production, consumption, trade, family relations, demographic trends, environmental problems, and many other components of human interaction.

Reviewing some of the basic mechanisms that led to women's economic marginalization is important for fully appreciating how much has changed in what is defined as economically productive activity and how it has been valued differently over time through various forms of property control. Well into the nineteenth century in most parts of the world, property relations were governed both legally and in practice by religious and other customary traditions rather than by secular legal codes.

Wealth was most often understood as linked to multigenerational familial ties and interests. With patriarchal notions of succession and inheritance already firmly in place in the premodern period in most places around the world, individual roles in the process of building and maintaining the interests of the family resulted in specific gendered norms. From Europe to Asia, most of these traditions placed women in a secondary position in the family as children, wives, and mothers, in terms of how much property they were entitled to inherit or own and how much control they had in disposing of such property as they saw fit.[7]

Christian traditions in Europe and other lands that had fallen under the colonial control of Christian empires provided a set of gender norms. These traditions often differentiated among categories of women, placing those of higher social standing in a more equitable position than those of the lower classes.[8] Women of the nobility could benefit from the privileges of their families' wealth if their fathers saw fit to support them. In practice thus, social standing and the lack of opportunities for social mobility among the lower classes rendered men and women of these large social categories more similar to each other in terms of property rights. The economic well-being of serfs and slaves was much more alike, regardless of gender, than any similarities women shared across social status.

Russia represents an important exception in this regard. In 1753 a law was passed to consolidate equality between men and women of the nobility in terms of control, use, and transfer of property.[9] The law provided a small but still sizable part of the female population with the ability to better control its economic well-being. Over time, however, this law came into increasing tension with marital law, which stipulated that women needed to remain subordinate to their husbands. As a recent study shows, over the nineteenth century this tension gave rise to practices that favored fathers and husbands over wives and daughters across all classes.[10] Dowries and immovable property began to be controlled by men rather than the women who nominally owned that property. The reality on the ground began to look more similar to other European states in terms of women's economic dependency.

Islamic societies from the Middle East to Africa had other traditions and somewhat different practices than those described above. In the Ottoman Empire siblings were entitled to equal inheritance. Women were allowed to control both property they brought into the marriage and wealth they accumulated while married.[11] Upon divorce, they would be able to recapture their entire dowry. In places like Tunisia, local interpretations of the Quran also dictated that they receive an additional gift from their husbands, a sort of settlement to assist them financially.[12] This only applied to Muslim women, however, rather than any other religious group over which the Ottomans ruled, such as Christians and Jews.

The interpretations and application of these laws differed, however, from place to place and over time. By the time reformers like the Tunisian Tahar Haddad (1899–1935) became active on behalf of women's rights in Islamic societies, their praise of the Quran's fair treatment of women was accompanied by a critique of the abusive and oppressive more recent practices that had brought women into a position of economic dependency on men.[13] Like other Islamic feminists, Haddad saw much potential in returning to "foundational" readings of the sacred texts as a path toward reconnecting with authentic Islamic beliefs.

The shift from a nonmonetized to a money economy started much earlier than the nineteenth century, but it only caught up in remote parts of the world as capitalism became globalized in the nineteenth century.[14] In virtually all countries around the world, secular laws governing control over property, both immovable and also monetary, started to define men more starkly as a category of people exclusively entitled to operate with full autonomy as signatories of contracts, owners of capital, managers of wealth, and heirs.[15]

These laws did not practically empower all men but gave them exclusive access to these opportunities. By gendering the identity of those who had economic autonomy, these laws also made it clearer than any previous traditional religious or customary legal practices that women were not entitled to these rights. Some women could and did benefit from forms of economic empowerment, but they were always at the hand of men. In some countries, women of the upper class continued to also enjoy privileges and wealth of the nobility from which they descended—that is, until legal civil codes became modernized in those states. At that point, they became legally subordinate to the fathers, husbands, and even sons in their lives.[16]

Through colonialism and the modernization of various states across the world, these new legal codes began to thoroughly redefine gender roles in the family in terms of financial responsibilities and rights, which radically altered women's position across all classes. The Napoleonic Code (1804) was hailed for a time as a progressive change that brought a more rational set of expectations in relations between citizens and in terms of the state's protection of its subjects.[17] In reality, the Napoleonic Code firmly empowered men to be the head of the family, financially speaking, rendering women legally and financially dependent on men. Over the nineteenth century, similar codes were passed in the Habsburg Empire (1811), Chile (1857), Italy (1865), Romania (1865), Portugal (1867), Argentina (1871), Spain (1899), and other countries.

The Napoleonic Code defined morality in gendered polarized terms and drew direct, inescapable connections between gender identity understood as a static, biological reality, and state protection for property rights. By defining men as the caretakers of the financial needs of the family, the new laws established the role of "head of household" more firmly than previous legal practices. They carefully detailed how wealth would pass from the father to sons and husbands, with daughters featured as infantilized vectors for moving control over property from one generation of men to the next. Women's role in the family and by extension society came to be defined legally as subordinate to the will of their fathers, husbands, and sometimes sons. Widows alone could aspire to actually controlling property nominally in their name. And until the twentieth century women tended to live shorter lives than men, so the category of widow was a small proportion of the population. As Carol Pateman has brilliantly shown, this new set of laws was the logical outcome of male domination over women, which she identifies as "sex-right," entwined with recent developments in capitalism, industrialization, and liberalism.[18] The feminist scholar argues that the contractual relationships that developed under capitalism to facilitate industrialization were set up to bolster men's "sex-right." Individual freedom, as defined predominantly in the liberal ideology of the nineteenth century in the West, was founded on similar assumptions about men's "sex-right" and stood in direct and explicit conflict with the feminist challengers of that period.[19]

Consolidating property so only one individual could fully control all assets generated increased capacity for the family to act as a unit, and that is precisely what the Napoleonic Code aimed to provide. Women could inherit the same amount as men, but as girls their property would be controlled by their father, as wives by their husband, and sometimes even as widows by their oldest son. By and large, only when their father and husband had died, as long as their sons did not dispute their rights, did women have the ability to control their own property, meaning property that had been placed in their name sometimes decades prior to assuming such control. Other related limitations imposed on women included their inability to sign contracts on their own, even when they were attempting to sell their own property.[20]

Needless to say, none of these restrictions applied to men as a category of people, with the exception of age: all children below a certain age (eighteen to twenty-four, depending on the place) would not be able to control assets in their names. The logic that undergirded these uneven gender roles was that (1) as procreators and homemakers, women needed protection and assistance, which men would be able to provide by consolidating all economic power in their hands; and (2) women were morally weaker and therefore unworthy of the same rights as men. The second assumption is best exemplified by the types of divorce granted under the Napoleonic Code. In general, only major crimes and infidelities, such as murder and moving into a home with one's mistress, would entitle a wife to seek divorce and still retain her dowry though not necessarily any of her husband's property. By contrast, something as little as spending one night under a roof that was not her husband's or parents' without his approval might provide the husband sufficient evidence to pursue a divorce and take away the wife's assets.

Over the nineteenth century this gender inequality in property relations became entrenched in much of the world. Most countries in Europe adopted a version of the Napoleonic Code (Britain and Scandinavia were exceptions), and many colonial territories in Asia and Africa did so as well. Although Islamic societies had their own very old traditions and legal codes, in places like the Ottoman Empire, Egypt, and Iran, proponents of modernization looked upon these newer ideas about marriage and property rights as a step toward bringing their societies onto a more equal footing with the West.[21]

In Africa, colonial visions of progress and property rights became imposed, sometimes very superficially, over very different practices and traditions.[22] Pastoral economies that did not include land enclosure, much less fixed and inheritable rights to the land itself, had generated different gender relations based more often on cooperation than subordination and focused primarily on the use of the natural resources on the land (trees, water, etc.). While scholars acknowledge these differences are important for policy makers seeking to address gender-equitable economic development, they also underscore the fundamental gender asymmetry in inheritance and ownership laws and practices dating back to precolonial times.[23] In areas where either Islam or Christianity had made long-term inroads in African societies, the view of these religions regarding property rights became important in addressing property transfers through inheritance and marriage. Overall, scholars have connected gender asymmetries in property transfer and actual control to women's lesser degree of economic autonomy and empowerment in the family.[24]

Reversing this trend was no small feat and it came about through the work of feminist activists around the globe. These were efforts largely started by elite women or those with significant education. Their experience had been of frustration at the hands of the restrictive laws that enabled their fathers, brothers, and husbands to reap the benefits of their family fortunes, but left these women in the position of powerless beneficiaries or supplicants.[25] The first significant challenges to this trend took place starting in the middle of the nineteenth century in the United States (1839) and in Great Britain (1870), where a number of laws were gradually passed to empower married women to gain complete control over property they brought into marriage and property they gained while married. Married women eventually gained the right to enter contracts on their own as well, though in practice blatant gender discrimination continued well into the twentieth century.[26]

By the beginning of the twentieth century there was increasing interest on the part of women from the higher echelons of society to control wealth that was far too often only nominally in their names. For most other women, however, such issues were of far less relevance than the sheer poverty they experienced. Laws undergirding gender differences in terms of property ownership, inheritance, and access to capital affected their lives as well, though not as directly.

Women living in rural areas were constricted more by local marriage practices and cultural—especially religious—traditions. Marriage remained an expectation for women, their value in these societies measured in terms of what they could bring into the marriage: purity, sexual and in terms of character; dowries, most of the time to be controlled by their fathers and husbands, respectively; and a hardy constitution that could withstand both reproductive and productive labor. For men, economic abilities and autonomy featured prominently, hand in hand with the assumption that they would be the head of their family in both moral and economic matters. Noncompliance with such expectations would result in punishments, but women had a lot more to lose than men if they strayed from the norms. Women often became ostracized, further marginalized, and impoverished to the point of starvation. Deviant men might lose the respect of some of their peers but were seldom banished from these communities. In places like Great Britain and the United States, the law courts were more likely to protect white married women from the economic neglect of their husbands, but in most other places around the world, women could expect little support from the legal system in curbing various forms of abuse or neglect on the part of their spouses.

At the beginning of the twentieth century, urban lower-class women suffered from the same lack of protection and economic autonomy in terms of property rights, but for them the context was very different from the traditions of the rural world. Unlike men, women were not as readily able to move to these areas unaccompanied by family (meaning, strictly speaking, a male figure of authority). Over time, with the growth of metropolitan areas, women became less constrained by these gendered expectations. The architecture and flow of people in and throughout these urban areas generated the promise of anonymity, even as it created the likelihood of less personal security for vulnerable populations, especially women and children.[27]

But the promise of greater choice was not necessarily followed by more empowering practices. As Shanghai grew into a major port and commercial center in the early twentieth century, it attracted increasing numbers of men and women from the Chinese countryside. Yet the entrenched gender customs of this society continued: a single woman was on the lowest rung of social respectability, with young married women just above that position. Women found themselves more often than not unable to find safe places to live and work without becoming indebted and sometimes virtually enslaved to men, other women, or families that hosted them. Marriage into an urban family often did not confer greater autonomy in terms of control over any property or income they garnered through work.[28] The daily life of one woman who moved to Shanghai on the eve of the Communist Revolution (1949) looked like this:

> Since her betrothal to Yeye at the age of fourteen in 1935, Nainai's life had been largely confined to the domestic sphere. . . . While Yeye attended schools, Nainai waited on her parents-in-law . . . from dawn to dusk. Her daily chores included cooking meals and "nourishing treats" such as white fungus with lotus seed, dusting and mopping all the rooms, washing her mother-in-law's feet and clipping her toenails, and serving her in-laws opium until they fell asleep. . . . When she cooked an egg for herself during her pregnancy, her mother-in-law scolded her.[29]

Starting in the 1930s laws provided women with greater economic autonomy in terms of inheritance, marriage, and divorce.[30] But practice was another matter, and women suffered great abuses in this area as a matter of mainstream behavior at the hands of their spouses, parents, in-laws, and often older women in the household.[31] Though many accept the narrative that women's economic autonomy improved after the communist takeover, recent scholarship offers a robust critique of whether practices on the ground were equitable and empowering for women, focusing on both the urban and especially much larger rural female population.[32] The slower pace of urbanization during the first period (1949–1978) of China's transformation under communism also meant that traditions of gender inequality in controlling property would continue here for decades. Recent scholarship identifies the period after the end of the Cultural Revolution in 1978 as the beginning of more effective reforms in eliminating persisting gender inequalities, and the 1990s as the decade when women truly began to gain access to the new types of capital available in the increasingly marketized economy.[33]

    In other communist regimes the process of addressing gender inequality in property relations followed the Soviet model. The Soviet Union was heir to a number of regions with very different traditions of property rights. After 1917 women made significant gains overall in terms of their legal equality with men in all matters pertaining to economic activity. Of course, the quality of these rights was framed by the larger context of abolishing private capital, which brought significantly greater losses for men. For most of the female population, who already lived in poverty and without control over capital, this was not as significant a change as for the men who had enjoyed those rights.

    Some positive qualitative changes for all women with regard to property rights did take place under this and other communist regimes. Women gained the exact same inheritance rights as men, were no longer bound by dowries, enjoyed the same rights to the fruit of the family labors in marriage and divorce, could open individual savings accounts whether married or not, and had access to cheap loans through a variety of funds provided by the state (e.g., through their place of work, labor union, or banks). Even though these rights did not amount to real possibilities for unlimited economic empowerment, they did provide important tools for women to act as autonomous economic agents rather than subservient second-class citizens.

In the case of other regions that came under Soviet direct or indirect control starting in World War II, changes in property rights were more mixed for women. In states where they had enjoyed strong protection, such as Estonia, their losses were more comparable to those of men. In places where serious legal gender disparities continued into the interwar period, such as Romania and Yugoslavia, communism took away less from women as a category of economic agents and instead equalized economic opportunities, as it did in the Soviet Union in the 1920s.[34] The same could be said of Cuba and North Korea.[35]

In countries where women began exercising voting rights after World War I, the question of full equality in terms of economic opportunities and property rights became articulated even more powerfully in the 1920s. From Germany to Australia and the United States, feminists continued to fight against forms of discrimination such as access to personal loans, divorce, inheritance, and professional development opportunities. In these societies, like much of the rest of the world, the notion that the male was the head of the household and thus responsible for the economic well-being of the family continued to pervade hiring and business practices well into the twentieth century. Married women were sometimes explicitly and more often implicitly prevented from pursuing paid work. If women wanted to take out loans, they might be required to have a male cosigner, or their chances of approval would go up significantly if they had one.[36]

Inequality between men and women with regard to property rights, as entrenched through the Napoleonic Code–inspired legal codes of the nineteenth century, was finally resolved over the second half of the twentieth century, as a result of a number of interrelated political developments. After winning voting rights, women began to question legal inequalities in other areas of public policy, such as property rights. The entry of a growing number of women into the legal profession ensured that discrimination against women in matters of property ownership would be addressed with greater attention than before. Women's access to education and new economic opportunities gave rise to a new category of voters and economic agents who spoke more assertively about continuing inequalities. As autonomous citizens, women's exercise of their economic self-interest had led to expanding the legal protection of their individual economic assets and to protection against gender discrimination in employment and property rights.

When, after 1945, liberation movements overtook colonial regimes, the question of property rights became an important matter resolved generally in nondemocratic ways by legislatures in which women played little, if any, direct role. With a few exceptions, such as Cuba, postcolonial regimes did not place a premium on gender equality in terms of access to capital or real estate or in terms of new civil codes, regardless of the ideological position the newly established political elites adopted (leftist versus more liberal or nationalist-traditional).[37] Just as important were continuing traditional or customary legal practices, which weakened the impact of broad postliberation institutional reforms.[38] In some cases, customary practices protected women from abuses on the part of state agents. In most cases, however, women have continued to suffer from fewer opportunities to become more economically self-sufficient.

Some scholars state that we still cannot speak about full legal equality between men and women at the beginning of the twenty-first century in matters of property ownership, protection, and access to capital in many states in Latin America, Africa, Europe, the Middle East, and Asia.[39] Yet the gap has been narrowed in virtually all states, with the exception of the resurgence of fundamentalist Islamic regimes in the Middle East and North Africa. In these countries, important strides women made in the twentieth century toward gender equality in property and political rights have been questioned by new generations of interpreters of Islam who negate the more women-friendly readings provided over the twentieth century by feminist Muslim thinkers.[40]

Looking at the twentieth century broadly, we don't have a good sense of what these legal changes have meant in terms of real wealth or freedom of choice in economic endeavors, because of the ways in which economists have chosen to analyze data. In his recent and much-discussed analysis of the future of capital and, by extension, property rights and wealth, Thomas Piketty spent virtually no effort in trying to understand the gender dimension of wealth accumulation through the acquisition and management of private property since the nineteenth century.[41] Historical data about the effect of property rights is difficult to interpret, given the unclear relationship between control on paper and control in real life. Sale of property rights held in women's names or inheritance and divorce documents would be able to provide us some measure of how women have or have not benefited from enhanced property rights. But research on such processes has not been a prominent topic in economic history overall, and we have little data that can be compared across the world. Still, one can observe that in 2017 significantly more women were moving autonomously in the world of economic activity than in the early 1900s, supported by laws that affirm legal gender equality and, in many cases, protect them against discrimination. Recent economic history research confirms this.[42] Concentrated efforts on producing reliable and comprehensive data on women's economic empowerment show a close correlation between strong protection for women's rights as property owners and women's ability to close the economic gender gap. [43]

WORK AND ECONOMIC POWER

The changing definitions of work and labor practices over the twentieth century provide another important insight into understanding how women have reshaped their societies in significant ways since 1900. This is a complicated story at the global level, and it is difficult to generalize about many specific changes. But a number of similar shifts across parts of the world can be distinguished: (1) the growing participation of women in the wage-earning workforce; (2) the strong correlation between women's education and economic empowerment; (3) the strong correlation between women's participation in the wage-earning workforce and the shift in the global economy from agriculture and industry toward the service sector; (4) and the growing inequalities among women due to the devaluing of caretaking work they tend to perform in all societies, like childcare, elderly care, and household work.

The gender gap in wage labor participation narrowed substantially over the twentieth century. In the United States, for instance, statistics show a growth in the percentage of women wage earners from 2.5 percent in 1890 to almost 60 percent a hundred years later. [44] This remarkable climb hides important nuances, however. To begin with, the percentage of women of color who worked outside their own households (sometimes remunerated, though initially not, as slaves), was much higher than that of white women: In 1900 17 percent of white women aged twenty to sixty-four were wage earners, by contrast with 42 percent of African American women. The gap narrowed significantly by 1983, showing growth for both categories—63 percent for white women to 64 percent of African American women. [45]

The race-based differential in how much women earn has also narrowed, by some measurements to nearly nil, and by others to a 7 to 9 percent difference. [46] The real issue into the future has to do with protection against discrimination for all women and equal access to the education and professional opportunities that could help eliminate the wage gap. After 1964, affirmative action programs in the United States helped address some of these issues, but the results are far from stellar and show that entrenched racism continues in areas of women's wage earning. [47]

In countries where capitalist economic regimes have remained in place throughout the twentieth century, the entry of women in the waged workforce came slowly and against strong opposition on the part of the male political class and labor organizations, which had become important institutions by the early twentieth century. [48] Women continued to be paid significantly lower wages (sometimes only half) than men for the same work. After World War I, when many women had the opportunity to step into higher-wage work, labor unions and politicians pushed for the replacement of women with men in the better-paid industries.

When the ILO was established after World War I as a measure for supporting and regulating workers' rights on a global scale, the universalist claims of this institution were immediately undermined by the resistance of many union leaders to bringing in a substantial female voice. [49] The International Congress of Women Workers that took place in 1919 in Washington, DC, highlighted these deficiencies and made a loud and persuasive argument for developing a women's section, if women's issues and voices were not to be fully integrated into ILO's other structures. [50]

As many historians have shown, labor movements most often started from the same premise of what work meant and who was responsible for the economic well-being of the family as the liberal framers of the property rights laws of the nineteenth century. [51] The notion of equal pay for equal work was beyond the pale for many of these labor leaders. These men could not fathom the notion of a woman being able and eager to perform the exact same tasks for the same amount of time and with the same results. If that might have been true for physically demanding jobs like mining and logging, the diversification of industrial production by the end of World War I created a more varied set of working conditions and demands. In addition, in World War I women had shown that they could handle many of these jobs when, for instance, they were called upon to work in ammunition factories. [52]

In the face of this opposition, women like Marguerite Thibert (1886–1982) played a crucial role in the international community in terms of keeping questions about women's employment and gender equality in the workplace a core component of the ILO's work and prominent in discussions at the League of Nations. Thibert was an unabashed socialist feminist and one of the first women to get a PhD in history. She was also the first woman to defend a history PhD with both a subject in nineteenth-century feminism and a feminist perspective on the matter. Thibert found the doors of academia shut and turned toward the ILO as a place of employment suitable for her expertise and as a platform for her feminist activism. [53] She helped produce many important reports on women's employment, both country-by-country and international, that pointed out the links between women's economic dependency on men and the unequal civil and political rights in most countries. These reports made specific recommendations to address the problems. Yet during the interwar period many of them remained without any follow-up, largely because of the lack of support by the top male leadership in both the ILO and the League of Nations.

As leader of the women and children's committee, Thibert also helped shape the position of the ILO in terms of protective legislation for working women, entering a long-term conflict with other feminist contemporaries who saw this perspective as undermining the quest for gender equality. In the eyes of the feminist Open Door International Council, protective legislation might have helped specific categories of women. But it ultimately served as a weapon against the broader quest on behalf of all women to secure entry into all professions as well as gain approval of the equal pay for equal work idea.[54]

After World War II Thibert came around to this position and became a strong proponent of the equal pay struggle. The UN, through its Commission on the Status of Women, has long drawn attention to the question of gender inequality in terms of access to wage labor and equal pay for equal work. And women like Dolores Huerta (b. 1930) in the United States and Anna Walentynowicz (1929–2010) in Poland became prominent labor activists in their respective countries, fighting for equal rights for all workers. But such rights remain elusive at the beginning of the twenty-first century and are some of the most entrenched forms of gender inequality in our world.

This problem has been compounded by the continued extensive practice of piecework done by women in many parts of the developing world.[55] Feminist activists in the ILO have drawn attention to women's vulnerability as workers in these working conditions of invisibility, low pay, and often physical abuse. Yet governments and international bodies like the World Trade Organization have refused to treat these abuses as serious problems.

The countries that made the greatest strides toward providing full access to women in all paid labor and addressing the issue of wage inequities are the communist regimes—the USSR, China, North Korea, Poland, Hungary, Czechoslovakia, East Germany, Romania, Bulgaria, Yugoslavia, Albania, Cuba, and Angola—and, after World War II, the most industrialized countries in Western Europe. In the case of the communist regimes, the ideological foundation that linked individual value with one's ability to work for the common good created a clear slate of expectations for both men and women: they would contribute to the productive economy and be rewarded for the same work in the same way as men.

Most of these countries were predominantly agricultural and rural[56] at the beginning of these radical transformations, so the effort to engage women in paid labor was part of a larger campaign to modernize and especially industrialize the economy, a fundamental tenet of communist ideology as operationalized by Lenin. Communist regimes established after World War II, either by force or through the support and the example of the Soviets, followed the lead provided by the policies initially laid out in the Soviet Union through the Zhenotdel (see chapter 2, "Politics"). They developed women-focused opportunities for paid labor not only in agriculture but increasingly in various industries. Such policies often con-

nected education or technical training with opportunities for employment in areas identified as suitable and in need. These governments
sought to alleviate caretaking burdens by developing childcare and after-
school programs, often in the vicinity of factories where mothers worked.
Canteens and other inexpensive services, such as laundering, were
opened up to assist working women.

Such developments were an unprecedented boon for women, though
the reality was less rosy than proclaimed by these communist regimes.[57]
Not all of them treated women in the same way, and there are differences
among these states in how far the goal of employing women and alleviat-
ing their traditional caretaking responsibilities went. Tension between
the stated goal of equality and the reality of women's double burden
defines every communist regime. According to a UNICEF report from
1999, women in the East European communist bloc worked around
seventy hours per week, fifteen more than in Western Europe. In 1990,
after forty-five or more years of policies proclaiming gender equality, the
percentage of women active in the labor force was significantly higher in
communist countries around the world in relation to the Arab world,
Latin America, and South Asia. But the regional percentages for the communist world were about the same as for North America, Western Europe, Sub-Saharan Africa, and East Asia.[58] More importantly, the gender
pay gap continued to be 20 to 30 percent between women and men.[59]
And the number of hours women continued to spend doing unremunerated work at home continued to be disproportionately larger than men's
in both communist and other countries.

Over the same period of time, women in Western Europe gained important economic rights and opportunities as part of the development of
the welfare state measures championed by many governments after
World War II, especially in Scandinavia, Germany, France, and Great
Britain. Southern European countries like Spain and Greece remained
less committed to these gender empowerment policies until decades later, when they were admitted into the EU in the 1980s. Over time, the EU
evolved to include more comprehensive checks and balances in terms of
individual rights in the member countries and developed specific policies
to combat economic discrimination, including gender.[60]

For several decades, until the recent recession of the 2000s, these policies helped bolster the growing feminist movements in member countries
and provided legal and financial opportunities for them to fight discrimination in their own countries or through international bodies such as the
EU human rights court. With legal protection against wage discrimination on the basis of gender and with attendant family leave policies becoming more widespread and gender-inclusive, some of the foundations
of economic gender inequality were being successfully addressed. However, the recent recession has had a devastating effect on some anti-dis-
criminatory gender policies. In Greece, the hardest hit member of the EU,

women's unemployment has continued to be higher than men's, with no efforts made to address it at the level of the EU. Some of the first expenditures to be cut from the budget in the name of austerity were programs addressing economic gender inequality, such as childcare support for working mothers.[61] In the face of great economic adversity, the promise of addressing discrimination and advancing gender equality as part of the larger principle of protecting individual rights has proven vulnerable in the EU.

The United States provides the most striking example of how industrialized states with a very large participation by women in the workforce and a huge national revenue base continue to refuse to consider caretaking needs as a core responsibility of public policy. Recently, the United States has come under severe criticism by the UN for its lack of support for working mothers.[62] A 2012 study on the economic gender gap in 128 countries places the United States thirtieth in rank, below all but a couple of industrialized states, as well as lower than nine postcommunist European countries.[63] A more recent publication (2016) places the United States forty-fifth in the world in terms of the economic gender gap, with Jamaica, Argentina, Laos, Burundi, South Africa, and most of the EU ranking higher.[64] Yet no comprehensive overhaul of its hands-off policies toward childcare, parental leaves, and elderly care is under way. Instead, as public education has come under increasing criticism at the state level, state legislatures are opening up funds earmarked for education, preschool, and kindergarten to individual vouchers, with the result of further privatizing childcare and education.[65] This trend has made it harder for working mothers to be able to afford childcare. Parental leaves continue to be short (twelve weeks), with no legal mandate to pay the employee for that time off.

Some private companies have become more forward-looking in this regard, as they have started to provide paid parental leaves and even childcare services for their employees.[66] But these practices remain uneven across industries, and they often cater to the highest-paid employees rather than the neediest ones.[67]

The data we have on women's paid employment for most of the world are spotty before 1945, when the establishment of the UN created new avenues for keeping statistics for all member countries and insisted on gendering the data. Before World War II, as already mentioned, the ILO attempted to create a more consistent form of keeping accurate data about women's employment, but the commitment to do so depended on the individual members, and though data were collected from around the world, they were by no means consistent enough to draw broad conclusions about global trends.

The crystallization of focus on gender inequality issues through the UN happened at the same time that many countries around the world were gaining independence from colonial rule. While many of these new states were slow in focusing on other forms of economic empowerment for women, such as property ownership, their focus on bringing women into paid labor was quicker and more thorough. This is why, by the 1990s, the percentage of women active in the labor force in countries from Sub-Saharan Africa was higher than most other places around the world, including Western Europe. In Tanzania, 89 percent of women ages fifteen to sixty-four were economically active, according to World Bank data for 1991–1995.[68] The male percentage for the same period is only slightly higher, at 91 percent. Other postcolonial countries, such as Rwanda and Vietnam, show equally impressive percentages of women participating in the labor force, surpassing women's participation in North America or Western Europe.

This, however, is not necessarily a sign of individual economic empowerment but more likely of economic mobilization into communities (most often kinship networks) that have become dependent on women's paid work. For many of these women, participation in labor has also been primarily in agriculture, where earnings and the possibility of gaining greater individual economic independence are low. In Tanzania in 1990, women's employment in agriculture counted for 90 percent of total women's employment.[69] By 2014 their participation in agriculture had gone down to 70 percent. This decrease represents a shift to the service industry, where a growing proportion of the world's active population, and especially women, has moved.

UNPAID LABOR

If women have continued to be paid less for their work than men, their contributions to the economy have also been consistently undervalued due to the definition of productive labor. Ever since modern states have taken on the responsibility of keeping statistics on economic production and the Gross Domestic Product (GDP), the question of what counts as productive labor has vexed economists: Would only work remunerated in cash be considered valuable? Or would the unpaid work of caretaking and performing routine household chores be also part of the equation of how "value" is economically defined? This question is key to understanding women's marginalization as a part of the labor force from the nineteenth century to the present.

As work moved into factories and agriculture became more commercially focused, the familial world of taking care of children, washing, clothing, feeding, cleaning, and overall keeping a household going every day came to signify the opposite of productive labor. Waged labor had value because of the money it could bring into the household for the purpose of taking care of various household necessities, such as rent, heating, and taxes. Household work contributed to similar needs, but more as process than raw materials (e.g., cooking, cleaning, sewing). Women's work became further devalued just as men's wage labor was becoming more universally the accepted norm of valuable work. In a cash-driven economy women's role was by definition secondary, auxiliary, rather than a primary economic force, even though the well-being of its families and societies would be greatly diminished without women's unremunerated contributions.

The question of how to account for women's unpaid work has preoccupied economists, politicians, and statisticians since the nineteenth century. It was there at the beginning of setting up national statistics on production, wealth, and employment. But, as economist Nancy Folbre pointed out in a recent book, the question of how women's unremunerated work could be counted in the larger scheme of productivity and wealth was slowly eliminated from discussion and continues to be so in most places around the world.[70] Feminist historians and economists have continued to push against gendered assumptions about "productivity" and "value" in defining forms of labor to be counted in national statistics. But their efforts have been at best barely audible, and at worst continuously ignored by the mainstream scholars and policy makers involved in measuring and interpreting the data. Recently, however, studies by the IMF and other powerful institutions have started to push this issue more directly in conversation with policy makers around the world.[71]

One important contribution in keeping these issues part of a global conversation on how to better represent the total contribution of working people has been that of New Zealander economist Marilyn Waring (b. 1952). Elected as a member of Parliament in 1975 at the age of twenty-three, she was appointed chair of the Public Expenditure Committee at a time when the conservative prime minister Robert Muldoon (1921–1992) was interested in enhancing government programs for women and education. He entrusted Waring with developing arguments and specific recommendations in these areas. The result was an overhaul in what counted as valuable labor in the country's GDP, with household unremunerated work and farm work both counting as active contributions to the economy. Waring used her experience in Parliament together with her own work as a farmer to build a broader case for how national and international economic agencies needed to change their assumptions about what should count as productive or valuable labor, by accounting for caretaking and other forms of unremunerated labor into GDP statistics.

Her landmark book, *If Women Counted: A New Feminist Economics* (1989), provided powerful stories, as well as a set of concrete critiques about the failures of the current accounting of work practices to measure women's work. The book was practical in also providing solutions for these inadequacies, solutions she took to the classroom, scholarly publications, and the UN, where she served on the Commission for the Status of Women. For more than a quarter of a century Waring has continued to address the UN to make the case for rethinking these national and international statistics. One has to commend her for this fortitude, but unfortunately the economists and politicians in charge of financial institutions have yet to take her criticisms and suggestions to heart, except in a handful of countries around the world, such as Finland and Australia.[72]

EDUCATION AND ECONOMIC POWER

Though today we take for granted the statement that educating girls is one of the best investments in the future of economic growth, the focus on women's education as a crucial factor toward empowering them economically became a global theme only in the 1970s, during the UN International Decade of Women.[73] Until then, with the exception of communist countries, international ideas and policies about economic development had focused on other macroeconomic factors and tied women's issues to these questions only through population policies.[74]

The results have been uneven globally, with Africa and the Middle East lagging significantly behind other parts of the world. But it is undeniable that the UN has played a crucial role in enhancing educational opportunities for women and enabling them to become more economically autonomous. The gender pay gap has started to close for women everywhere in the world where they have had the same educational opportunities as men and where there is no discrimination in professional opportunities. In places like North America, China, and Europe, women today surpass the number of men attending institutions of higher education and have been successful in challenging male prerogatives in every professional endeavor, including the military. But these are very recent accomplishments, dating less than a generation ago, which suggests that the impact of growing educational gender parity on economic empowerment will become more noticeable into the future.

This is not the case for the rest of the world. Even with policies and investment in women's education by a number of organizations, such as the Bill and Melinda Gates Foundation and the UN, in many countries across the world, from Africa to the Middle East and South Asia, the literacy rate among girls is significantly lower than that of boys.[75] Girls tend to be taken out of school more often than boys for cultural/religious reasons, from concern with exposure to sexual danger to early marriage and caretaking responsibilities around the home. The educational gender gap has been closing especially since the 1980s, but continues to be quite significant in Sub-Saharan Africa and South Asia.[76] In Sub-Saharan Africa, in particular, there has been regression in this area since the late 1990s.

MIGRATION

Another set of changes that shaped economic disparities around the world centers around migration practices and policies, especially over the last three decades of the twentieth century. Though at the beginning of the twentieth century international migration was strongly gendered masculine, by the 1970s women began to close the gap. At the beginning of the twenty-first century women reached near parity in this area of human activity.

Migration is correlated with a number of other changes, such as population growth and economic empowerment opportunities.[77] If migration is partly about which states count people as "theirs," it is also about what choices individual citizens can make regarding their professional and personal lives. These choices eventually impact other aspects of migrants' lives, like marriage and birth rates. But the research on this matter, especially with regard to women's lives, has not been a subject of sufficient interest across the world to generate good transnational data and analyses.[78] Some recent work allows us, however, to speculate about possible connections between women's migration as a new phenomenon in the twentieth century and women's economic empowerment.

To begin with, we now know that women began to constitute a growing component of the migrant population after 1900. By the end of World War I women had come to represent almost 30 percent of global migration and grew to almost 45 percent by the end of the century.[79] This is a remarkable shift, but how is it historically significant beyond this numerical growth? The ability to move across borders is connected to both the porousness of the borders as established by sovereign states and the international order at that time, as well as to the legal and economic ability of individuals to move freely. These factors have changed independently of each other in the twentieth century, so it is impossible to generalize globally about the relationship between them and women's growing participation in migration. Still, some scholars argue that economic globalization itself is a cause of this increase.[80]

The porousness of borders decreased significantly over the twentieth century, with the number of states growing and the redrawing of citizenship rules becoming increasingly restrictive in terms of who can have a passport, as well as how, when, and where one can use it. This phenomenon started after World War I, at a time when women activists were beginning to push in a concerted transnational effort to enable women to gain greater autonomy in declaring and retaining their citizenship regardless of marital status and the citizenship of their husbands.[81] At the end of the war many women found themselves defined as displaced persons, given the shifts in borders and the massive casualties among soldiers. Many of them were living in territories that had ceased to be empires and were in the process of being declared part of new states (e.g.,

Poland, Estonia, Czechoslovakia). These international factors help explain the spike in migration at that point. It was less that these women
moved than that the map was redrawn around them.[82]

Women's movement across borders continued to grow into the 1920s
and 1930s, but less as a factor of external massive shifts than as a personal
choice they could make. In countries where they gained the vote, women
also obtained different civil rights, such as the ability to move around
without consent from men. In some cases, women who had pursued
public careers during the war found themselves frustrated in their ambitions by the preferential treatment given to soldiers returning from the
front. They sought economic opportunities commensurate with their experience and qualifications by moving elsewhere. In other cases, especially the Soviet Union in the years after the Bolshevik Revolution, the massive emigration of families to Europe (e.g., France) and Asia (e.g., China),
counted for an important component of women's participation in this
phenomenon.[83]

After World War II regulations regarding visas and control over borders continued to increase, especially with the polarization of international relations over the Cold War. In terms of allowing immigrants to
relocate in the host country, these policies showed a preference for families and against single male laborers. In short, when applying for visas to
move to another country, families (couples or parents with children)
came to be viewed as more of an asset than single men.[84] These preferences had important consequences for women's mobility, and they enhanced the economic prospects of married men even as they disadvan-
taged single men and women. For married women who were part of
migrant families, moving to countries that had greater employment opportunities, more legal protections for women's rights, and greater access
to birth control overall significantly enhanced their economic agency. For
the United States, the country with the largest number of immigrants
during that period, in the 1960s fewer than 40 percent of these women
migrants worked outside the home; by 1990 around 65 percent were
active in the labor force.[85]

During the 1960s a new phenomenon emerged in the industrialized
world: the preference for bringing in women as part of migrant or guest
worker programs. By 2000 women made up 90 million of the 159 million
international labor migrants.[86] In the United States, women represented
54 percent of the total. This is a remarkable phenomenon and begs for a
comprehensive explanation. At first glance, these statistics point toward
greater opportunities for women through the lowering of international
barriers. Yet the reality of these migrants' lives is far more complicated.
While women have been able to make more choices regarding employment, these are not necessarily more unconstrained options than staying
in one's country of citizenship, nor are they necessarily a sign of women
being able to follow professional or economic personal ambitions. In

short, they have not helped enhance women's economic power universally.

For many women with strong professional training who came from authoritarian regimes like China or the Soviet Union, migration to Western Europe, North America, or Australia between 1945 and 1989 meant greater economic and social opportunities. Since the 1980s, however, most women migrants have come from the Caribbean, Latin America, or Southeast Asia to developed countries without their families or strong professional training that they could easily translate into secure well-paid jobs in the host country. These women often choose to travel overseas because of the lack of economic opportunity in their home countries and as a way to take care of their family's basic economic needs in places like the Philippines, Vietnam, or Ecuador. Their jobs have been predominantly in caretaking or service industries, from elderly care and childcare to sex work and the garment industry. The wages are low and the work often unprotected by any transparent oversight, thus open to abuse by the employers.[87]

This surge in women's economic migration from poor to rich countries and the parallel growth in the need for elderly care and childcare in these richer countries are not coincidental. As women in developed economies have become better educated and gained access to jobs that pay well and make higher demands on their time because of greater responsibilities, they have had to make different choices about their professional life in relation to their parental and other caretaking needs. The double burden has continued to rest unequally on their shoulders, due to continuing assumptions that household chores are primarily women's work. In some states, predominantly Western Europe and Canada, public programs for parental leave and childcare became a core component of the state's responsibilities toward its citizens, especially starting in the 1970s. But even there, the supply and demand do not match, and families in which both parents work have sought other means to cover their caretaking needs (for children, household, and sometimes elderly parents).[88]

Since the most significant common change in these families has been women's growing participation in the economy and their earning power, it would be facile to point toward them as the cause for generating a greater demand for vulnerable women immigrants as domestic workers. But a growing body of scholarship reframes such correlations: individual decisions to employ migrant workers are connected to the lack of adequate state planning, both in terms of policy and also financially.[89] If there are no affordable public programs for childcare and elderly care, and if their male partners continue to view household responsibilities as primarily women's business, the choices women have remain quite restricted: they can either work and hire someone they can afford, or they can choose to be the caretaker and forgo the professional, personal, and financial benefits afforded by employment.

Where women play a more directly oppressive role vis-à-vis migrant female workers is on the plane of how, as employers, they treat domestic workers. A 2016 report provides worrisome conclusions about current trends in this area.[90] Immigrants to the United States who work in this sector, almost exclusively women, reported significantly more forms of abuse than domestically born workers: 31 percent of undocumented immigrants performed work outside of their job description by contrast with 19 percent of US-born workers; 77 percent of undocumented immigrants reported working while sick, injured, or in pain, compared to 56 percent of the US-born.[91] And 85 percent of the undocumented immigrants who experienced abuse at work did not complain, out of fear they would be deported.[92] There are no good statistics on the gender breakdown of employer abuse except in the area of sexual abuse, where men are almost exclusively the abuser. But it is fair to say that in such informal employment settings, women can and have been the perpetrators of abuse both directly, by asking domestic workers to perform work not assigned, not allowing enough rest, and other forms of abuse, and indirectly, by not standing up to spouses who perpetrate abuses.

In response to these conditions women have started to play a more prominent role as workers and voting citizens in relation to their elected officials as well as to employers. Some have also engaged in activism on behalf of immigrant domestic workers who do not have the political rights or economic power to engage in this sort of activism. During the first decade of the twenty-first century, domestic workers began to organize and sought forms of legal support to codify their work through contracts, standardized regulations regarding work hours, conditions, pay, and the like, as well as against discrimination and specific forms of abuse.[93] Starting in 2010, the passage of the Domestic Worker Bills of Rights in New York, California, Hawaii, Massachusetts, and Illinois was an important step toward addressing abuses on a legal level in the United States. In the EU, the second largest market for female migrant domestic workers, ILO Convention no. 189, "concerning decent work for domestic workers," has provided the template for an ongoing discussion about guidelines for all member states.[94] Women's NGOs have been working with migrants to enhance their legal protection and work conditions, but the results have fallen short of full recognition of these workers as deserving protection and the same benefits as other types of work in the service sector.[95]

By voting for politicians and policies that support their needs as workers and mothers, and by opting to work for employers who pay attention to these issues, women are starting to alter the conversations about these caretaking responsibilities and turn them into socially and policy-relevant questions rather than private familial concerns. Yet in periods of financial constraint, like the recent global recession, the programs that get squeezed out first are those focusing on working women's caretaking needs. Even in the most legally protected region, the EU, women's needs as workers and mothers became recast more easily into "luxuries" by contrast with the salaries and benefits of government employees or the military, for instance.[96] In short, despite having their views and interests more visibly represented, women still fall short of drawing the same attention as workers and taxpayers as men, even in countries where they have reached near parity in level of employment.

Furthermore, in countries where migrant women have entered the labor force in significant numbers, female citizens of the host countries have found themselves in a more complex setting of competing interests and definitions of rights, priorities for government policies, and gender norms. This is a major challenge for the near future, especially with globalization of the labor force growing, even as protection for workers inside states fails to keep up with these fast-paced shifts. Women—as workers, employers, citizens, and the category of humans still disproportionately shouldering the burden of caretaking needs in most families around the world—will have a crucial role in negotiating these policies.

In many places around the world where migrant women work in other parts of the service sector in large numbers, legal protection is even less available and abuses abound. This is especially the case in the loosely defined category of "entertainment." Often this includes sex work without clear definitions of what such services entail and what sorts of vulnerabilities the workers encounter, and overall it offers no protection against human trafficking, primarily because sex work continues to be illegal in most countries. In Japan, for instance, a significant part of the migrant female labor force has been employed in the entertainment industry as singers and dancers, under a category of visas that provides few protections against abuses by employers. Some of these workers have been trafficked as sex workers. The coercive and illegal nature of these work situations and the lack of protection for the workers translate into vulnerable and economically dependent positions for the migrants.[97]

Sex trafficking of women has been an ongoing international issue since before the twentieth century. The League of Nations was the first international organization to draw attention to sex trafficking by undertaking an extensive undercover research mission in the 1920s. At the urging of Grace Abbott (1878–1939), who became a member of the Advisory Committee on the Traffic of Women and Children in 1923, the League set out to document all such illicit activities. The resulting reports provided a detailed picture of practices and networks in sixty major urban centers across thirty countries.[98] Unfortunately, there was no significant follow-up from this major documentation effort, and the problem remains poorly addressed today.

Sex trafficking continues to go underreported because sex workers fear retribution from the traffickers, and the societies where they operate refuse to discuss such problems openly. The result has been poor statistics and a lack of understanding by policy makers of the magnitude of this global problem. A study published by a French foundation in 2012 provides the closest thing to global statistics, placing the total number of sex workers around the world at forty to forty-two million.[99] Seventy-five percent of the workers are thirteen to twenty-five years old—in other words, many of them are children—and 80 percent are female.[100] The United States, Brazil, Spain, China, India, Thailand, Morocco, and Ukraine are among the countries with the highest percentages.

With sex work considered illegal in most of these countries, the trade remains open to great abuses by illicit businesses. Considered a less violent crime than drug or arms trafficking, sex trafficking has remained largely tolerated by international agencies like Interpol. A 2014 report by Interpol secretary general Jürgen Stock stated that 5,400 victims and 2,700 offenders had been identified in recent years, out of 4.5 million victims of sexual exploitation, or a tiny 0.12 percent out of the total.[101] Feminist activists have become more forceful in bringing to light the abuses suffered by sex workers, but there is little international coordination on how to tackle this problem: some want greater enforcement of existing laws; others would like to change the legislation to afford more visibility and protection to sex work.[102] As long as international agencies that have the human and financial resources to combat sex trafficking remain uninterested in devoting more of their attention to this problem, it will continue to fester. Since men are the primary perpetrators and also enforcers of such crimes and women are the primary victims, only strong, international leadership by feminist policy makers is likely to change this pattern.

CONSUMPTION

A sweeping change around the world in the twentieth century has centered around the shift of most economic activity from agriculture and industry to the service sector. In Western Europe and the colonial regimes Europeans established elsewhere, what we call consumer culture today had already begun to develop as an important aspect of both sociocultural and especially economic life in the eighteenth and especially nineteenth centuries.[103] Over the twentieth century these trends became global, as colonialism retreated and the newly independent states began to take consumer culture as a mark of modernity. Starting in the 1960s, the communist bloc began to compete for international and internal legitimacy in relation to access to consumer goods.[104] It is a striking change with implications in every aspect of human interaction, from education and employment to environmental concerns and political movements. And it would not have happened without women playing a central role.

Consumer power exists only for individuals who have sufficient buying or production power to exercise choices over consumption, and where the markets offer them the option of choosing. At the beginning of the twentieth century, most women's buying power was limited by factors already detailed in this chapter—such as limited property rights and unequal access to paid labor, professional development, and education. Women from elite economic classes as far back as the eighteenth century were already enjoying the ability to manifest this power in places like Britain and Russia. But they did not necessarily manifest this power on behalf of all women and especially not on behalf of those who were on the lower end of economic well-being.[105]

As women's economic autonomy and buying power grew over the twentieth century in other places, where restrictions against employment and property rights began to be eliminated, the choices women made in the market began to have greater impact on their societies and not just in their own lives or family. In the United States, segregation reinforced the political racist aspects of consumption, which women activists in the civil rights movement turned into an important means of educating the African American population and of empowering women. Ella Baker (1903–1986) played a particularly important pioneering role in this regard starting in the 1930s, when she began teaching courses on consumer politics at the Rand School.[106] By the 1960s these themes and strategies for empowerment had started to impact the civil rights movement at its core. Sitting at a counter to eat a piece of pie, riding a bus, drinking from a water fountain—all forms of consumption had been turned into focal points of political protest that questioned racist privilege. The participation of so many women in the civil rights movement was a result in part of the intimate knowledge they had about the impact of segregation on their own ability to act in the marketplace with the same rights and responsibilities as their white neighbors.

In the long run, in capitalist countries, the growing economic and political power of women as producers, employees, and consumers translated into greater consumer choices as well as more opportunities to shape what was produced and sold. The proliferation of appliances for the household took place in part as a result of women's greater ability to make purchases aligned with prevailing gender norms. Class and race/ethnic differences have been important in how these choices have been framed and whom they actually benefit. Thus consumer politics have been at times a unifying issue, and at other times divisive in terms of mobilizing specific groups of people.

With the globalization of economic processes, consumer choices have started to include more important hidden caveats, especially as production became further removed from the sale and consumption of goods. Labor abuses hidden behind glossy labels have gained more visibility in the last two decades.[107] Even as women with greater economic agency started making choices between thrift and savings, on the one hand, and socially responsible purchases on the other hand, they began to play a more direct and substantial role in determining the future directions of the service economy.

This is nowhere clearer than in the areas of international labor protection and environmental sustainability. Free trade, which emerged as a hegemonic global doctrine in the twenty-first century, has been challenged by consumer and labor activist alliances, for whom the dignity of the most vulnerable workers, many of them women, is as important as access to inexpensive consumer goods. Feminist activists have played a crucial role in maintaining this as a focus of negotiations in international agreements. The National Organization of Women opposed the Trans-Pacific Partnership legislation in the US Congress when it was brought up for a vote in 2015.[108] Speaking on behalf of women workers and consumers of the developed world, it deemed the law a feminist issue insofar as it would enable countries that continue to have gender discriminatory practices to benefit from the lack of tariffs without having to address these problems. In short, free trade still hides important forms of discrimination. The abolitionists knew that in the nineteenth century. As fully empowered citizens, women in parliamentary democracies have started to assert their responsibility to address these forms of discrimination.

As consumers and still primary caretakers in household matters, women remain the main agents for choosing products in terms of cost versus other considerations, such as carbon footprint. In Africa women have played a central role in shaping government policy, working through NGOs, educating younger generations, and making choices as both producers and consumers of goods. The work of Wangari Maathai in Kenya to reverse the disastrous results of deforestation has already been mentioned here (chapter 2). As a very large proportion of the working population in economies that are shifting from agricultural production to service industries, women are shaping that transition through their own engagement with new opportunities as entrepreneurs and managers of their own households.[109]

A Pew Research Center study from 2015 shows that in the countries with the highest pollution emission, women tend to be significantly more concerned about their impact on environmental problems at the global level than men. If 75 percent of women in the United States believed they needed to change their lifestyle to address these environmental problems, only 57 percent of men did. In Germany, 81 percent women versus 70 percent men had this view, while in South Korea the gender differential was eleven points (89 percent of women versus 78 percent of men).[110] Moving from attitudes to action, a recent EU report, "The Gender Dimension of Climate Justice," called on international organizations (e.g., the UN) and national governments in the EU to "improve the participation of women in decision-making on climate change mitigation and adaptation policies and do more to make their climate policies gender-sensitive."[111]

Pressure from above has been backed up by pressure from below. At the UN Climate Change Summit in Paris in December 2015, gender was a hot-button issue. Feminist activists from many places but especially the global South presented passionate arguments for the need to rethink economic development policies and priorities.[112] Many were connected to longer traditions of feminist international networks created over the twentieth century, such as the peace movements, and regional and global organizations like the UN Permanent Forum on Indigenous Issues. As such, they spoke on behalf of women as producers and citizens and also to represent indigenous groups whose very existence is being threatened by deforestation, limited access to water, and other economic practices.[113] Established female leaders in the environmental movement, such as Costa Rican diplomat Christiana Figueres (b. 1956) and Filipino activist Victoria Tauli-Corpuz, UN Special Rapporteur on Indigenous People, played a crucial role in organizing the Paris climate talks and drawing attention to gender and indigenous people's specific relationship with environmental problems. Members of FRIDA (Flexibility, Resources, Inclusivity, Diversity, Action)—a global network of young feminist activists—and other international networks of young feminists brought concerns with gendered aspects of climate change to the streets and hallways of the conference through boisterous protests.[114] The final document included three specific references that connect gender and environmental policy making, moving forward, among them:

> Acknowledging that climate change is a common concern of humankind, Parties should, when taking action to address climate change, respect, promote and consider their respective obligations on human rights, the right to health, the rights of indigenous peoples, local communities, migrants, children, persons with disabilities and people in vulnerable situations and the right to development, as well as *gender equality, empowerment of women* and intergenerational equity.[115]

The Paris agreement explicitly acknowledged gender equality and women's empowerment as global goals linked to climate change only because of pressure by feminist activists inside the forum and on the street.[116]

In communist regimes, consumer politics took on different nuances starting in the 1960s. The first generation of newly empowered women workers focused their energies on shifting from unpaid to paid labor. For the subsequent generations of women who had come to take for granted gender equality at work, the privations in consumer goods and services they experienced as caretakers of the home, children, and the elderly began to translate into greater burdens on their time and energies.[117] If the communist regimes promised access to modernized means of energy, the reality often fell short of those goals. Electrification in rural areas took place faster than the introduction of running water. Purification of the water systems was uneven and often took a back seat to other projects deemed more urgent by the predominantly male leadership of these regimes. As a result, even as they spent a lot more time outside the home as paid workers, women often returned home to backbreaking household chores like washing, cooking, and cleaning, in which men by and large did not participate and therefore saw as secondary to other projects. In places like Poland, women showed their disapproval of these failures on the part of the communist regime through strikes and other forms of protest.[118]

The most direct and long-term consequence of the double burden and lack of necessary goods and services imposed by the communist regimes on women was their refusal to embrace motherhood. Under communist rule the birth rate plummeted to levels that provoked a complete rethinking of the population policies in the Soviet Union, Bulgaria, Romania, and Hungary.[119] Women voted with their wombs and, in the absence of consumer goods and services that would enable them to make better choices in the work-life balance, denied the state the labor force it had hoped to generate.[120] By the fall of the communist regimes, these countries had some of the lowest birth rates in the world, whereas at the beginning of the communist regimes, they had registered some of the highest birth rates in the world.

The political intricacies of women's behavior as consumers with increasing economic power constitute an area that is likely to expand as the twenty-first century progresses. It is a place of relative gender empowerment that deserves greater attention, especially since some of this empowerment is taking place at the expense of other women.[121]

INNOVATION AND LEADERSHIP

Oprah Winfrey (b. 1954), Meg Whitman (b. 1956), Sheryl Sandberg (b. 1969), and Qunfei Zhou (b. 1970): What do they have in common? They are among the most famous and wealthiest women in the world. They are also self-made successful businesswomen in entertainment, online sales, social media, and touch screen manufacturing, respectively.[122] This group highlights the extraordinary accomplishments women have been able to achieve in the last hundred years in the field of economic enterprise, as well as the ways in which gender continues to be an important element in the economic obstacles and opportunities people around the world face structurally. Their extraordinary stories exemplify the great enhancements women have brought over the past hundred years to the global economy and societies in which they live.

Known around the world simply as "Oprah," Winfrey is not the first African American woman to become extremely successful exclusively through her ideas, hard work, and business acumen. Sarah Breedlove (1867–1919), better known as Madame C. J. Walker, was born in Louisiana a couple of years after the end of the Civil War, the first in her family to be free at birth. Her family had been slaves on a plantation and both of her parents died when she was seven. She started working as a domestic servant as a child and had a hard life of manual work and moving around the country until she was able to research, produce, and start selling hair products designed specifically for African Americans. Walker rose to become the most successful self-made businesswoman in the world by the time of her death. She was able to do so by figuring out a unique niche for her sales, doing great marketing and research, and by developing an extensive network to sell her product all over the United States and the Caribbean. She also benefited from strong familial support.

Affirmative action did not exist at the dawn of the twentieth century, and no rich philanthropist helped Walker get started. She did it on her own and over time accumulated a fortune the equivalent of $8 million today. Just as importantly, she created a business model and trained a large number of other African American budding entrepreneurs, and she spent a significant part of her fortune on important social causes, such as the NAACP antilynching fund.

Born almost a century later, Winfrey's story has a lot in common with Walker's. She came from a very poor background in the South and as a child moved to Milwaukee. Growing up, she experienced much abuse at home and in society. Her professional and financial success are attributable exclusively to her talents, ambition, and hard work, with even less support from anyone in her family than Walker had enjoyed. But two significant differences between the two need to be noted. In the 1960s and '70s, Winfrey benefited from newly established affirmative action programs, such as Upward Bound, which facilitated her access to an elite high school. By the mid-1970s, Winfrey also experienced somewhat greater acceptance of African American faces and voices in mainstream media programming than in the harsh world that Walker lived in. Both women remain extraordinary in terms of the extent of their economic success among African American women in the United States. [123]

Winfrey has directed much of her extensive philanthropic work and wealth (over $400 million in gifts) toward eliminating gender inequality. By providing generous funds toward girls' education in Africa, she chose to support the long-term empowerment of some of the most vulnerable populations in the world. By donating more than $1 million to the Green Belt movement, she helped sustain the work of women environmental leaders.

The opportunities open to Meg Whitman and Sheryl Sandberg were quite different from those described above. Whitman came from a well-to-do family, with well-educated parents. Her mother had even served as a mechanic in World War II. She was supported by her family, had access to elite educational institutions, and made use of these connections to advance her business career. Her successes in various businesses are based on the talents and skills she built up. But entry into the boardroom was also a function of her class and race. Sandberg, though from a more modest background, came from a family of highly educated and nurturing parents. As part of a younger generation, she benefited from greater interest on the part of Ivy league business schools at that time to admit women.

How these two women chose to use their wealth suggests relations with the communities in which they live that are different from Winfrey's. Whitman donated a very large sum to her alma mater, Princeton, to have a building named after her, a philanthropic endeavor like many other alumni donations, with no particular focus on women's empowerment. She also spent a sizable part of her wealth running for governor of California against a progressive candidate who supported women's issues. Sandberg made an equally large donation to her own philanthropic organization, which focuses on gathering already successful partners in networking together, to celebrate their empowerment and become a model for others.

On the opposite side of the globe, Qunfei Zhou provides a strikingly different example of a woman's economic success. Born into a poor family in the midst of the Cultural Revolution, Zhou was orphaned at five and quit school when she was fifteen to eke out a living. She worked hard and doggedly pursued higher education part-time, where she excelled in every discipline, from commercial driving to computer science. By 1993 she had saved enough to open a small business, with the help and enthusiastic support of several family members. With the growth of mobile phone production in China, she found a niche for developing high-quality touch screens and by 2015 was worth $10 billion.

Zhou's success could not have happened without an extraordinary work ethic and talents. As she built her empire, she learned to operate every machine on the factory floor. But her ability to prevail over her humble beginnings is also connected to the environment in which she grew up. Communist China opened the door for women to gain equal access to education. It did not provide any special facilities for women, but it also did not openly discriminate against women's access to these opportunities, as had been the case before. Zhou's luck was to be of the generation that came of age just as the communist leadership was starting to liberalize business opportunities. She was there at the very beginning of this process, with both significant savings and also great skills to take advantage of these new circumstances. Zhou is not known as a philanthropist.

These portraits serve to highlight important changes and continuities in the world of business leadership in terms of the glass ceiling women still confront. Today there are real differences among categories of women with regard to access to the education and connections that helped open doors for them to become leaders in the business world. In the United States, though women make up more than 40 percent of the students pursuing MBAs at prestigious schools, they comprise 4 percent of the CEOs of S&P companies. Of those 40 percent, women of color are a minority and African American women a small proportion. The situation is not rosier around the world, with the exceptions of the postcommunist world and China, where women have reached near parity with men in terms of choosing business careers and education. Yet as leaders of major businesses, women are still conspicuous through their absence.

Some successful entrepreneurs like Winfrey believe it is incumbent upon those who made it to the top to support those who are struggling in a gender-biased business world. So does Christine Lagarde (b. 1956), the first woman to head the IMF. For the first time since its founding in 1945, under Lagarde the IMF started to focus on closing the economic gap between men and women. It initiated a forceful conversation and substantial research on the causes of the economic gender gap and has started to point toward policies that could begin to address this problem in a nuanced fashion.[124] Member countries are starting to be assessed on their level of performance toward closing the gender gap, with the goal of tying success in this area to access to IMF funds. The message Lagarde has been delivering since 2011 is clear: when more women work, are better educated, and bring into the economy their talents and energies, society as a whole benefits. In short, women's advancement is not a threat to the male workforce, but a boon to society. Lagarde is not known as a softie but rather as a no-nonsense leader for whom this project is about fairness in the interest of the common good and not about addressing women's victimization through some form of reparations. In her view, investing in women makes business sense, and the costs involved, such as enhancing parental leaves and other services, are necessary in order to build a loyal and successful labor force.

Some advanced economies, especially in the EU, are taking even more drastic measures to address the gender gap in the boardroom. In November 2013 the European Parliament passed the rule that companies listed in the EU would need to have 40 percent female members on their nonexecutive boards, to come into effect after national legislations would endorse the move. Norway, Spain, France, Iceland, and Germany have passed such legislation, with Italy voting for a more modest (30 percent) ratio and the UK establishing a nonbinding practice of also 30 percent. No such initiatives exist elsewhere in the world. It will take a much broader and sustained engagement on the part of those who have become successful, men and especially women, to make a significant, long-lasting change in this area.

* * *

The economic gender gap has narrowed considerably over the twentieth century. More women today than ever before lead economically independent lives and make greater contributions to the world economy than at any other point in time. Still, economic inequalities between men and women continue both at the legal and policy level and especially at the implementation level. The greatest challenge today is to eliminate cultural practices and mentalities that translate into denying girls the same educational and professional development opportunities, as well as rendering the work of reproduction a private matter. Without a comprehensive process of rethinking how to support women to become more productive workers in parallel with offering affordable childcare and elderly care, women's economic empowerment will continue to lag behind men's, and the societies in which they live will fail to live up to their full economic potential.[125]

NOTES

1. DeAnne Aguirre et al., *Empowering the Third Billion: Women and the World of Work in 2012* (New York: Booz & Company, 2012).
2. Katrin Elborgh-Woytek et al., "Women, Work, and the Economy: Macroeconomic Gains from Gender Equity," IMF Discussion Note, September 2013, accessed August 17, 2017, https://www.imf.org/external/pubs/ft/sdn/2013/sdn1310.pdf.
3. Ibid.; Isaac Chotiner, "Lagarde-ian of the Galaxy," *Huffington Post*, October 2, 2015, http://highline.huffingtonpost.com/articles/en/lagarde-interview.
4. Here I define the workforce as all individuals economically active in production, reproduction, and services, whether paid or not.
5. Thomas Piketty, *Capital in the Twenty-First Century* (Cambridge: Belknap Press, 2014).
6. Himani Bannerji, Shahrzad Mojab, and Judith Whitehead, eds., *Of Property and Propriety: The Role of Gender and Class in Imperialism and Nationalism* (Toronto: University of Toronto Press, 2001).
7. Donald R. Kelly, "Property Rights," in *The Oxford Encyclopedia of Women in World History*, ed. Bonnie Smith (Oxford: Oxford University Press, 2008).
8. Ibid. See also Michelle Lamarche Marrese, *A Woman's Kingdom: Noblewomen and the Control of Property in Russia, 1700–1861* (Ithaca, NY: Cornell University Press, 2002); Amy Louise Erickson, *Women and Property in Early Modern England* (London: Routledge, 1993).
9. Marrese, *A Woman's Kingdom*, chapter 2.
10. Barbara Alpern Engel, *Breaking the Ties That Bound: The Politics of Marital Strife in Late Imperial Russia* (Ithaca, NY: Cornell University Press, 2011).
11. Judith E. Tucker, *In the House of the Law: Gender and Islamic Law in Ottoman Syria and Palestine* (Berkeley: University of California Press, 1998).
12. Christina Jones-Pauly, *Women Under Islam: Gender, Justice and the Politics of Islamic Law* (New York: I. B. Tauris, 2011).
13. Tahar Haddad, *Our Women in the Shari'a and Human Society (Imra'ana fil shari'a wal mujtama)* (Tunis: Dar at tunisiya lil nashr, 1985), as discussed in Jones-Pauly, *Women under Islam*.
14. Felix Martin, *Money: The Unauthorized Biography* (New York: Alfred A. Knopf, 2014).

15. Carol Pateman, *The Sexual Contract* (Stanford, CA: Stanford University Press, 1988).

16. Hungary is a very interesting example of this gradual disempowerment over the nineteenth century. See Anna Loutfi, "Legal Ambiguity and the 'European Norm': Women's Independence and Hungarian Family Law, 1880–1913," *L'Homme* 13 (2006): 507–15.

17. Steven Englund, *Napoleon: A Political Life* (Cambridge, MA: Harvard University Press, 2005), 337.

18. Pateman, *The Sexual Contract*.

19. The best known of these challengers were Harriet Taylor Mill (1807–1858) and her partner John Stuart Mill (1806–1873).

20. This only applied to bills of credit. Simple cash transactions, such as the exchange of a pair of earrings for money, were not governed by these restrictions.

21. Jones-Pauly, *Women under Islam*.

22. Susana Lastarria-Cornhiel, "Impact of Privatization on Gender and Property Rights in Africa," *World Development* 25, no. 8 (1997): 1317–33.

23. Ibid.

24. Ruth S. Meinzen-Dick et al., "Gender, Property Rights, and Natural Resources," *World Development* 25, no. 8 (1997): 1303–15.

25. Leonore Davidoff and Catherine Hall, *Family Fortunes: Men and Women of the English Middle Class, 1780–1850* (Chicago: University of Chicago Press, 1991).

26. Jean H. Baker, *Women and the U.S. Constitution, 1776–1920* (Washington, DC: American Historical Association, 2008); Christine Bolt, *The Women's Movements in the United States and Britain from the 1790s to the 1920s* (Amherst: University of Massachusetts Press, 1993).

27. Walkowitz, *City of Dreadful Delight*; Kali Gross, *Colored Amazons: Crime, Violence, and Black Women in the City of Brotherly Love, 1880–1910* (Raleigh, NC: Duke University Press, 2006); Nathaniel Wood, *Becoming Metropolitan: Urban Selfhood and the Making of Modern Cracow* (Dekalb: Northern Illinois University Press, 2010).

28. Susan L. Glosser, *Chinese Visions of Family and State, 1915–1953* (Berkeley: University of California Press, 2014).

29. Jie Li, *Shanghai Homes* (New York: Columbia University Press, 2014), 62.

30. Kathryn Bernhardt, *Women and Property in China, 960–1949* (Stanford, CA: Stanford University Press, 1999).

31. Rubie S. Watson and Patricia Buckley Ebrey, eds., *Marriage and Inequality in Chinese Society* (Berkeley: University of California Press, 1991).

32. Sally Sargeson, "Gender as a Categorical Source of Property Inequality in Urbanizing China," in *Unequal China: The Political Economy and Cultural Politics of Inequality*, ed. Wanning Sun and Yingjie Guo (New York: Routledge, 2015), 168–83.

33. Günseli Berik, Xiao-yuan Dong, and Gale Summerfield, eds., "Gender, China, and the World Trade Organization," special issue, *Feminist Economics* 13, nos. 3–4 (2007).

34. Maria Bucur, "Gender, Citizenship, and Property Regimes in Twentieth-Century Romania," in *Gender and Citizenship in Historical and Transnational Perspective*, ed. Anne Epstein and Rachel Fuchs (Basingstoke, UK: Palgrave, 2016), 143–65.

35. Nicola Murray, "Socialism and Feminism: Women and the Cuban Revolution, Part One," *Feminist Review* 2 no. 1 (1979): 57–73; Sungyun Lim, "Enemies of the Lineage: Widows and Customary Rights in Colonial Korea, 1910–1945" (PhD diss., University of California, Berkeley, 2011).

36. France is an interesting exception here. French women did not gain the right to vote until 1945, but they had gained the right to open bank accounts in 1881 (single women) and 1886 (married women). By contrast, women in the United States and Great Britain did not gain the right to open bank accounts until almost a century later.

37. Murray, "Socialism and Feminism: Women and the Cuban Revolution, Part One," and Nicola Murray, "Socialism and Feminism: Women and the Cuban Revolution, Part Two," *Feminist Review* 2, no. 3 (1979): 99–108.

38. Muna Ndulo, "African Customary Law, Customs, and Women's Rights," *Indiana Journal of Global Legal Studies* 18, no. 1 (Winter 2011): 87–120; Susan H. Williams, "Democracy, Gender Equality, and Customary Law: Constitutionalizing Internal Cultural Disruption," *Indiana Journal of Global Legal Studies* 18, no. 1 (Winter 2011): 65–85.

39. See the individual subentries under "Codes of Law and Laws," in *Oxford Encyclopedia of Women in World History*, ed. Smith; Elborgh-Woytek et al., "Women, Work, and the Economy."

40. Najmabadi, *Women with Mustaches and Men without Beards*.

41. Piketty, *Capital in the Twenty-First Century*.

42. Matthias Doepke, Michele Tertilt, and Alessandra Voena, "The Economics and Politics of Women's Rights," *Annual Review of Economics* 4, no. 1 (2012): 339–72.

43. Elborgh-Woytek et al., "Women, Work, and the Economy," 20.

44. James P. Smith and Michael P. Ward, "Women's Wages and Work in the Twentieth Century," a report funded by the Rand Corporation and prepared for the National Institute of Child Health and Human Development, October 1984, accessed August 18, 2017, https://www.rand.org/content/dam/rand/pubs/reports/2007/R3119.pdf, xv.

45. Cathy Scarborough, "Conceptualizing Black Women's Employment Experiences," *Yale Law Journal* 98, no. 7 (May 1989): 1457–78.

46. Reynolds Farley and John Haaga, eds., *The American People: Census 2000* (New York: Russell Sage Foundation, 2005), 68, state that there still is a 4 to 9 percent differential between white women and women of color; Smith and Ward, "Women's Wages and Work," claim the wage differential was becoming insignificant by the 1990s.

47. Marta Russell, "Backlash, the Political Economy, and Structural Exclusion," in *Backlash against the ADA: Reinterpreting Disability Rights*, ed. Linda Hamilton Krieger (Ann Arbor: University of Michigan Press, 2003), 254–96.

48. Mary H. Blewett, *Men, Women, and Work: Class, Gender, and Protest in the New England Shoe Industry, 1780–1910* (Urbana: University of Illinois Press, 1990).

49. Eileen Boris and Jill Jensen, "The ILO: Women's Networks and the Making of the Women Worker," Alexander Street, 2012, accessed December 24, 2017, http://search.alexanderstreet.com/view/work/bibliographic_entity%7Cbibliographic_details%7C2476919.

50. Gerry Rodgers et al., eds., *The International Labour Organization and the Quest for Social Justice, 1919–2009* (Ithaca, NY: Cornell University Press, 2009).

51. Geoff Eley, *Forging Democracy: The History of the Left in Europe, 1850–2000* (Oxford: Oxford University Press, 2002); Blewett, *Men, Women, and Work*.

52. Margaret R. Higonnet et al., eds., *Behind the Lines: Gender and the Two World Wars* (New Haven, CT: Yale University Press, 1989).

53. Françoise Thébaud, "What Is a Transnational Life? Some Thoughts about Marguerite Thibert's Career and Life (1886–1982)," in *Gender History in a Transnational Perspective: Networks, Biographies, Gender Orders*, ed. Oliver Janz and Daniel Schönpflug (New York: Berghahn, 2014), 167–68.

54. Ibid., 170.

55. Eileen Boris, "Difference's Other: The ILO and 'Women in Developing Countries,'" in *The ILO from Geneva to the Pacific Rim: West Meets East*, ed. Nelson Lichtenstein and Jill M. Jensen (New York: Palgrave and the International Labour Organization, 2016), 134–58.

56. East Germany, Czechoslovakia, and to some extent Poland and Hungary were more industrialized at the time of the communist takeover.

57. On China, see Anna M. Han, "Holding Up More Than Half the Sky: Marketization and the Status of Women in China," in *Global Critical Race Feminism: An International Reader*, ed. Adrien Katherine Wing (New York: New York University Press, 2000), 392–408; on Cuba, see Berta Esperanza Hernandez-Truyol, "Feminismes sans Frontieres? The Cuban Challenge—Women, Equality and Culture," in *Global Critical Race Feminism*, ed. Wing, 81–94; on Angola, see Henda Ducados, "An All Men's Show?

Angolan Women's Survival in the 30-Year War," *Agenda: Empowering Women for Gender Equity* 16, no. 43 (2000): 11–22.

58. See data provided by the World Bank, accessed August 18, 2017, http://databank.worldbank.org/data/reports.aspx?Code=SL.TLF.TOTL.FE.ZS&id=2ddc971b&report_name=Gender_Indicators_Report&populartype=series.

59. Anna Pollert, "Women, Work and Equal Opportunities in Post-Communist Transition," *Work, Employment and Society* 17, no. 2 (2003): 331–57.

60. For current legislation and other initiatives at the EU level, see European Commission, "Gender Equality," accessed August 18, 2017, http://ec.europa.eu/justice/gender-equality/index_en.htm.

61. Maria Karamessini and Jill Rubery, eds., *Women and Austerity: The Economic Crisis and the Future for Gender Equality* (New York: Routledge, 2014).

62. Laura Bassett, "The U.N. Sent 3 Foreign Women to the U.S. to Assess Gender Equality. They Were Horrified," *Huffington Post*, December 16, 2015, http://www.huffingtonpost.com/entry/foreign-women-assess-us-gender-equality_us_566ef77de4b0e292150e92f0.

63. Aguirre et al., "Empowering the Third Billion," 33–34. The countries ranked higher than the United States were, in descending order: Australia, Norway, Sweden, Finland, New Zealand, Netherlands, Canada, Germany Belgium, France, Denmark, Lithuania, the United Kingdom, Iceland, Spain, Hungary, Switzerland, Ireland, Latvia, Portugal, Austria, Estonia, Luxembourg, Poland, Slovenia, Israel, Bulgaria, Moldova, and the Slovak Republic.

64. "Global Gender Gap," accessed August 18, 2017, http://reports.weforum.org/global-gender-gap-report-2016/rankings.

65. Sonya Michel and Rianne Mahon, eds., *Child Care Policy at the Crossroads: Gender and Welfare State Restructuring* (New York: Routledge, 2002).

66. Susan Wojcicki, "Paid Maternity Leave Is Good for Business," *Wall Street Journal*, December 16, 2014, http://www.wsj.com/articles/susan-wojcicki-paid-maternity-leave-is-good-for-business-1418773756.

67. Rachel Gillett, "The Science Behind Why Paid Parental Leave Is Good for Everyone," *Business Insider*, August 5, 2015, http://www.businessinsider.com/author/rachel-gillett.

68. "World Bank Data," accessed December 24, 2017, https://data.worldbank.org/indicator/SL.TLF.CACT.FE.ZS.

69. 1990 is the only year for which the World Bank has figures for the 1990s.

70. Nancy Folbre, *Greed, Lust, and Gender: A History of Economic Ideas* (New York: Oxford University Press, 2009).

71. Elborgh-Woytek et al., "Women, Work, and the Economy," 8–9.

72. Margunn Bjørnholt and Ailsa McKay, eds., *Counting on Marilyn Waring: New Advances in Feminist Economics* (Bradford, ON: Demeter Press, 2014).

73. Valentine M. Moghadam, "Economic Development," in Smith, ed., *Oxford Encyclopedia of Women in World History*.

74. Solinger and Nakachi, eds., *Reproductive States*.

75. Elborgh-Woytek et al., "Women, Work, and the Economy."

76. Ibid., 11.

77. Lutz and Ren, "Determinants of Human Population Growth."

78. Ibid.

79. Katharine M. Donato and Donna Gabaccia, *Gender and International Migration: From the Slavery Era to the Global Age* (New York: Russell Sage Foundation, 2015), 106.

80. Colette V. Browne and Kathryn L. Braun, "Globalization, Women's Migration, and the Long-Term-Care Workforce," *Gerontologist* 48, no. 1 (2008): 16–24.

81. See the discussion about the League of Nations in chapter 2.

82. Donato and Gabaccia, *Gender and International Migration*.

83. Cynthia J. Buckley and Blair A. Ruble, eds., *Migration, Homeland, and Belonging in Eurasia* (Baltimore: Johns Hopkins University Press, 2008).

84. Donato and Gabaccia, *Gender and International Migration*, chapter 5. This preference was not the case everywhere. In places like West Germany, for instance, the guest worker program was open more to individual workers.
85. Ibid., 165.
86. Browne and Braun, "Globalization," 19.
87. Department of Economic and Social Affairs, Division for the Advancement of Women, *2004 World Survey on the Role of Women in Development: Women and International Migration* (New York: United Nations, 2006).
88. Ute Gerhard, Trudie Knijn, and Anja Weckwert, eds., *Working Mothers in Europe: A Comparison of Policies and Practices* (Cheltenham, UK: Edward Elgar Publishing, 2005).
89. Amalia L. Cabezas, Ellen Reese, and Marguerite Waller, eds., *Wages of Empire: Neoliberal Policies, Repression, and Women's Poverty* (New York: Routledge, 2016).
90. National Domestic Workers Alliance, "Home Economics: The Invisible and Unregulated World of Domestic Work," accessed August 18, 2017, https://www.2016.domesticworkers.org/homeeconomics/key-findings.
91. Cabezas, Reese, and Waller, eds., *Wages of Empire*, 32.
92. Ibid., xii.
93. Nicole Constable, ed., *Migrant Workers in Asia: Distant Divides, Intimate Connections* (New York: Routledge, 2010).
94. International Labour Office, "For the ILO Convention no. 189," accessed August 18, 2017, http://www.ilo.org/wcmsp5/groups/public/---asia/---ro-bangkok/documents/genericdocument/wcms_208561.pdf; for the current discussion in the EU, see European Parliament, *Report on Women Domestic Workers and Careers in the EU*, April 5, 2016, accessed December 24, 2017, http://www.europarl.europa.eu/sides/getDoc.do?type=REPORT&mode=XML&reference=A8-2016-0053&language=EN.
95. Nicola Piper, "Feminization of Labor Migration as Violence against Women: International, Regional, and Local Nongovernmental Organization Responses in Asia," *Violence Against Women* 9, no. 6 (June 2003): 723–45.
96. Karamessini and Rubery, eds., *Women and Austerity*.
97. Mizuho Matsuda, "Japan: An Assessment of the International Labour Migration Situation: The Case of Female Labour Migrants," GENPROM Working Paper No. 5 (Geneva: International Labour Organization, 2002); Rhacel Parreñas, *Illicit Flirtations: Labor, Migration, and Sex Trafficking in Tokyo* (Stanford, CA: Stanford University Press, 2011).
98. Jean-Michel Chaumont, Magaly Rodriguez Garcia, and Paul Servais, eds., *Trafficking in Women (1924–1926): The Paul Kinsie Reports for the League of Nations*, 2 vols. (Geneva: United Nations Publications, 2017).
99. Most of Africa and much of the Middle East are absent from the statistics, which were gathered based on the willingness of in-country officials to provide them.
100. Yves Charpenel, ed., *Rapport mondial sur l'exploitation sexuelle: La prostitution au coeur de crime organisé* (Paris: Economica, 2012).
101. Jürgen Stock, "Opening Address," Third INTERPOL Global Trafficking in Human Beings Conference, November 12, 2014, Lyon, https://www.interpol.int/en/content/download/26990/364281/version/3/file/Final%20Opening%20Address_3rd%20THB%20Conference_12NOV14.pdf. I note that the total number of victims identified by Interpol does not come close to the total number of sex workers (forty to forty-two million) identified in the 2012 French report mentioned above. It is not clear why that is the case, as no study or other database is referenced in the Interpol report. Most likely, the Interpol only counted the number of underage sex workers reported to them by national agencies, together with some of the illegal migrants operating as sex workers. As I stated above, the total number of sex workers who are being abused is grossly underreported due to victims' fear of retribution.
102. Jennifer K. Lobasz, "Beyond Border Security: Feminist Approaches to Human Trafficking," in *Gender and International Security: Feminist Perspectives*, ed. Laura Sjoberg (Abingdon, UK: Routledge, 2010), 213–35.

103. Victoria De Grazia and Ellen Furlough, eds., *The Sex of Things: Gender and Consumption in Historical Perspective* (Berkeley: University of California Press, 1996).
104. Paulina Bren and Mary Neuburger, eds., *Communism Unwrapped: Consumption in Cold War Eastern Europe* (New York: Oxford University Press, 2012).
105. Britain is an excellent example of these conflicting consumer politics: Matthew Hilton, "The Female Consumer and the Politics of Consumption in Twentieth-Century Britain," *Historical Journal* 45, no. 1 (March 2002): 103–28.
106. Barbara Ransby, *Ella Baker and the Black Freedom Movement: A Radical Democratic Vision* (Chapel Hill: University of North Carolina Press, 2003).
107. Michelle Micheletti, ed., *Political Virtue and Shopping: Individuals, Consumerism, and Collective Action* (Basingstoke, UK: Palgrave Macmillan, 2003).
108. Marandah Field-Elliot, "Issue Advisory: Free Trade and Feminism—How the TPP Will Hurt Women," National Organization for Women, accessed August 18, 2017, http://now.org/resource/issue-advisory-free-trade-and-feminism-how-the-tpp-will-hurt-women.
109. Ruth S. Meizen-Dick et al., "Gender, Property Rights, and Natural Resources," *World Development* 25, no. 8 (August 1997): 1303–15.
110. "Women, More Than Men, Say Personal Changes Needed to Combat Global Warming in Major Polluting Nations," Pew Research Center, November 2, 2015, accessed August 18, 2017, http://www.pewglobal.org/2015/11/05/2-public-support-for-action-on-climate-change/climate-change-report-06.
111. Anne Bonewit, "The Gender Dimension of Climate Justice," European Parliament, accessed August 18, 2017, http://www.europarl.europa.eu/RegData/etudes/IDAN/2015/536478/IPOL_IDA(2015)536478_EN.pdf.
112. "Women Present Key Demands for World Leaders at UN Climate Talks in Paris," Asia Pacific Forum on Women, Law and Development, December 1, 2015, accessed August 18, 2017, http://apwld.org/women-present-key-demands-for-world-leaders-at-un-climate-talks-in-paris.
113. Mary Annette Pember, "Indigenous Climate Activists Descent on Paris for COP21," Indian Country Today, November 27, 2015, http://indiancountrytodaymedianetwork.com/2015/11/27/indigenous-climate-experts-descend-paris-cop21-162573.
114. Maria Alejandra Rodriguez Acha, "How Young Feminists Are Tackling Climate Justice in 2016," *Huffington Post*, July 3, 2016, http://www.huffingtonpost.com/maria-alejandra-rodriguez-acha/how-young-feminists-climate-justice_b_9369338.html.
115. *Paris Climate Agreement*, accessed August 18, 2017, https://unfccc.int/files/meetings/paris_nov_2015/application/pdf/paris_agreement_english_.pdf; my italics.
116. Nabeelah Shabbir, "Women and Climate Change Injustice: Thoughts from the Paris Talks," *Guardian*, December 10, 2015, https://www.theguardian.com/global-development/2015/dec/10/women-injustice-climate-change-thoughts-from-the-paris-talks.
117. Malgorzata Fidelis, *Women, Communism, and Industrialization in Postwar Poland* (Cambridge: Cambridge University Press, 2010); Donna Harsch, *Revenge of the Domestic: Women, the Family, and Communism in the German Democratic Republic* (Princeton, NJ: Princeton University Press, 2007).
118. Fidelis, *Women, Communism, and Industrialization in Postwar Poland.*
119. Mie Nakachi, "Liberation without Contraception? The Rise of the Abortion Empire and Pronatalism in Socialist/Post Socialist Russia," in *Reproductive States*, ed. Solinger and Nakachi, 290–328; Kristen Ghodsee, *The Left Side of History: World War II and the Unfulfilled Promise of Communism in Eastern Europe* (Raleigh, NC: Duke University Press, 2015); Kligman, *The Politics of Duplicity*; Lynne Haney, *Inventing the Needy: Gender and the Politics of Welfare in Hungary* (Berkeley: University of California Press, 2002).
120. China constitutes an important exception to this trend for reasons connected to the size of the population at the beginning of the communist regime, and to the deeply held traditions regarding the role of children in the family economy. See Tyrene

White, "China's Population Policy in Historical Context," in *Reproductive States*, ed. Solinger and Nakachi, 329–68.

121. Andi Zeisler, *We Were Feminists Once: From Riot Grrrl to CoverGirl®, the Buying and Selling of a Political Movement* (New York: PublicAffairs, 2017).

122. According to *Forbes Magazine*, in 2017 Oprah Winfrey was the third wealthiest on the list of self-made rich women in the United States, her fortune coming from the media empire she built. Meg Whitman, who was the CEO of eBay and subsequently Hewlett-Packard, stood at number six. Sheryl Sandberg, the COO of Facebook, was twelfth on the same list. *Forbes* also named Zhou Qunfei, the worker-turned-founder of the Chinese touch screen manufacturing company Lens Technology, the richest self-made woman in the world; her fortune was listed at $7.4 billion. Chloe Sorvino, "The World's 56 Self-Made Women Billionaires: The Definitive Ranking," *Forbes*, March 8, 2017, https://www.forbes.com/sites/chloesorvino/2017/03/08/the-worlds-56-self-made-women-billionaires-the-definitive-ranking/#232c00bc68a2, and https://www.forbes.com/self-made-women/#465ca9cd6d96. Of the three ranked in relation to how "self-made" they are, with 10 as the coefficient of greatest self-reliance, Winfrey ranked above the other US women in the top twenty. Zhou, though not ranked by such a coefficient in the separate index, would also rank as a 10. Whitman had a coefficient of 6. Sandberg did not have a coefficient of self-reliance, but based on the definitions used in the ranking, she would most likely stand at 8 (Mark Zuckerberg had the same coefficient). See Agustino Fontevecchia, "The New Forbes 400 Self-Made Score: From Silver Spooners to Bootstrappers," *Forbes*, October 2, 2014, http://www.forbes.com/sites/afontevecchia/2014/10/02/the-new-forbes-400-self-made-score-from-silver-spooners-to-boostrappers/#45433a047d40.

123. On the 2017 Forbes list of the top fifty self-made, wealthiest women in the United States, there are only three African Americans, the equivalent of 6 percent. The other two names are Sheila Johnson (b. 1949), founder and owner of Black Entertainment Television, and Beyoncé Knowles (b. 1981), the musician.

124. Elborgh-Woytek et al., "Women, Work, and the Economy."

125. According to Elborgh-Woytek et al., "Women, Work, and the Economy," 4, bringing about gender parity in employment levels would help elevate the GDP of the United States by 5 percent, Japan by 9 percent, United Arab Emirates by 12 percent, and Egypt by 34 percent.

FIVE

Knowledge

Never doubt that a small group of thoughtful, committed citizens can
change the world. Indeed, it is the only thing that ever has.
—Margaret Mead[1]

There are few areas in which women's contributions have been more
stunning and profound in reshaping humanity in the twentieth century
than knowledge making. If around 1900 fewer than 6 percent of all PhDs
in the United States were awarded to women, by 2010 women held 49
percent of all PhDs.[2] The highest ratio was 58 percent in Lithuania, with
women at parity or higher in fourteen out of the fifty-six states ranked by
the National Science Foundation.[3] Half of these high-ranking countries
had been part of the communist bloc before 1991, and only five of these
countries are part of the developed world without a communist past.[4]
When differentiated by disciplines, women had become 50 percent or
more of PhD holders in thirty-two of the fifty-six states in the humanities,
social, and behavioral fields; only four countries ranked at parity or
above for science. The lowest representation of women remains in engineering, where the highest percentage of women with PhDs was 39, in
Turkey. Despite remaining disparities especially in science fields, these
statistics are nothing short of spectacular and show how important wom-
en's contribution to knowledge making became by the beginning of the
twenty-first century. This chapter brings into focus some of the important
qualitative aspects of this huge quantitative shift.

The philosophical foundations of how we make sense of life, social
relations, economic processes, our beliefs, and our identities were predominantly masculinist until the twentieth century.[5] There is evidence of
cultures and societies that do not fit this picture. Native American tribes
like the Iroquois had a matrilineal society that provided men and women
different norms and opportunities for development than what the Euro-

peans forced them to adopt during colonization.[6] Similar differences can
be noted with matrilineal tribes in Africa, Asia, Europe, and South America.[7] Yet most of these societies were eventually reshaped by the encounter with patriarchal colonizers, and their values and beliefs were eventually snuffed out.[8] Where matrilineal practices (e.g., Judaism) continued
into modern times, they lost their social power as expressed in political or
economic rights.[9]

Over time, one can find examples of brilliant critiques of patriarchal
hegemony, such as the unfortunate daring position of Hypatia (c.
360–415) as a philosopher and teacher in ancient Alexandria and the ele-
gant assessments made by Daoyun Xie (c. 340–c. 399) during the Jin dy-
nasty.[10] Yet their contributions were eventually buried or marginalized
until they were slowly rediscovered or rather rendered visible and valuable again late in the twentieth century.

It was in the twentieth century that feminist challenges began to make
an important impact on hegemonic patriarchal thinking. In most parts of
the globe today, it is impossible to imagine the world of ideas without
women's contribution to it. From Simone de Beauvoir (1908–1986) to Judith Butler (b. 1956), from Hannah Arendt (1906–1975) to Gayatri Spivak
(b. 1942), women thinkers reshaped what we consider to be the object of
philosophy, the assumptions that undergird philosophical thought, and
the methods for approaching research. Not all these contributions are
overtly feminist. But feminist approaches to critiquing masculinist epistemologies have helped recast the contribution of all women knowledge
makers, whether feminist or not, into a different, more expansive framework of analysis.[11] In particular, feminist epistemologists have shown
how women's contributions are significant not only for what they overtly
claim, but also for where they are situated, inclusive of gender norms and
practices.

Recasting women's production of knowledge through various feminist frameworks has led to critiques of these knowledge makers. Toward
the end of the twentieth century, as postcolonial and non-Western female
intellectual elites became better integrated in the web of scholarly and
intellectual dialogue, they brought attention to the racial/ethnic, class,
religious, and other important differences that helped frame many of the
Western feminist critiques of patriarchy.[12] Today, feminists have become
very diverse and sometimes combative in their interactions with each
other along some of these divisions. Few celebrate a sense of sisterhood,
even though their impact on society and academic communities has a lot
in common.

The accumulation of women's contributions to every scholarly discipline and area of knowledge making is in itself a revolutionary act, regardless of the specific politics and self-identification of these individuals
with any kind of feminist aspirations or with each other's struggle. This
chapter examines some of the most significant shifts that have taken

place in the way we understand the nature, past, and future of humanity. If my focus in this chapter is disproportionately on Europe and North America, it is because women in these regions have made disproportionately longer strides toward gender inclusiveness in academia.[13]

HISTORY: GENDERING THE PAST

The beginnings of deconstructing masculinist epistemologies happened in historical research and writing before most other areas of knowledge making.[14] Since premodern times the efforts of women with access to education and libraries, something rare everywhere around the world, developed women-centered approaches to understanding the past.[15] That might be why this is the first field where women made inroads in the twentieth century, even though history academic programs have been some of the slowest to accept the feminist challenges introduced by women historians.[16]

For many feminists at the beginning of the twentieth century, looking into the past for traces of women's lost social and political power was a logical and appealing step in constructing arguments about the present and the future. If women had once been more fully integrated in contributing to the well-being of their societies, that would indicate they could again become fully empowered members of the citizenry. If there was evidence of women's oppression in the past, one could draw a contrast between that situation and the feminist aspirations of the present. In 1900 history held a central role in academic discourse in many places around the world, from Japan to Greece. Other social sciences, like anthropology and sociology, were just developing. And philosophy, which is where political theory was situated, was a discipline with a much more decisively masculinist profile than history.[17]

Thus, for a number of women around the world involved in political activism, making visible a past in which women were dynamic historical agents and an important subject of analysis became means for legitimating their own political aspirations. Some did so from positions of marginality in academia, and most as outsiders. The male academic establishment often derided women's work as dilettantish, regardless of the success some women historians enjoyed as published authors.[18]

The Japanese socialist historian Kikue Yamakawa (1890–1980) offers an excellent example of how intellectual passion and scholarly research fed and were nurtured by intense political activism.[19] As a young woman, Yamakawa became a zealous activist in the young communist movement in Japan. In the 1920s she focused on developing a platform for women's issues inside the Japanese Communist Party, at times coming to blows with her male partners over concerns such as condemning prostitution (she did; they didn't). When the movement was driven underground by the fascist regime of the 1930s, Yamakawa turned her attention to writing history, partly out of economic need. In 1940 she was commissioned to write a book on women's daily lives from a historical perspective and she jumped at the chance, which offered the opportunity to continue her feminist activism in a more concealed manner.

Her *Women of the Mito Domain: Recollections of Samurai Family Life* (1943), which became internationally known, offered a nuanced depiction of everyday life and traditional gender norms in Japanese families. The book beautifully exemplified new methodologies for accessing historical evidence and placed the reality of women's daily occupations and relations with each other in the realm of significant topics for historical research. For instance, she recast the practice of ikebana as an outcome of specific government and social dynamics, rather than a mere flourish on the edges of significant historical processes. Throughout, she drew a clear and striking contrast between the world of the male samurai and the lives women were forced into inhabiting by virtue of the prevailing masculinist norms of that society. Though generally unable to exercise a substantial role in the political life of the country, Yamakawa represented women's actions in the household as socially significant. The wives of the large samurai class managed most of the lived environment with very limited financial resources. They also facilitated relations with other such families, thus enhancing alliances and shoring up the social status of this class. Overall, she drew attention to the importance of the private sphere as a site of social agency and to women's contribution to these processes. [20]

At that time, though women were still underrepresented among the members of the historical profession in Western Europe and North America, they were starting to make some inroads toward recognition in print, through academic appointments, as well as in professional organizations. [21] British Eileen Power (1889–1940) became an internationally respected economic historian in her lifetime. [22] Focusing on medieval Europe, her research was guided by feminism, pacifism, and internationalism. Having traveled extensively throughout the world in the early 1920s, Power brought that knowledge to her comparative exploration of medieval social relations. Her focus on everyday life and the domestic sphere helped usher in a new type of economic history, which looked at production and reproduction as linked processes and accounted for women's roles in society as a matter of course. Power's work also drew attention to class differences among women in terms of both law and social practices. Written in an appealing literary style filled with delightful details alongside data-driven analysis, Power's work became popular and remained a model for subsequent generations. [23]

Yet women historians continued to be a minority in the profession and especially in terms of academic appointments. In the United States Nellie Neilson (1873–1947) became the first woman president of the

American Historical Association (AHA, established in 1894) in 1942, in the midst of World War II, when the female membership was growing and had come to be more balanced due to the absence of many male members fighting in the war. It would take thirty-five years for another woman to gain such professional recognition and authority. In 1987 Natalie Zemon Davis (b. 1928) became the second woman president of the AHA in its first century of existence. She has been followed by a number of other women, a sure mark that the historical profession has turned a page in terms of embracing women as members and especially leaders.

By 2016 there had been thirteen female presidents out of 130.[24] The overall figure doesn't look encouraging, but over the last twenty years ten women have been presidents, bringing the gender ratio to full parity. Therefore, by the end of the twentieth century, we can speak about history catching up to other disciplines in terms of gender parity in the United States. While the more recent history of this professional organization shows greater sensitivity to gender equity, one cannot say the same regarding ethnicity and race. Vicky Ruiz, president of the AHA in 2015–2016, was the first woman of color to serve in this capacity.

If in 1980 fewer than 15 percent of history professors in the United States were women, by 2007 their proportion rose to 35 percent. While this is clearly progress, one needs to understand the growth in the context of larger trends. For the humanities overall, by 1930 the proportion of women faculty was 38 percent and by 1990 it had crossed the 50 percent mark, revealing history as a laggard discipline. Even when counting all disciplines, inclusive of the hard sciences, the proportions are higher on average than for history in particular.[25] In the meantime, women have become a majority of students in both undergraduate and graduate studies.

This growing female presence has translated into a growing diversity of approaches to traditional fields as well as the emergence of new fields. One of the most important pioneers in rendering women's history a legitimate field of historical research and teaching was Gerda Lerner (1920–2013). An immigrant from fascist Austria, Lerner was committed throughout her life to bringing to light the lives of marginalized people. Having once noted that all of the historians interested in women's history "could have fit into a telephone booth," Lerner dedicated her professional career to developing the first graduate program in women's history, writing about race and gender in the United States, and introducing new methods and types of evidence as important sources for historical research.[26] Starting in the 1980s, social history was further altered through Davis's biographical approach and rich literary style.[27] Barbara Weinstein (b. 1954), another president of the AHA, helped transform research on race and class relations under colonial rule in South America by bringing in questions about gender norms and roles among both colonizers and colonized.[28] Historians like Luise White (b. 1945) helped complicate our understanding of African history through investigations of material culture in which women were constantly present and thus important historical agents. [29]

The fields of women's history, gender history, and history of sexuality as distinct areas of specialization developed starting in the 1970s, when significantly more women began to enter this profession in conjunction with the growth of feminist movements around the world. This is also the period when the Berkshire Conference of Women Historians started to take off, creating a "room of their own" for this growing variety of women's and gender historians. The conference grew from a small gathering to a large meeting of thousands of participants, whose makeup and interests became significantly more international by the 1990s.

A related development during this period was the founding of the International Federation for Research in Women's History (IFRWH) in 1987, which aimed, as a vehicle for collaboration and comparative research in the field, to connect historians of women and gender. The IFRWH has become larger and more representative of global trends in the past two decades, hosting conferences in Bulgaria, Ireland, and China, and leading to the publication of some of the first collections of historical studies on race and gender in a comparative perspective. [30]

The contributions of historians from around the world to growing these fields are too expansive to offer anything other than a cursory discussion here. Some of the major contributions range from powerful statements by Joan Scott (b. 1941) about the need to consider gender as a core category of historical analysis with its own historicity to Susan Stryker (b. 1961) and her queering of the history of sexuality. Scott's 1986 seminal essay, "Gender: A Useful Category of Historical Analysis," encapsulated the moment of shifting from women's history to a broader set of questions about what it meant to "add women and stir" in terms of broader historical epistemological assumptions. [31] Her work opened the way toward new subfields, from gender history to the history of masculinity. [32]

Stryker and other historians coming of age in the 1990s used Scott's insights and other theoretical reconceptualizations, offered by Eve Kosofsky Sedgwick (1950–2009) and Judith Butler (b. 1956), among others, to open up the definition and study of gender and sexuality beyond hegemonic binaries (e.g., male/female, hetero-/homo-) and embrace the notion of fluid, performative identity. [33] Queer history has flourished into its own field, initially with a concentration on the United States and eventually branching out to focus on other places around the world, such as East Asia and Great Britain. [34]

The work of women historians dealing with questions of race and empire covers a wide spectrum of topics, such as the research of Mrinalini Sinha (b. 1960) on twentieth-century India and the contributions of Evelyn Brooks Higginbotham (b. 1945) on US history. Sinha has played an important role in bringing into conversation postcolonial studies with gender analysis, when it comes to fully understanding the articulations of power between colonizers and the colonized in the modern period.[35] Higginbotham has been an influential pioneer in gendering African American history and helping address the complex intersection of race and gender in how political, economic, and cultural changes have unfolded in the history of the United States.[36] Younger generations of historians of women and gender have embraced the turn toward analyzing the intersection of gender and race/ethnicity, bringing about new important insights into the history of colonization, politics, and capitalism, as well as anticolonial and postcolonial struggles.[37]

These historians, who have their staunch critics and supporters, have planted the seeds of further insights into the gendered elements of every aspect of human interaction from the past and into the future. They and many other historians have also asked broader questions about the gendered nature of assumptions historians make when framing questions, looking for historical evidence, and interpreting that evidence. Their broader queries about authenticity, experience, and historical agency have helped push even further the ways in which knowledge makers reflect on humanity's meanings.

NATURAL SCIENCES: FROM SEXOLOGY AND EUGENICS TO AIDS RESEARCH

Just as historians helped bring women into the focus of research about the past, around the dawn of the twentieth century biologists and doctors helped recast the object of their studies into a different mold. The relationship between biology and gender became an increasingly intense and contested focus of much biological research over the twentieth century, leading to important advancements in medicine and other related fields.

Some of the earliest attempts to draw scientific correlations between biology and gender came from supporters of eugenics, starting in the 1880s.[38] At that time, few women had access to any science education, so it is no wonder that what were defined as biologically "normal" gender traits revolved around masculinist assumptions about such norms. The first generation of eugenicists aimed to create an irrefutable framework for understanding gender roles and attributes as a hereditary polarity of characteristics. Eugenics was anchored in both Darwinian biology and the racist ideas about identity in the mainstream of scientific research at that time. This theory valued some women (of "healthy stock") but restricted their role to the reproduction of a healthy population, with the possibility of including some types of education as sociopolitically useful. Thus, in the larger framework of how eugenicists imagined the state becoming more directly involved in restricting and enhancing gender roles, some women would in fact stand to gain greater state support in areas such as public health and education.[39] But part and parcel of this theory was the notion that individual freedom was not valuable except in the service of biopolitics.

By the turn of the century, as more women began to enter higher education in science and medicine, a new generation of supporters of eugenics came to the fore, with women now helping articulate the relationship between biology, gender identity, and politics. Around the same time, sexology appeared as a subdiscipline of biology, fueled in part by the eugenics movement. The life and writings of Marie Stopes have already been discussed in chapter 3 ("Population"). Her ideas helped push against established social norms, as well as toward rethinking the definition of women's sexuality. Moving against the established Victorian gender norms of her time, Stopes promoted a view of women as naturally interested in sex for pleasure and not just as conjugal duty.

Given the speculative rather than clinical nature of her evidence, Stopes did not develop her own scientific theory about gender and sexuality. It wasn't until Alfred Kinsey's massive study of sexual behavior in humans in the 1940s and early '50s that accepted science methods were deployed to demonstrate the range of sexual behaviors in females and males that profoundly altered normative thinking at that time about "normal" sexuality.[40] Kinsey, however, did not develop clinical studies of sexuality but limited himself to a sociological collection of large sets of data that he treated statistically.

It was primarily through the work of a next generation of sexologists, especially the team of William H. Masters (1915–2001) and Virginia E. Johnson (1925–2013), that sexology turned toward direct clinical research on sexual activity focusing on both men and women. By observing more than ten thousand sexual encounters in a clinical environment, Masters and Johnson were able to make more incontrovertible claims about gender and sex. Their research overturned many previous assumptions about women's sexual arousal and ability to climax.[41]

The Masters and Johnson team was remarkable for a number of reasons. Masters understood the crucial need to bring in a female perspective in framing and analyzing the data if they were to be gender-inclusive. He was willing to hire as his partner a woman without formal training in biological research, a great risk in the world of science. Though coming from this risky background of mostly informal training, Johnson was an engaged partner and at times disagreed strongly and vocally with Masters's conclusions.[42] The result was a large body of data and publications that became the most important scientific findings for framing cultural discourse and public policy about sexuality beginning in the 1960s, just as the sexual revolution was getting started. Their work gained worldwide notoriety, with several of their books translated into as many as thirty languages.

The Masters and Johnson team made some problematic claims, however, helping vilify homosexuality as a psychological condition. In the 1960s the work of the institute had focused on identifying triggers and centers of sexual pleasure as well as on therapy for men and women who were not able to achieve sexual satisfaction. The therapy was grounded in the assumption that heterosexuality was normal and sexual satisfaction in women, for instance, was connected to their encounters with men. By 1968 the team began to explore sexual dissatisfaction in homosexuals, but the therapy focused exclusively on enabling heterosexual encounters as a corrective. The assumption undergirding this work was that individuals, though born heterosexual, were nurtured into a variety of gender norms and thus might develop homosexual preferences. [43]

The publications that developed out of this research helped fuel a debate about the AIDS epidemic starting in the late 1980s. [44] Masters pushed for the notion that homosexuals could be "cured" through heterosexual therapy, thus reducing the likelihood of spreading the HIV virus. Though she remained loyal to him, Johnson later expressed serious reservations about the study, whose findings have been proven scientifically unsound. [45]

Another woman who has played a major role in addressing the AIDS epidemic is Françoise Barré-Sinoussi (b. 1947), a French virologist who in 1983 identified the HIV virus as the cause of AIDS and was later awarded a Nobel Prize for this discovery. Her research paved the way toward better isolating the virus and identifying means to combat the symptoms of AIDS and eventually finding a cure for it, one of the most important medical achievements of the twentieth century, given the deadly effects of the virus.

In her youth, Barré-Sinoussi had a difficult time accessing the means for pursuing her passion for research in biological sciences: spots in labs where one could get started learning the necessary skills for basic virological research were carefully guarded by almost exclusively male scientists. Few of them wished to extend the opportunity for hands-on learning to young women, and it took Barré-Sinoussi a lot of persistent searching to find a willing patron. [46] This initial support enabled her to take her passion into the lab, where she built a successful team, mentoring new generations of women and men scientists toward future advances in medicine.

In 2008 Barré-Sinoussi became one of only twelve women to receive the Nobel Prize in Medicine out of 210 awardees. Over the first hundred years of the prize (1901–2001), only six women won this award. The progress of women in the sciences can be measured by the fact that in the following fifteen years, out of the thirty-five awardees, six have been women, two of them from the United States and the others from Australia, China, Israel, and Norway. This geographic diversity suggests that talented women scientists started to enjoy greater access to academic research environments in more parts of the world than had been the case just fifty years before. It is also the case that these are countries known for their strategic interest in science research and substantial financial commitment on the part of the government to fund science research.

How is Barré-Sinoussi's gender relevant in terms of her scientific contributions? There is no clear direct connection, and one doesn't need to be established to make the following point: extraordinary minds and talents like hers would have likely been wasted a century before, exceptions like Marie Curie notwithstanding. The contributions she and other successful women scientists have made over the twentieth century are in themselves proof that, by eliminating gender discrimination in science training and nurturing the curiosity and talents of all students, such contributions will only increase in the future, enhancing our ability to understand humanity and solve complex science questions. [47]

Barré-Sinoussi placed her reputation and notoriety in the service of public health policy making, something many star scientists show little interest in. She pressed tirelessly for providing access to treatment for the poorest people affected by AIDS, especially in Africa. As president of the International AIDS Society (IAS), she pushed against the stigmatization of the most vulnerable populations afflicted by the disease—gay people, drug users, sex workers, and the poor. In her last address as IAS president, Barré-Sinoussi stated forcefully, "We need again to shout out loud that we will not stand idly by when governments, in violation of all human right principles, are enforcing monstrous laws that only marginalize populations that are already the most vulnerable in the society." [48]

Barré-Sinoussi's career resembles the path of many other women around the world in science and technology fields. [49] I have already mentioned the difficulties and great achievements of Wangari Maathai in environmental science and activism in chapter 2 ("Politics"). Like Barré-Sinoussi, Maathai struggled with lack of acceptance, first as a student and then as a faculty member and researcher, in the male-dominated science research and teaching environment in Kenya. Her success came from the same dogged pursuit of her scientific interests and finding a willing supporter inside the science academic community.

These issues became a focal point of discussions inside the science community starting in the 1980s and amplifying in the 1990s. In 1985 a US Public Health Service Task Force on Women's Health Issues issued a report that stated unequivocally that "the historical lack of research focus on women's health concerns has compromised the quality of health information available to women as well as the health care they receive." [50] Over the next decade concern for these problems began to engage a wider audience. [51]

These discussions had a direct impact on addressing some of the fundamental problems in science design and funding prevalent at the time. In 1991 Bernadine Healy (1944–2011) became the first woman director of

the National Institutes of Health (NIH), one of the two largest government organizations that provide funding for basic science research in the
United States.[52] Though my focus here is on a US agency, similar problems existed at that time in leading centers of medical research in Europe.
Until recently, these scientific communities led the way and influenced
the design and development of medical research elsewhere in the world.
China and India have become important centers in the past two decades.

Healy's appointment was a game changer in the design and funding
of medical science research both in the United States and overseas, with
women now as a crucial element of focus. To begin with, having provided funding for medical research for more than a century, the NIH had
not seen fit to include research on women as part of the requirements for
doing clinical studies. On the contrary, women had been both habitually
and eventually explicitly excluded, in part because of fear of possible side
effects for subjects of childbearing age, who eventually might become
pregnant after participating in clinical studies.[53] Doing clinical studies
exclusively on men was not only acceptable but it became the undisputed
norm. The consequences of this insufficiency are easy to grasp today:
certain conditions having predominantly or exclusively to do with wom-
en's physiology (e.g., breast cancer) were not a priority for research and
funding.[54] In addition, clinical studies on everything from blood pressure
to smoking or depression often did not consider gender a core variable,
leading to erroneous conclusions and recommendations. For instance,
trials with pharmaceuticals defined "average" weight and metabolism in
relation to men's physiology, leading to problems with dosage for wom-
en patients. In the sense of making clinical trials more authentically reflective of the population, 1991 is an important departure, a kind of reset
in science research.

Healy also introduced a major new program, the Women's Health
Initiative, which continues today. The initial funding set aside for this
project was $625 million and involved longitudinal research on 150,000
women. This unprecedented level of funding and of reaching out to female subjects for science research created a boon for future biomedical
scientists to begin fully investigating what elements of gender identity
(e.g., social, physiological, genetic) correlate with certain behaviors, including the relationship between sex and gender.

By 2016 more than 270 major studies resulted from this funding, on
topics such as diet/nutrition, cardiovascular disease, cancer, dementia,
and incontinence.[55] Over time the questions have become more sophisticated and harder to tease out. Doctors, psychologists, and biologists continue to debate to what extent gender is a set of behaviors that are learned
and to what extent it is a set of biological attributes that impact medical
conditions.[56] And a pushback against this trend has also been visible in
the past decade. Some scientists claim that requiring equal numbers of
men and women for any NIH-funded study is a "huge waste of re-

sources," because "modifying experiments to include both males and females costs money and requires a duplication of time and effort . . . that is rarely practical or scientifically warranted."[57] Many other scientists disagree with this assessment. Feminist biologists in particular have continued to demonstrate the significance of gender hereditary and behavioral elements for understanding human physiology, behavior, and medical conditions. Under pressure from the Office of Research on Women's Health established by Healy in 1993, in 2015 the NIH passed a new regulation that "all grant applications involving studies of vertebrate animals or humans have to account for sex as a biological variable."[58]

Today, clinical studies that aspire to NIH funding continue to be designed in radically different ways than in the pre-1991 era. Healy's leadership and the work of other women scientists supported through the Women's Health Initiative have fundamentally altered the landscape of science research: with gender at the core of asking questions about human behavior and physiology, the research has broadened and become more complicated. It has come to reflect the complexity of our humanity more closely, with overall beneficial results for our society.

While clinical research conducted in the United States with funding from the NIH and other government sources has been altered positively under pressure from women scientists and feminist activists, these new gender-inclusive guidelines have had perverse and worrisome effects in the global South. With growing regulations and costs for doing research, scientists using US government funding and a growing array of private foundation sources (e.g., the Bill and Melinda Gates Foundation) have opted to test drugs on vulnerable populations, especially women and children, in parts of South Asia and Africa. These women are often poor and join such trials under false premises or even unknowingly. Some of them have suffered long-term, dire side effects.[59] For example, for years Letrozole was given to women in India who had fertility problems, without informing the participants in trials that the drug was designed for breast cancer and had not been tested in any lab environment for fertility. Side effects for the participants included severe genetic abnormalities among the babies born to the participants, a fact that was not communicated to the subjects. In October 2011 the Indian government finally banned the use of the drug for enhancing fertility.[60]

Despite advances, the world of science remains disproportionately male-dominated. Fewer women than men pursue science education, and only 28 percent of science researchers around the world are women.[61] If broken down by region, the averages show a much larger proportion of women in places like Central Asia (47 percent) and Latin America (44 percent) than in the most developed regions of the world, North America and Western Europe (32 percent). A larger proportion of women are part of the science community in Egypt (43 percent) than in Germany (27 percent). This huge difference doesn't necessarily mean that women scientists are well respected in Egypt and not in Germany. Both statistics suggest, in fact, different forms of institutional sexism in their respective societies. In the case of Egypt, women are active in fields that receive little research support from the state and where the pay is lower than in other areas of knowledge making, such as dentistry versus biotechnology.[62] In the case of Germany, women have much more choice in their educational and professional paths. But the funding mechanisms for advanced science research and the parallel social expectations that women spend more time with their small children than men translate into restrictive choices for women who want to pursue an ambitious science research path.[63] They can either pursue their professional passion and not have children or bow to societal pressures and forgo developing a research portfolio at a time when they need it most for long-term professional advancement. These pressures translate into other choices made professionally, such as who to collaborate with and how much risk to take in their research projects, all of which render women riskier lab partners and less cutting-edge than their male counterparts.[64]

While these disparities can be explained in relation to both gender factors and other national institutional differences, countries across the world share important elements of continuing gender inequity: (1) The proportion of women pursuing science careers becomes smaller and smaller as one moves up the educational and academic ladder; and (2) women scientists tend to work in the public sector, while men tend to work in the private sector, where salaries and opportunities for promotion are greater. Starting in 2015 UNESCO identified the underrepresentation of women in the sciences and technology as a priority area and is currently developing better data and tools for measuring gender disparities as a means to develop more locally impactful policy recommendations.[65]

PSYCHOLOGY

Around the same time that sexology began to develop as a branch of biology, scholars started to inquire how the mind is conditioned to make sense of biology and gender norms. Psychology is known as the brainchild of a group of male scientists, among them Wilhelm Wundt (1832–1920) in Germany, G. Stanley Hall (1846–1924) in the United States, and Sigmund Freud (1856–1939) in Austria-Hungary. The inequitable access for women to higher education in the sciences explains the reason for the dominant male voices in this discipline at the very outset.

Yet women scientists joined in the dialogue about these issues and made remarkable contributions to shaping psychology very early on, using it to treat various conditions and build new systems of education. One of the first challenges to the male establishment came from Mary

Whiton Calkins (1863–1930), who was trained by several scholars at Harvard.[66] Though she was allowed to attend classes in the 1890s, Harvard never accepted Calkins as a student. In a class she audited, all male students de-enrolled. When her mentor, the chair of the experimental psychology program, wrote the president of Harvard to petition for her admission into the doctoral program as the most talented student he had seen in all his years teaching at that institution, the response was no. Later on, Calkins's professors attempted a second petition to award her a PhD based on her exceptional research and analytical abilities, which she amply demonstrated during the time she audited with all of them and worked in their labs, but the professors were again turned down. Calkins went on to become the first woman president of the American Psychological Association (1905), but Harvard never acquiesced to awarding her a PhD.

Calkins was the first psychologist to challenge the gender assumptions of some of the dominant theories in the field at that time. Though she did not self-identify as a feminist, she criticized the notion postulated by other psychologists that biological differences explained the variety of word usage between men and women. Instead, she pointed toward environmental factors, such as education, as a cause. Her writings, which helped establish the field of "self-psychology," questioned the notion that identity was grounded in the metaphysical, and she focused instead on the self as grounded in "totality, identity, change, uniqueness, and of relatedness, or consciousness."[67] Despite these contributions, with the exception of feminist psychologists, historians of the field of self-psychology continue to ignore Calkins.[68]

The field of feminist psychology developed out of the efforts of Karen Horney (1885–1952), a German-born contemporary of Freud's. Horney spent her life advocating for understanding neuroses and a variety of other psychological dysfunctions as learned behavior, a function of sociocultural norms and relations rather than of biological sexual attributes. She was the first self-identified feminist psychologist, and she focused on cultural assumptions regarding gender and biology at the center of her theories and criticism of other schools of psychology. To Freud's theory about penis envy as an explanation for women's specific gender identity, Horney counterposed the notion that men could have "womb envy," pointing toward women's abilities to be caretakers and men's inadequacies in this realm.[69] Overall, Horney questioned Freud's uncritical assumptions about male sexuality as a norm and women's as derivative. She rightly identified them as unscientific and grounded in cultural norms about gender roles rather than physiology or the psyche.

Horney was able to pursue her ambition of becoming a doctor because she happened to be among the first generation of women admitted to medical school and able to take the medical examinations when German medical schools lifted interdictions for women to sit for these exams, around 1900.[70] Unhappy with the research climate in her field and due to personal problems, she moved to the United States in the mid-1920s, first to Chicago and eventually to New York. She founded the Association for the Advancement of Psychoanalysis to create a professional network for the kind of approach and theories she advocated, in explicit contrast to Freud's followers, and eventually established the *American Journal of Psychoanalysis*. As Freud's following (predominantly men) grew, Freudian theories about gender norms and sexuality gained prominence while Horney's critiques became sidelined. Her arguments and ideas were slowly marginalized in subsequent courses and textbooks until the second half of the twentieth century.

Though Horney's contributions to psychoanalysis remained neglected for decades, other women psychologists managed to shape entire fields, especially educational psychology. The Italian Maria Montessori (1870–1952) became the most successful woman scientist in that field and left behind a transformative legacy in the area of early-childhood educational psychology and pedagogy. Passionate about science from childhood, Montessori initially wished to pursue engineering and eventually attended the University of Rome, graduating in 1896 with a degree in medicine. Her research focused on children with mental disabilities. After working for five years as a volunteer with such children, who were housed in asylums around Rome, Montessori began to develop a new theory for how to educate these abandoned children.

Over the next decade, Montessori further expanded her experimental ideas about scientific pedagogy and began to modify them to include all children, starting in an orphanage whose curriculum she helped revolutionize between 1906 and 1911. What today is known internationally as the Montessori method is the fruit of her research and experimentation during that period, synthesized in the book *The Montessori Method of Scientific Pedagogy: As Applied to Child Education in the Children's Houses*.[71] Montessori advocated abandoning the rote learning methods that emphasized retention through discipline and repetition. Instead, she showed that critical thinking and overall cognitive abilities would develop better if children were less constrained physically and if they mixed more freely in the classroom with other peers of different ages. Rather than disciplining with an iron fist, she believed teachers could be more effective by gently guiding children's self-paced process of individual discovery.

Montessori continued to refine her ideas about effective early-childhood education and train generations of teachers throughout her career. By the time she passed away, she had helped set up more than four thousand Montessori-method classrooms around the world.[72] Her ideas about learning through play helped open up whole new areas of psychological and educational research still vibrant today.

Feminist psychology saw a revival in the 1970s, around the same time that we see a flourishing of feminism in sexology, history, and other academic disciplines.[73] It has spearheaded organizations, publications, and overall a lively discussion about the nature of individual identity in relation to sex and gender. Important differences developed between clinical psychologists whose methods and studies emphasized biological difference when examining gendered phenomena, and those who have defined sociocultural gender norms as crucial factors for explaining psychological experiences. The biology-as-destiny school of thought has helped reinforce the notion of gender polarities. Many feminists have seen that as a problem because it enables misogynists to point toward science as evidence for women's biological limitations in taking on leadership positions in politics, the military, or any other area of human activity. On the other hand, the cultural deconstructionist argument has led to a relativism that other feminists have seen as eviscerating any possibility for effective political action and improvement of women's position in society.[74] These differences and other questions of class, race, and other variables still anchor debates over the meaning of gender and biology in terms of individual and social psychology.[75] Through the twentieth century, female scholars in this discipline have played an essential role in pushing against continuing masculinist assumptions about what is normal and how to frame research projects.

In recent decades this research has extended into questioning the very notion of gender as a clear and polarized set of attributes and behaviors. Feminist psychologists have become engaged in researching the possibility that gender represents an evolving mix of biological hard predispositions, learned behavior, and personal preferences. The work of Anne Fausto-Sterling (b. 1944), for instance, has illuminated the extent to which caretakers' behavior greatly influences the attitudes and self-presentation of specific gendered attributes in infants and toddlers.[76] This research is pushing the boundaries of our understanding about gender in new directions. We are starting to look at gender as a complex set of elements that include cognition, attitude, self-presentation, and relations with others. These elements do not necessarily align in unison in a polarized fashion but are part of a spectrum of possibilities. They evolve over one's lifetime in relation to each other and other external stimuli. As more individuals begin to self-identify explicitly with these various possible attributes, our long-held social and scientific assumptions about gender roles as dichotomous are being questioned.[77] It is possible that within a generation, a new theory about gender might emerge.

GENDER AND SOCIETY: ANTHROPOLOGY AND SOCIOLOGY

The disciplines dedicated to better understanding how human beings function in their societies—anthropology, sociology, demography, economics, and political science—have grown tremendously over the twentieth century and have been fundamentally altered by the rising numbers and diversity of women scholars in terms of research design and methods, framing questions, and analysis. None is more emblematic of these changes than Margaret Mead (1901–1978), the famous anthropologist.[78]

A student of Franz Boas (1858–1942), considered the founder of American anthropology, Mead found in anthropology a lifelong passion that surpassed any other commitments in her life. She wrote twenty-three books based on extensive field research, with a focus first on the Pacific (Samoa) and eventually closer to home, in North America.[79] Mead spent her professional career (1926–1978) as a curator at the American Museum of Natural History, moving through the ranks and becoming one of the most prominent scientists in residence at the museum. Mead was broadly influential as a scholar, shaping the field of cultural anthropology to include a more clearly and forcefully articulated gendered perspective than her predecessors. Several of her works, most prominently *Sex and Temperament* (1935) and *Male and Female: A Study of the Sexes in a Changing World* (1949), grappled with the relationship between biology and gender identity by examining how gender norms developed among a variety of rather isolated societies. Her conclusions shifted over time, giving more credit to the ways in which biological, especially reproductive, attributes shaped behavior. But Mead remained insistent that gender attributes were ultimately rendered meaningful through social norms and cultural traditions. Her work influenced future generations of feminist anthropologists, such as Sherry Ortner (b. 1941) and Gayle Rubin (b. 1949), as well as feminist activists especially in the United States starting in the 1960s.[80]

Mead's reputation as a scholar won her many prestigious awards, among them election as president of the American Association for the Advancement of Science. In 1975 she became only the second woman to hold this position in the Association's 127 years of existence and the first to deal with questions about gender in her scientific work. This accomplishment seemed perfectly timed with the UN International Women's Year. Mead made use of her prestige as a scientist to speak forcefully about global advances made on behalf of women's economic empowerment, access to birth control, and education. She also used her expertise and popularity to present to a broad audience continuing problems, especially in parts around the world where women were still predominantly the agricultural workers and were being replaced by machines, without any plans in place with regard to the future of these displaced laborers.[81] Mead defined the situation in 1975 as a global crisis that tied all people to each other's fate: the growing disparity between the economic needs of an exploding population, on the one hand, and the ability to sustain economic growth within the existing systems of production, on the other hand, was giving rise to an untenable situation and begged for new ways of thinking about the common good. She placed women as active social agents at the center of the solutions to be developed, because of their underused talents and their crucial role in reproduction.

Like Mead, Zora Neale Hurston (1891–1960) sought to understand culture as a comprehensive system of various traditions and actions, but with a focus inward.[82] She was a contemporary of Mead and studied with some of the same people, but unlike her more fortunate white colleague, Hurston did not complete graduate studies.[83] With a prestigious Guggenheim fellowship, she went into the field and began testing her ideas about the culture of the communities in which she had grown up: Hurston was particularly fascinated by cultural links, from religion to music, with the Caribbean, especially Jamaica and Haiti. She was not the first anthropologist to individually, through deep immersion, seek to understand these communities, but she was the first woman of color to do so.[84] Hurston also helped develop the concept of the African diaspora as a culturally vibrant and intergenerational connection element of African American values and behavior. The role of voodoo and women's place in this society were core elements in her analysis.[85] Unfortunately, like many other scholars of color who lacked the formal training of their white counterparts, Hurston fell into obscurity and has yet to be recognized for her contributions to the field, even as she has become a celebrated figure of literary modernism in the Harlem Renaissance.[86]

Anthropology has become one of the most gender-balanced scholarly disciplines, and women have played an increasingly central role in shaping it. Generations of scholars since the pioneering days of Mead and Hurston have pushed further into fully integrating a gendered understanding of all aspects of social interaction and structures, from sexuality to the division of labor and technological development. Some of their most important developments in the late twentieth century have been to connect scholarship about indigenous cultures and people with policy to protect and empower them, especially in the face of environmental degradation.

In 1992 Rigoberta Menchú Tum (b. 1959) was awarded the Nobel Peace Prize for her activism in fighting for the livelihood and rights of indigenous Mayan people in Guatemala.[87] By 1995 the Gender Working Group of the UN Commission on Science and Technology Development published what has become an important watershed in recognizing the work of women like Menchú Tum as valuable not only locally, but also as a path toward global sustainability in the face of rising ecological problems.[88] The work of the UN Gender Working Group and the international recognition brought by the Nobel Peace Prize have helped shake up the relationship between knowledge making and academic training. In essence, these women scholars and activists have underscored the importance of moving beyond academia and the rules established over the twentieth century in terms of objectivity, accepted disciplinary methods, and analysis. Deep, engaged observation in a community, together with actions that aim to identify and address real social problems, like lack of access to education, clean water, and healthcare for the poorest are becoming recognized as uniquely valuable knowledge.

As tensions grow between globalizing processes of production and consumption, on the one hand, and the local environmental conditions produced by globalization, on the other hand, a gender dynamic has become apparent in understanding and resolving growing ecological problems. Women, as the predominant workforce in agriculture in the global South, are the individuals who see what is happening to the soil, plants, and fauna they tend to every day. These women have had to struggle with local solutions to these problems, from deforestation to global warming. Their voices are being heard louder than ever before through scientists, activists, and government servants.

The leader who brought all 195 country participants to the negotiation table at the Paris Climate Summit in 2015 was Christiana Figueres, Executive Secretary of the UN Framework Convention on Climate Change between 2010 and 2016. An anthropologist by training, Figueres entered the world of diplomacy, following in the steps of her prominent father, three times president of Costa Rica, and mother, also a diplomat. Figueres also served in the Costa Rican government. Starting in 1995 she dedicated herself to developing long-term strategies for curbing pollution and enabling more environmentally friendly forms of energy. Using her position at the UN, she worked tirelessly to bring the global North and South together and change the attitudes of those around her through her infectious "relentless optimism."[89] Scholars and politicians alike view her leadership as crucial to arriving at the historic Paris agreement: "[Her] contribution to international climate negotiations over the [past] six years has been really extraordinary. . . . She is gifted with an outstanding ability to see where we need to go as a world and to bring people together. [Figueres] is one of the great leaders of our time. She no doubt has much more to contribute in the coming years. The challenge for everyone is to build on her achievements."[90]

If women's participation in anthropology facilitated a more gender-nuanced approach to fieldwork and understanding of cultural dynamics across the world, the gendering of sociology has led to our ability to identify gender problems on a massive scale. It is not difficult to see the huge jumps we have made in this regard. We simply need to glance at the ways in which large sets of data were collected in 1900 and compare them with today's data sets. Breakdown by gender of any number of elements, from education to income level and employment, was simply not a factor of interest at the beginning of the twentieth century anywhere around the world. Questions about marriage, divorce, and birth rate were implicitly gendered, but not always explicitly so. But virtually no other elements that describe human activity were counted by gender, leading to an inability to detect correlations between gender and various social phenomena. In 1948, when the UN issued its first *Demographic Yearbook*, the compilers were forced to state that "the comparability of the statistics for men is, in general, much better than that of statistics for women," adding that women were also often undercounted because they were participants in informal types of economic activity (i.e., not paid).[91]

The situation changed when sociologists, economists, and statisticians began to articulate reasons for having gender as an explicit category of analysis. In addition, feminists questioned the utility and completeness of studies that failed to address gender when examining any social activity. My discussion of Marilyn Waring in chapter 4 ("Economics") has already highlighted the extent to which traditional economists undercounted women's productive work due to such oversights.

Feminist sociologists have played an especially impactful role in how we understand the change in kinship and family structures beyond established societal traditions throughout the twentieth century as a dynamic social phenomenon.[92] Radical critiques of the nuclear family as a fundamental unit in society have been ongoing since the publication of Engels's famous *The Origin of the Family*, in 1884.[93] Socialist and communist feminists starting with Clara Zetkin and Alexandra Kollontai had incorporated the debates about the future of the family within their larger ideological discussions about oppression and equality. Yet little changed in social expectations regarding familial relations well into the 1950s throughout the world.

By the 1970s, however, it had become clear that many more families were shifting in composition and relations among members. There were many more single and divorced parents, with children more likely to stay with their mothers than ever before. There were more unmarried couples raising children and more children being raised by at least one nonbiological parent. By the 1990s new types of kinship relations, especially among same-sex couples as well as through informal multigenerational living arrangements, were becoming more common. These variations were present to different degrees in various parts of the world. Overall, feminist sociological research unraveled any fantasy of the "normal" family unit as husband and wife with two or three children.[94] Chapter 7 ("Kinship") discusses these issues in greater detail.

Initially the sociological establishment questioned the relevance of studies on these variations as quirky, small, or even "melodramatic."[95] But the passage of time has revealed how important it is to understand these long-lasting shifts in gender norms in societies across the world, in order for policy makers, doctors, teachers, and countless other professionals to successfully tackle evolving social issues. The gendering of sociological research has led to greater nuances in understanding specific social phenomena and addressing problems such as criminal behavior, educational achievement, and economic agency. Disagreements continue over the nature and meaning of specific gender variables, but current social scientists have become much more cognizant and accepting of the need to take them into account.

THE POLIS: POLITICAL THEORY

Over the twentieth century, some remarkable women thinkers, not all interested in feminism or the question of gender equality in particular, have shaped how we understand political processes today. Thinkers like the Polish Rosa Luxemburg (1871–1919) and the German Hannah Arendt established themselves as prominent voices in movements dominated by men, Luxemburg in politics and Arendt in philosophy.

Near the beginning of the twentieth century, Marxist political economist and theorist Rosa Luxemburg became a fiercely independent critic of the direction taken by the prominent thinkers and organizers of the movement. She was uncompromising in her view of the socialist movement, which she saw as a dead end and capitulation to capitalism, rather than the path toward social revolution. She criticized the Russian Bolshevik Revolution as well, describing it as a compromise with the bourgeoisie, rather than a clean and necessary break from the past.

Luxemburg is best known for her theory of imperialism, which engaged critically with Karl Marx. In *The Accumulation of Capital: A Contribution to an Economic Explanation of Imperialism* (1913), she greatly expanded what Marx had posited about the relationship between imperialism and capitalism.[96] By enlarging the focus from origins to impact, she offered a harsh picture of the effect of capitalist imperialism on precapitalist societies, prefiguring many postcolonial critiques of the late twentieth century. For Luxemburg, violence was at the heart of capitalism, and nowhere did it become more readily apparent than in the ways capitalist expansion was destroying precapitalist economies. The international systems of loans and alliances between advanced capitalist states and newly formed ones in the nineteenth century became "the surest ties by which the old capitalist states maintain their influence, exercise financial control and exert pressure on the customs, foreign and commercial policy of the young capitalist states."[97]

Due to her violent death during the short-lived communist revolt in Germany at the end of World War I, Luxemburg soon became more of a symbol of communist struggle than a continuing intellectual powerhouse in the ideological debates of the interwar period. She was subsequently "rediscovered" by postcolonial Marxists and economists and continues to be the subject of much scholarly attention.[98]

Born a generation after Rosa Luxemburg, Hannah Arendt became one of the most prominent political philosophers of the twentieth century through her theory of political action in defining the human condition and her writings on totalitarianism.[99] A student of Martin Heidegger (1889–1976) and later a refugee from the Nazi regime, Arendt made her mark on political theory starting in the 1950s with *The Origins of Totalitarianism* (1951). The book provided the first comprehensive theory of the political tragedies of fascism and communism as outcomes of forces of modernity, such as the rise of mass politics.[100] It became a blueprint for critiquing the development of communist regimes in real time, even though Arendt herself was not a self-avowed anticommunist.

Critics and disciples have tried to pigeonhole Arendt in terms of her political leanings, but she remains a true original whose intellectual complexity reaches beyond strict ideological lines. In *The Human Condition* (1958), arguably her most influential work, Arendt developed a theory that laid the way forward beyond the excesses of modernity analyzed in *The Origins of Totalitarianism*. Arendt identified active participation in the life of the *polis* through engaged citizenship as the noblest form of being human, calling for individuals to reimagine their relationship with each other and with the common good. For Arendt, each individual had the immanent power to influence politics through his or her ability to speak and act, and reconciliation of differences would be the embodiment of such power in the service of the common good. Critics have pointed toward her lack of analysis of inequality and injustice as structurally imposed by those who control political processes. But Arendt has also inspired leftist thinkers and activists. Some have seen in her a humanist whose aspirations are not naïve but instead aim to reinstate hope and faith in the human race in the face of despair and decay.[101]

Feminists sometimes vilified Arendt for her lack of attention to misogyny and other times attempted to appropriate her insights into the nature of modern politics.[102] These debates have continued for over four decades, suggesting the staying power of Arendt's originality and depth as a thinker. Her ideas have shaped how feminist political theorists subsequently conceptualized the relationship between gender and citizenship under neoliberal regimes.[103]

Feminist thinkers like Ruth Lister (b. 1949) and Nancy Fraser (b. 1947) have expanded the notion of citizenship as constitutive of our modern humanity to include questions about social discrimination and the need to engage in political action to address such problems.[104] Most notably, feminist political theorists have pointed toward the need to reexamine the responsibilities of the modern state toward its citizens in terms of eliminating forms of discrimination that depart from claims of full gender equality. They have also called upon women as citizens to act on solving these problems, to bring the diversity of their experiences to bear upon our understanding of universal rights.

FEMINIST EPISTEMOLOGY AND THEOLOGY

The nature of humanity has been the core subject of philosophical thought and religious systems of belief. Whether looking at what makes us essentially what we are as people, or trying to imagine the relationship between the here and now and the spiritual or the afterlife, until the twentieth century, philosophers and theologians primarily pondered on humanity from a perspective that seldom critiqued its masculinist, epistemic foundations.

Significant pre–twentieth-century critiques came from thinkers like Christine de Pisan (1364–c. 1430), Mary Wollstonecraft (1759–1797), Bibi Khanoom Astrabadi (1858/1859–1921), and Harriet Taylor Mill, to name just a few.[105] Sadly, many more contributions were lost, buried, and, generally speaking, forcefully forgotten, so we don't really have a good archive of women's contributions to knowledge making until the advent of a strong feminist movement, access to education, and the publication of works by women.

This is even more the case for women knowledge makers outside of Europe, especially in areas where European colonialism helped articulate patriarchal social and political regimes that pushed the knowledge making of indigenous women even further underground. The resurfacing of historical legacies in these parts of the world has been a slow and uneven process, with Western feminists sometimes acting as the vectors of marginalization of local women's knowledge.[106] What is most impressive about women's contributions to shaping knowledge in the twentieth century is the sheer diversity of perspectives they have offered to multiple audiences.

Simone de Beauvoir's *The Second Sex* (1949) is considered the modern foundational text for the development of feminist epistemology in the twentieth century, especially in the West. The book has gone through several editions and has been translated into many languages.[107] De Beauvoir was the first philosopher to combine a broad historical overview with arguments plucked from biology, literature, and other disciplines in order to construct an extended argument about the ways in which the category of "woman" had come to be constructed and was being reconstructed, with each generation as the "other" or secondary to the category of "man." Though at times confusing, the book forcefully exposed the impact of masculinist epistemology for what it was—a tool for oppressing all women without any way out. However, de Beauvoir was not prepared to develop an original philosophical system out of this critique. Instead, she aimed to situate her findings within existentialism, the philosophical system developed by her partner, Jean-Paul Sartre (1905–1980).

Yet her writings had a ripple effect throughout the women's movement and especially among future generations of feminist scholars. Starting in the 1960s, from *The Feminine Mystique* (1963) by Betty Friedan (1921–2006) to *The Female Eunuch* (1970) by Germaine Greer, feminist thinkers took de Beauvoir's work as a starting point and inspiration for further critiquing patriarchy. These and other such books became best sellers and radicalized many women.

As feminist epistemology was becoming its own field, feminists began to engage in robust critiques of each other's work.[108] One important set of critiques came from women of color like the Indian scholar Gayatri Chakravorty Spivak, whose essay, "Can the Subaltern Speak?" (1988), helped redefine postcolonial studies.[109] Building on the work of trailblazer Audre Lorde (1934–1992), Kimberlé Crenshaw (b. 1959) introduced into feminist theory the concept of "intersectionality" with the aim of complicating and rendering more nuanced our understanding of gender oppression in a racialized state like the United States.[110] These scholars challenged the privileging of gender analysis to the exclusion of other factors, like class, religion, sexuality, or race. Without self-reflexivity about the complex webs of power relations that help constitute the identity of the scholar and the subject of study, knowledge makers can only reproduce uncritically the categories of meaning they seek to understand.

If scholars and activists of the 1970s felt an urgency to generate broad analyses and provide universal answers to the problems of misogyny and gender inequality, that picture has changed dramatically since then. The proliferation of feminist interpretations of the challenges and solutions to patriarchy came from many places around the world, encouraged by the concept of situated knowledge popularized during that period. In addition, the encounters among feminists from vastly different places and perspectives grew through the institutional support provided by the UN during the Decade of Women (1975–1985).

It was also during this time that post-structuralism and postmodernism became mainstream trends, in disciplines such as philosophy and literary studies. As the study of identities and discourse became more prominent at the expense of the study of actions, feminist epistemologies also became increasingly fragmented and deconstructivist. The most prominent scholar of this wave of feminist thought is Judith Butler, whose book *Gender Trouble* (1990) became very popular and widely cited throughout the world. Focusing on the performative aspects of how gender is constructed, Butler helped develop the new field of queer studies, further dislocating normative binary assumptions about the relationship between biology, sexuality, and gender identity.

While most of these feminist thinkers were secular and remained preoccupied with the social and political, a smaller but still significant set of feminists developed original interpretations of the transcendental. Feminist theologians have pushed against masculinist interpretations and especially the religious institutionalization of men as the exclusive gatekeepers in especially the major monotheistic religions of the world. Mary

Daly (1928–2010) became a trailblazer among the first generation of feminist philosophers in the twentieth century to offer a radical critique of patriarchy through the lens of theology.

Her first two books, *The Church and the Second Sex* (1968) and *Beyond God the Father: Toward a Philosophy of Women's Liberation* (1973), offered a thorough and unforgiving critique of Catholicism, the religion she was raised in, and monotheistic religions in general, from the perspective of a disenchanted believer and radical feminist. Her philosophical and theological studies led Daly to see these religions as means for misogynist oppression and violence against women. She called on women to become liberated by rejecting the major established religions as she did. After declaring herself a post-Christian, Daly's philosophy shifted toward imagining ways in which women could develop a more nurturing relationship with each other by removing themselves from the omnipresent forms of patriarchal oppression in contemporary society.[111]

Some feminist thinkers of the 1970s were inspired by Daly's rejection of patriarchal monotheistic religions to develop a nostalgic notion of women's original spiritual superiority and the need to articulate a separate, female-focused religion.[112] Some of these ideas were anchored, for instance, in theories about matriarchy and patriarchy that challenged the history of Christianity. By inserting alternative female-centered retellings of events in the New Testament, these feminist theologians expressed a longing toward women's full presence and participation in the spiritual life of their communities.

Other feminist theologians focused more closely on altering the ideas and practices of existing religions.[113] The most successful have been those in Protestant denominations who advocate enabling women to serve as officiators/priests: today, women can serve in the same capacity as men in Episcopalian churches. The Catholic Church has yet to open up the road toward such changes, but a conversation about women as deacons has recently been reignited.[114] For Orthodox Christians, Jews, and Muslims, where theological debates play a smaller role than the institutionalized authority of the clergy, feminist challenges have been present but without the impact on reforming ideas and practices as for Protestant Christians. One feminist thinker of prominent influence in the Islamic world is Fatema Mernissi (1940–2015). Mernissi was not a theologian, but her sociological analyses of women's position in Islamic societies focused on the contrast between the position women occupied in the present and the ideas about women's role in society as expressed in the Quran: "If women's rights are a problem for some modern Muslim men, it is neither because of the Quran nor the Prophet, nor the Islamic tradition, but simply because those rights conflict with the interests of a male elite."[115]

Feminist epistemology has become segmented even further and offers many opportunities for criticism as well as engaged scholarship. These thinkers have pushed us to think more carefully about the complex nature of human institutions and practices that have generated various forms of gender inequality, including the oppression of women by other women. They draw different conclusions about the origins and effect of how societies, states, and individuals act. Some still consider biological differences fundamental for understanding motivations of our desires, fears, and needs—in short, how we relate to each other. But the impact of human-made environments on rendering these differences meaningful has also become much clearer in every area of knowledge making. If we continue to perpetrate misogyny, it is not out of ignorance or naiveté. At the very least, it is out of sheer carelessness; more likely, it is out of fear of being dislocated from positions of comfort and/or privilege. The charge of the next generation of knowledge makers will be how to translate epistemological fragmentation and discomfort into a productive partnership rather than a competitive struggle for power.

* * *

Feminist scholars have been crucial in bringing greater attention to questions about the gendered nature of social, economic, and political processes. Some have stressed the importance of understanding presumed radical differences between men and women in order to create the possibility for women's emancipation and full participation in all aspects of human activity. Others have focused on the social construction of such differences, with the goal of questioning and eventually eliminating them. These debates continue today, having been rendered more complex by other similarly difficult questions related to the nature of difference among people.

A related, continuing debate introduced in large part by feminist knowledge makers and other women thinkers has been how to connect identity and action, especially when we seek to understand power relations and forms of discrimination. For some scholars, categories of identity—gender, sexuality, race, and class among them—have become the building blocks for understanding the past and present. Actions taken by individuals need to be placed in the context of how such identity categories illuminate power relations. For other thinkers, like Hannah Arendt, the focus has been on the actions taken (or not) by individuals as a first line of examining social and political communities.

The extent of gendering broad fields of inquiry, such as economic development, has grown over time and remains uneven. Yet today, research models in any social science need to address the relevance of gender as a category of knowledge making if they wish to uphold current academic standards. From linguistics to economics, from demography to ethnography, scholars are chipping away at the relevance of models for understanding the world that assume an unquestioned masculinist "normal."

Gender disparities remain highest in science fields and especially engineering, as the statistics at the beginning of this chapter show. Overall, even in countries with high percentages of women holding PhDs, the economic gender gap remains significant. For instance, in Israel, 51 percent of PhD holders are women, yet the wage gender gap is 22 percent.[116] The disparities are even greater in Estonia: women are 53 percent of all PhDs, while the wage gender gap stands at 32 percent. Of the fourteen countries listed at the beginning of this chapter in which more women hold PhDs than men do, New Zealand is the only example of a country that has also achieved near wage gender parity, with the difference narrowing down to 5.6 percent. The future challenge for women is to achieve gender parity in having their contributions to knowledge making fully and fairly translated into economic power.

NOTES

1. Though the exact origins of the quote are disputed, this is a source that references it: Nancy C. Lutkehaus, *Margaret Mead: The Making of an American Icon* (Princeton, NJ: Princeton University Press, 2008), 261.

2. Holding a PhD is not a guarantee for the production of impactful knowledge, nor is it the only way to measure creativity and innovation in many fields. Still, with the growth of higher education programs since especially World War II and with the increasing institutionalization of how innovation is translated into production, holding a PhD has become a widely accepted measurement of how we understand the advancement of knowledge.

3. "How Nations Fare in PhDs by Sex," *Scientific American*, https://www.scientificamerican.com/article/how-nations-fare-in-phds-by-sex-interactive1.

4. The fourteen countries are, in descending order of women's PhDs: *Lithuania*, Thailand, *Mongolia*, Argentina, *Kyrgyzstan, Ukraine*, Finland, New Zealand, *Estonia*, Italy, *Croatia, Macedonia*, Israel, and Australia (postcommunist countries are italicized).

5. Michele Le Doeuff, *The Sex of Knowing* (New York: Routledge, 2004).

6. Merlin G. Myers, Fred Eggan, and M. Sam Cronk, *Households and Families of the Longhouse Iroquois at Six Nations Reserve* (Lincoln: University of Nebraska Press, 2006).

7. Oyewumi Oyeronke, *The Invention of Women: Making African Sense of Western Gender Discourses* (Minneapolis: University of Minnesota Press, 1997).

8. Evelyn Blackwood, *Webs of Power: Women, Kin, and Community in a Sumatran Village* (Lanham, MD: Rowman & Littlefield, 2002).

9. In Israel, though Jewish heritage can be traced in a matrilineal way in cases of a non-Jewish father, women remain subordinated to men on matters of marriage and divorce. For instance, a man only needs to declare his intention of marrying a woman in front of a witness to be able to proceed with such action, while a woman cannot do the same. Frances Raday, "Equality, Religion and Gender in Israel," in Jewish Women's Archive, http://jwa.org/encyclopedia/article/equality-religion-and-gender-in-israel.

10. Maria Dzielska, *Hypatia of Alexandria* (Cambridge, MA: Harvard University Press, 1995); Lily Xiao Hong Lee and A. D. Stefanowska, eds., *Biographical Dictionary of Chinese Women: Antiquity through Sui, 1600 B.C.E.–618 C.E.* (Armonk, NY: M. E. Sharpe, 2007).

11. Lucy Tatman, *Knowledge That Matters: A Feminist Theological Paradigm and Epistemology* (Cleveland, OH: Pilgrim Press, 2001).

12. See, for instance, Ratna Kapur, "The Tragedy of Victimization Rhetoric: Resurrecting the 'Native' Subject in International/Post-Colonial Feminist Legal Politics," *Harvard Human Rights Journal* 15 (Spring 2002): 1–38.

13. It is also the case that, with English, French, and German as the main languages for disseminating knowledge starting in the nineteenth century, the impact of any studies in other languages, with the exception of Russian, Mandarin, and Spanish, has been more limited.

14. For a more in-depth discussion of the impact of gender analysis on the historical craft over the last half-century, see also the bibliographic essay at the end of this book.

15. Mary Spongberg, *Writing Women's History since the Renaissance* (Basingstoke, UK: Palgrave, 2002).

16. On the United States, see Peter Novick, *That Noble Dream: The 'Objectivity Question' and the American Historical Profession* (Cambridge: Cambridge University Press, 1988); on global trends, see Daniel Woolf, *A Global History of History* (Cambridge: Cambridge University Press, 2011).

17. A recent encyclopedia entry on the history of feminist philosophy places the beginnings of a robust critique of misogyny in philosophical thought and writing in the 1980s, with the parallel "discovery" of a number of women philosophers and feminist critique of the philosophical canon, starting with Aristotle and Plato. A relevant observation is that a 1967 *Encyclopedia of Philosophy* with nine hundred entries included not a single female philosopher. By contrast, the 1998 *Routledge Encyclopedia of Philosophy* included entries on Hannah Arendt, Mary Wollstonecraft, and Simone de Beauvoir, among other women philosophers. Charlotte Witt and Lisa Shapiro, "Feminist History of Philosophy," in *The Stanford Encyclopedia of Philosophy*, ed. Edward N. Zalta (Palo Alto, CA: Stanford University Press, 2016), http://plato.stanford.edu/archives/spr2016/entries/feminism-femhist.

18. Bonnie Smith, *The Gender of History: Men, Women, and Historical Practice* (Cambridge, MA: Harvard University Press, 1998).

19. E. Patricia Tsurumi, "The Accidental Historian, Yamakawa Kikue," *Gender & History* 8, no. 2 (August 1996): 258–76. Though Tsurumi brands Yamakawa an "accidental" historian, in fact she was thoughtful and purposeful in her decision to write *Women of the Mito Domain: Recollections of Samurai Family Life* (Palo Alto, CA: Stanford University Press, 2002).

20. Yamakawa, *Women of the Mito Domain*.

21. Smith, *Gender of History*.

22. For instance, Marc Bloch of the Annales School wrote appreciative reviews of her work and collaborated with Power on an edited volume. Natalie Zemon Davis, "History's Two Bodies," *American Historical Review* 93, no. 1 (February 1988): 1–30.

23. Maxine Berg, *A Woman in History: Eileen Power, 1889–1940* (Cambridge: Cambridge University Press, 1996).

24. Two early male presidents served for two terms.

25. The percentages for all fields are 32 percent and 42 percent in 1988 and 2007, respectively. See Robert B. Townsend, "What the Data Reveals about Women Historians," *Perspectives on History* 48, no. 5 (May 2010), https://www.historians.org/publications-and-directories/perspectives-on-history/may-2010/what-the-data-reveals-about-women-historians.

26. Linda Greenhouse, "A Graduate Program Sets Out to Find History's Women," *New York Times*, March 20, 1973, http://www.nytimes.com/1973/03/20/archives/a-graduate-program-sets-out-to-find-historys-women-we-need-to-learn.html.

27. Natalie Zemon Davis, *The Return of Martin Guerre* (Cambridge, MA: Harvard University Press, 1983).

28. Barbara Weinstein, *The Color of Modernity: São Paulo and the Making of Race and Nation in Brazil* (Durham, NC: Duke University Press, 2015).

29. Luise White, *The Comforts of Home: Prostitution in Colonial Nairobi* (Chicago: University of Chicago Press, 1990).

30. Ruth Roach Pierson and Nupur Chaudhuri, eds., *Nation, Empire, Colony: Historicizing Gender and Race* (Bloomington: Indiana University Press, 1998); Julia Clancy-Smith and Frances Gouda, eds., *Domesticating the Empire: Race, Gender, and Family Life in French and Dutch Colonialism* (Richmond: University of Virginia Press, 1998).

31. Joan Scott, "Gender: A Useful Category of Historical Analysis," *American Historical Review* 91, no. 5 (December 1986): 1053–75. It is the most widely cited article from the journal.

32. See the forum "Revisiting 'Gender: A Useful Category of Historical Analysis,'" *American Historical Review* 113, no. 5 (December 2008): 1344–430.

33. Susan Stryker and Jim Van Buskirk, *Gay by the Bay: A History of Queer Culture in the San Francisco Bay Area* (San Francisco: Chronicle Books, 1996); Eve Kosofsky Sedgwick, *Epistemology of the Closet* (Berkeley: University of California Press, 1991); Judith Butler, *Gender Trouble: Feminism and the Subversion of Identity* (New York: Routledge, 1990).

34. Heike Bauer and Matt Cook, eds., *Queer 1950s: Rethinking Sexuality in the Postwar Years* (Basingstoke, UK: Palgrave, 2012); Mark McLelland, *Queer Japan from the Pacific War to the Internet Age* (Lanham, MD: Rowman & Littlefield, 2005); Brian Lewis, ed., *British Queer History: New Approaches and Perspectives* (Manchester: Manchester University Press, 2013).

35. Mrinalini Sinha, *Specters of Mother India: The Global Restructuring of an Empire* (Durham, NC: Duke University Press, 2006).

36. Evelyn Brooks Higginbotham, "African-American Women's History and the Metalanguage of Race," *Signs* 17, no. 2 (Winter 1992): 251–74; John Hope Franklin and Evelyn Brooks Higginbotham, *From Slavery to Freedom: A History of African Americans* (New York: McGraw Hill, 2010). John Hope Franklin wrote the first edition of this book in 1947. Higginbotham's coauthorship brought significant revisions that helped enhance the analysis toward a comprehensive understanding of the gendered aspects of this narrative.

37. Jean Allman, Susan Geiger, and Nakanyike Musisi, eds., *Women in African Colonial Histories* (Bloomington: Indiana University Press, 2002); Ann Stoler, *Carnal Knowledge and Imperial Power: Race and the Intimate in Colonial Rule* (Berkeley: University of California Press, 2002); Anne McClintock, *Imperial Leather: Race, Gender, and Sexuality in the Colonial Contest* (New York: Routledge, 1995).

38. Wendy Kline, *Building a Better Race: Gender, Sexuality, and Eugenics from the Turn of the Century to the Baby Boom* (Berkeley: University of California Press, 2005).

39. Annette F. Timm, "Biopolitics, Demographobia, and Individual Freedom: Lessons from Germany's Century of Extremes," in *Reproductive States*, ed. Solinger and Nakachi, 33–62.

40. Kinsey et al., *Sexual Behavior in the Human Female*.

41. William H. Masters and Virginia E. Johnson, *Human Sexual Response* (Toronto: Bantam Books, 1966).

42. Johnson had a degree in sociology and used skills developed through that formal training to help design and interpret some of the research projects of the Masters and Johnson Institute.

43. M. F. Schwartz and William H. Masters, "The Masters and Johnson Treatment Program for Dissatisfied Homosexual Men," *American Journal of Psychiatry* 141, no. 2 (February 1984): 173–81.

44. William H. Masters, Virginia Johnson, and Robert Kolodny, *Crisis: Heterosexual Behavior in the Age of AIDS* (New York: Grove Press, 1988).

45. Thomas Maier, "Can Psychiatrists Really 'Cure' Homosexuality?" *Scientific American*, April 22, 2009, http://www.scientificamerican.com/article/homosexuality-cure-masters-johnson.

46. Melissa Davey, "Françoise Barré-Sinoussi on the History and Future of HIV Research," *Guardian*, July 25, 2014, http://www.theguardian.com/society/2014/jul/25/francoise-barre-sinoussi-on-the-history-and-future-of-hiv-research.

47. On some of these contributions, see Rachel Swaby, *Headstrong: 52 Women Who Changed Science—and the World* (New York: Broadway Books, 2015). Forty-four out of the fifty-two women portrayed in the book lived at least part of their professionally active life in the twentieth century.

48. Françoise Barré-Sinoussi, "Opening Address," Twentieth International AIDS Conference, Melbourne, Australia, July 20, 2014, http://www.aids2014.org/webcontent/file/AIDS2014_Opening_Addresses_FBarre-Sinoussi.pdf.

49. Marilyn Ogilvie and Joy Harvey, eds., *The Biographical Dictionary of Women in Science: Pioneering Lives from Ancient Times to the Mid-20th Century* (New York: Routledge, 2000).

50. Anna C. Mastroianni, Ruth Faden, and Daniel Federman, eds., *Women and Health Research: Ethical and Legal Issues of Including Women in Clinical Studies* (Washington, DC: National Academies Press, 1994), 1:43.

51. A 1993 issue of the internationally popular journal *Science* was dedicated to women in science and brought into discussion everything from the notion of a "female style" of doing science to the structural problems that created an uneven playing field for women interested in the sciences. See *Science* 260, no. 5106 (April, 16, 1993): esp. 384–93. The journal reaches more than a million readers across the world, and its articles consistently rank among the world's most cited science research.

52. The NIH was founded in 1887.

53. In 1977 the FDA issued guidelines that explicitly forbade clinical trials on women of childbearing age, out of fear of possible long-term problems in both their health and their children's health. See Mastroianni, Faden, and Federman, eds., *Women and Health Research*, 41.

54. Ibid.

55. "Women's Health Initiative Publications," accessed August 18, 2017, https://www.nhlbi.nih.gov/whi/references.htm.

56. Anne Fausto-Sterling, *Sexing the Body: Gender Politics and the Construction of Sexuality* (New York: Basic Books, 2000).

57. R. Douglas Fields, "Vive la Différence," *Scientific American* 311, no. 3 (September 2014): 14.

58. "Consideration of Sex as a Biological Variable in NIH-funded Research," National Institutes of Health, June 9, 2015, https://grants.nih.gov/grants/guide/notice-files/NOT-OD-15-102.html.

59. Fiona Fleck, "Clinical Trials without Ethical Review under the Spotlight," *Bulletin of the World Health Organization*, March 2004, http://www.who.int/bulletin/volumes/82/4/feature0404/en.

60. Sunita Sharma et al., "Congenital Malformations among Babies Born Following Letrozole or Clomiphene for Infertility Treatment," *PLOS ONE* 9, no. 10 (2014), https://doi.org/10.1371/journal.pone.0108219.

61. UNESCO, "Women in Science," accessed December 26, 2017, http://uis.unesco.org/apps/visualisations/women-in-science.

62. Nagwa El-Badri, "Women and Science in Post-Revolution Egypt: The Long Road Ahead," *Nature: Middle East*, March 2013, http://www.natureasia.com/en/nmiddleeast/article/10.1038/nmiddleeast.2013.31; see also American Association for the Advancement of Science, "Profiles of Women in STE in Egypt," accessed August 18, 2017, http://www.aaas.org/page/profiles-women-ste-egypt.

63. Agnieszka Majcher, "Gender Inequality in German Academia and Strategies for Change," *German Policy Studies/Politikfeldanalyse* 2, no. 3 (2002), https://www.questia.com/library/journal/1G1-110081125/gender-inequality-in-german-academia-and-strategies.

64. Elsevier, *Mapping Gender in the German Research Arena, 2015*, https://www.elsevier.com/__data/assets/pdf_file/0004/126715/ELS_Germany_Gender_Research-SinglePages.pdf.

65. UNESCO, "Women, Agents of Change," accessed August 18, 2017, http://www.unesco.org/new/en/natural-sciences/priority-areas/gender-and-science.

66. Elizabeth Scarborough and Laurel Furumoto, *Untold Lives: The First Generation of American Women Psychologists* (New York: Columbia University Press, 1987).

67. Mary Whiton Calkins, "Autobiography of Mary Whiton Calkins," in *History of Psychology in Autobiography*, ed. Carl Murchison (Worcester, MA: Clark University Press, 1930), 1:45.

68. For an appreciative description of Calkins's contributions to self-psychology, see Janis S. Bohan, "Sex Differences and/in the Self: Classic Themes, Feminist Variations, Postmodern Challenges," *Psychology of Women Quarterly* 26, no. 1 (2002): 74–88; for a recent discussion of the development of self-psychology that completely ignores Calkins, see Allen M. Siegel, *Heinz Kohut and the Psychology of the Self* (New York: Routledge, 1996).

69. Barbara Engler, *Personality Theories* (Belmont, CA: Wadsworth, 2014), 110–34.

70. Switzerland and France were the first countries to allow women admission to medical training schools in the second half of the nineteenth century. Suzanne Le-May Sheffield, *Women and Science: Social Impact and Interaction* (New Brunswick, NJ: Rutgers University Press, 2006), 109–10.

71. The book was published in Italian in 1909 and translated into English in 1912. Within a few years it became known throughout the world, from Spain and the Netherlands to Romania and Japan. See Rita Kramer, *Maria Montessori* (Chicago: University of Chicago Press, 1976).

72. P. Lillard, *Montessori Today: A Comprehensive Approach to Education from Birth to Adulthood* (New York: Pantheon Books, 1996).

73. Nancy Chodorow, *Feminism and Psychoanalytic Theory* (New Haven, CT: Yale University Press, 1989).

74. Sue Wilkinson, "Prioritizing the Political: Feminist Psychology," in *Critical Social Psychology*, ed. Tomás Ibáñez and Lupicinio Íñiguez Rueda (New York: Sage, 1997), 178–94.

75. L. Jussim, *Social Perception and Social Reality: Why Accuracy Dominates Bias and Self-Fulfilling Prophecy* (New York: Oxford University Press, 2012); Laurie A. Rudman and Peter Glick, *The Social Psychology of Gender: How Power and Intimacy Shape Gender Relations* (New York: Guilford Press, 2008).

76. Anne Fausto-Sterling et al., "Multimodal Sex-Related Differences in Infant and in Infant-Directed Maternal Behaviors during Months Three through Twelve of Development," *Developmental Psychology* 51, no. 10 (2015): 1351–66.

77. Anne Fausto-Sterling, "Against Dichotomy," *Evolutionary Studies in Imaginative Culture* 1, no. 1 (2017): 63–66.

78. Mead was the object of both adulation and relentless criticism throughout her career and after her death. Some critics' views had ideological underpinnings, but other scholars argued her research methods were not up to the standards of her profession. A few critics went so far as to consider some of her arguments as "hoaxes." More recently, younger generations of scholars have revisited these debates and argued that Mead was by no means a careless or fraudulent researcher. For criticism of Mead as "hoaxed," see Derek Freeman, *The Fateful Hoaxing of Margaret Mead: A Historical Analysis of Her Samoan Research* (New York: Basic Books, 1999). For a more recent appreciative view of Mead that questions such criticisms, see Paul Shankman, *The Trashing of Margaret Mead: Anatomy of an Anthropological Controversy* (Madison: University of Wisconsin Press, 2009).

79. Lutkehaus, *Margaret Mead*.

80. Sherry Ortner, *Making Gender: The Politics and Erotics of Culture* (Boston: Beacon Press, 1996); Gayle Rubin, "The Traffic of Women: Notes on the 'Political Economy' of Sex," in *Toward an Anthropology of Women*, ed. Rayna R. Reiter (New York: Monthly Review Press, 1975), 157–210.

81. "Interview with Margaret Mead on International Women's Year," United Nations, January 1, 1975, accessed September 29, 2017, http://www.unmultimedia.org/classics/asset/C205/C2058.

82. The technical term in anthropology is *emic*.

83. In 1928 Hurston became the first African American woman to graduate from Barnard. She started doctoral studies at Columbia (1934–1935) but never completed them. The gender and color barriers were insurmountable at that time.

84. Ellen Lewin, ed., *Feminist Anthropology: A Reader* (Oxford: Blackwell, 2006).

85. Irma McClaurin, *Black Feminist Anthropology: Theory, Politics, Praxis, and Poetics* (New Brunswick, NJ: Rutgers University Press, 2001).

86. Valerie Boyd, *Wrapped in Rainbows: The Life of Zora Neale Hurston* (New York: Simon & Schuster, 2003).

87. Rigoberta Menchú Tum's work has given rise to debates among anthropologists and historians of Guatemala, some of whom questioned her methods and use of sources. Other scholars have shown that, despite elements of speculation in her analysis, Menchú Tum's work was both truthful and also extremely valuable as an insight into understanding the dynamics in her society and the violence perpetrated by the Guatemalan military during the civil war. See Victoria Sanford, "The Silencing of Maya Women from Mama Maquin to Rigoberta Menchú," *Social Justice* 27, no. 1 (2000): 128–43; David Stoll, *Rigoberta Menchú and the Story of All Poor Guatemalans* (New York: Westview Press, 1999); Victoria Sanford, "Between Rigoberta Menchú and La Violencia: Deconstructing David Stoll's History of Guatemala," *Latin American Perspectives* 26, no. 6 (November 1999): 38–46.

88. Gender Working Group, United Nations Commission on Science and Technology for Development, eds., *Missing Links: Gender Equity in Science and Technology for Development* (Ottawa: International Development Research Centre, 1995).

89. Christiana Figueres, "The Inside Story of the Paris Climate Agreement," TED, accessed August 18, 2017, https://www.ted.com/talks/christiana_figueres_the_inside_story_of_the_paris_climate_agreement?language=en.

90. Quote by the climate economist and politician Nicholas Stern in Matt McGrath, "UN Climate Chief Christiana Figueres to Step Down," BBC News, February 19, 2016, http://www.bbc.com/news/science-environment-35612559.

91. United Nations, *Demographic Yearbook 1948*, http://unstats.un.org/unsd/demographic/products/dyb/dybsets/1948%20DYB.pdf, 19.

92. Maxine Baca Zinn, "Feminism and Family Studies for a New Century," *Annals of the American Academy of Political and Social Science* 571, no. 1 (September 2000): 42–56.

93. Friedrich Engels, *The Origin of the Family, Private Property and the State* (Chicago: Charles H. Kerr, 1902 [1884]).

94. Judith Stacey, *Brave New Families: Stories of Domestic Upheaval in Late-Twentieth-Century America* (Berkeley: University of California Press, 1998).

95. Jonathan Riede, "Surprising the Sociologist," *New York Times*, November 18, 1990, http://www.nytimes.com/1990/11/18/books/surprising-the-sociologist.html.

96. Rosa Luxemburg, *The Accumulation of Capital: A Contribution to an Economic Explanation of Imperialism* (London: Routledge, 1951); George Lee, "Rosa Luxemburg and the Impact of Imperialism," *Economic Journal* 81, no. 324 (December 1971): 847–62.

97. From Luxemburg, *The Accumulation of Capital*, as quoted in Lee, "Rosa Luxemburg," 851–52.

98. Riccardo Bellofiore, Ewa Karwowski, and Jan Toporowski, eds., *The Legacy of Rosa Luxemburg, Oskar Lange and Michał Kalecki*, vol. 1 (Basingstoke, UK: Palgrave, 2014); Peter Hudis and Kevin B. Anderson, eds., *The Rosa Luxemburg Reader* (New York: Monthly Review Press, 2004); Norman Geras, *The Legacy of Rosa Luxemburg* (New York: Verso, 2015).

99. Seyla Benhabib, *The Reluctant Modernism of Hannah Arendt* (Lanham: Rowman & Littlefield, 2003).

100. *The Origins of Totalitarianism* is one of the most often cited books and certainly the most often cited work of political theory in the literature focusing on the history of communism.

101. Benhabib, *The Reluctant Modernism of Hannah Arendt*; Elisabeth Young-Bruehl, *Why Arendt Matters* (New Haven, CT: Yale University Press, 2006).

102. Seyla Benhabib, "Feminist Theory and Hannah Arendt's Concept of Public Space," *History of the Human Sciences* 6, no. 2 (1993): 97–114; Kimberly Maslin, "The Gender-Neutral Feminism of Hannah Arendt," *Hypatia* 28, no. 3 (Summer 2012): 585–601; Maria Markus, "The 'Anti-Feminism' of Hannah Arendt," *Thesis Eleven* 17, no. 1 (May 1987): 76–87.

103. Patricia Moynagh, "A Politics of Enlarged Mentality: Hannah Arendt, Citizenship Responsibility, and Feminism," *Hypatia* 12, no. 4 (Fall 1997): 27–53.

104. Nancy Fraser, *Unruly Practices: Power, Discourse, and Gender in Contemporary Social Theory* (Minneapolis: University of Minnesota Press, 1989); Nancy Fraser, *Fortunes of Feminism: From State-Managed Capitalism to Neoliberal Crisis* (New York: Verso Books, 2013); Ruth Lister, *Citizenship: Feminist Perspectives* (New York: Routledge, 1997).

105. Le Doeuff, *The Sex of Knowing*. On Astrabadi, see Najmabadi, *Women with Mustaches and Men without Beards*.

106. Antoinette Burton, "'History' Is Now: Feminist Theory and the Production of Historical Feminisms," *Women's History Review* 1, no. 1 (1992): 25–39.

107. The book was translated into English in 1953 and became an inspiration for Betty Friedan in writing *The Feminine Mystique*. It was translated into Polish in the 1970s, into Mandarin in 1986, and into Russian in the 1990s.

108. Rosemarie Tong and Tina Fernandes Botts, *Feminist Thought: A More Comprehensive Introduction*, 5th ed. (New York: Westview Press, 2017).

109. Rosalind Morris, ed., *Can the Subaltern Speak? Reflections on the History of an Idea* (New York: Columbia University Press, 2010).

110. Kimberlé Crenshaw, "Mapping the Margins: Intersectionality, Identity Politics, and Violence against Women of Color," *Stanford Law Review* 43, no. 6 (July 1991): 1241–99.

111. Mary Daly, *Gyn/Ecology: The Metaethics of Radical Feminism* (Boston: Beacon Press, 1978). Daly came under criticism, most prominently from Audre Lorde, for her inattention to questions of race in her depiction of patriarchy.

112. Elisabeth Schussler Fiorenza, *In Memory of Her: A Feminist Theological Reconstruction of Christian Origins* (New York: Crossroads, 1992).

113. Rosemary Radford Ruether, *Goddesses and the Divine Feminine: A Western Religious History* (Los Angeles: University of California Press, 2005).

114. Elisabetta Povoledo and Laurie Goodstein, "Pope Francis Says Panel Will Study Whether Women May Serve as Deacons," *New York Times*, May 12, 2016, http://www.nytimes.com/2016/05/13/world/europe/pope-says-hes-open-to-studying-whether-women-can-serve-as-deacons.html.

115. Fatema Mernissi, *The Veil and the Male Elite: A Feminist Interpretation of Women's Rights in Islam* (New York: Basic Books, 1987), ix.

116. "Gender Wage Gap," OECD, accessed August 18, 2017, http://www.oecd.org/gender/data/genderwagegap.htm (site discontinued).

SIX

Culture

In this decrepit, moribund, and evil society where patriarchal power is so strong, there is no truth for women.
— Wei Bai, 1936[1]

It is easier to conjure up images of women playing a vibrant role in the creation of culture throughout history than in almost any other human endeavor. Whether spinning tales about mythological creatures, singing songs, creating a beautiful living environment, or dancing at a festive gathering, women have participated in the making of cultural artifacts and practices as much as men have. However, there is a significant difference in how women versus men have been able to follow their creative impulses into socially acceptable outlets, and how much recognition they have garnered as creative spirits. Therefore, although less unprecedented than gaining political or civil rights, women's participation in shaping culture is still an important development in generating a greater diversity of aesthetic forms, as well as specifically articulating feminist art, literature, theater, film, music, dance, architecture, and other forms of cultural self-expression.

It is impossible to provide any overarching large data sets for the entire world that demonstrate changes in gender ratios in the production or popularity of any type of cultural artifact. There is no dearth of "top 100" lists, but they are generated by a wide variety of outlets that make comparisons or aggregation impossible. However, they have a few specifics in common: they are strongly biased toward Western culture, especially in music, film, and television; they feature a handful of female producers of culture in a sea of men; and they rarely agree on who those top female producers are, even as they tend to agree more on the male producers of culture.[2]

Rankings that draw attention to women producers of culture have started to be compiled only recently. One such research project from 2017 that focuses on albums by women musicians, "Turning the Tables," shows a very different array of featured artists: the genres of music are broader than most other "top 100" lists and the geographic diversity significantly greater than in most of them.[3] Women of color from every continent are featured on this list rather than just white artists who are produced by the largest labels in the industry. My discussion of music draws upon this ranking, but other sections do not have parallel data sets.

The multitude of outlets for cultural expression is far too great to touch on significantly in this chapter. Therefore, my approach is to illustrate selectively in most major areas of cultural creativity as a way to evoke, without being exhaustive, the impact of women as cultural producers in reshaping aesthetic norms, the value of culture in society, and overall how we understand, celebrate, and challenge our humanity through the arts.

WORDS

Literature and storytelling have long been gendered in terms of production and tropes. In societies with very low levels of literacy, which encompassed most of the world until well into the twentieth century, oral transmission of stories was an important element of constructing identity and community spirit and shaping the meaning of love, duty, and a host of other values. Many Scheherazades participated in shaping these narratives, both as bedtime stories that mothers told small children as well as tales women told each other while spinning, weaving, and doing any number of other household tasks.

The rise of "national" literature in the nineteenth century was a masculine affair, prompted primarily by the emphasis on educating boys before girls and more deeply by gendered assumptions about genius, creativity, and overall literary talent.[4] However, as female literacy increased, so did women's appetite for reading and writing. In Europe and North America in particular, female authors became increasingly published and known. Women writers developed a particular style of cloaking frustrations or desires not acceptable by the gender norms of the day into successful literary devices.[5] In addition, with the development of different forms of print culture, such as the serialized novel, we see a rise in readership among both men and women. Where women's writing had difficulty getting published due to editorial preferences for male writers, women and their allies created publications of their own. This is a nearly universal trend around the dawn of the twentieth century, from Greece to China.

Little known outside of her native Greece, Kalliroi Parren (1861–1940) is one of the most prominent figures of the first generation of feminists in that country, where she has been acknowledged for her editorial work as well as literary production. She was born in Rethymno, Crete, into a middle-class family that encouraged her to become educated. She eventually went on to become a teacher. After working overseas for Greek diaspora schools, she settled in Athens at the end of the 1880s, where in 1887 she founded the first women's publication in Greece, *The Women's Journal*.

Parren became a beacon of the emerging feminist movement in Greece. Her publication featured women's voices exclusively and came out as a weekly. The efforts Parren put into making this publication representative of women's notions of citizenship and gender roles in Greek society were tremendous and have remained largely unappreciated in the history of modern Greece. Her strongly held ideas about women's potential for shaping their society were close to other maternalist feminists from that period. She wished to bring to women the political rights she believed they deserved as the moral compass of their families.[6]

In addition to her educational efforts and political activism, Parren produced a number of original and successful works of fiction. Between 1900 and 1902 she published a trilogy entitled *The Books of Dawn*, which featured strong female characters and an unabashedly feminist perspective, a novelty in the local literary culture. The book came out in serialized form in *The Women's Journal* and was widely read, bringing visibility to the journal as well as to Parren's ideas. By 1907 the trilogy had been adapted for the stage and attracted an even wider audience, as it featured one of the most popular actresses of the time in the main role.[7]

Though they were not necessarily supportive of her feminist ideas, contemporary literary critics spoke highly of Parren's contribution to developing an original type of social novel.[8] Her writing did much to render women's issues and gender norms legible to a wide audience. Her construction of strong female characters with a positive agenda turned out to be appealing, opening wider imaginary horizons for how gender roles might develop into the future.

In China, where there was a very old tradition of women writers, the twentieth century saw a different gendered shift, the emergence of a decidedly and even combative feminist literature as part of the progressive movement that animated significant political and social activism, especially after the May Fourth era (1915–1921).[9] This period of intense intellectual and political mobilization against Western imperialism coalesced into several important new movements, among them nationalism, communism, and modernism. Feminist issues in the literature of that period resonated with a growing audience of urban, educated women, as well as male writers and especially leftist political activists. The "Woman Question," as portrayed in novels and plays from the 1920s onward, became a frequent theme in articulating broader critiques of Chinese society and traditions.[10]

One of the most radical voices of that generation was Wei Bai (1894–1987), who became successful as a playwright and penned a bold feminist autobiography that spelled out how the personal was political in Chinese society. Though leftist in her political outlook, Bai balked at the criticism of her male communist fellow travelers, who depicted autobiographical writing as inherently bourgeois because of its focus on the self rather than the social.[11] Instead, she crafted a narrative that turned the focus on the self into a social critique of gender roles and exposed the hidden pain many women suffered without any public acknowledgment. Having contracted syphilis from her lover, she endured a life of shame and pain that shaped her sense of worth and view of gender roles in Chinese society. Her work rejected the masculinist premises of the left-wing male writers of her day and instead provided a powerful counter-model for other women writers to continue to critique social and political problems through autobiographical writing.

In neighboring Japan, Akiko Yosano (1878–1942) became one of the most celebrated poets of the "tanka" tradition during the first half of the twentieth century.[12] Yosano produced more than twenty thousand such poems over her lifetime, her most widely read collection being the first she published, in 1901: *Tangled Hair*. Though originally depicted as greatly influenced by several tanka male masters, Yosano has come to be seen as an original: "Like a wolf in sheep's clothing, the early Akiko was an innovative new-style poet clad in the delicate modesty of the tanka form, its colors heightened by infusions from several other genres and arts."[13] Though a focus on women's interior lives had been a theme of tanka poetry, Yosano brought a feminist sensibility and force to the genre. Her vision rendered portrayals of women's loves, sexuality, and everyday life more vivid than her predecessors.

Yosano became a household name because of her early success as an author. She used this prominence to bring various issues of political and social prominence to the attention of her readers. Until the 1930s she was a militant pacifist, vocally critical of the militaristic culture in Japan at that time. She was also dedicated to freeing women from the isolation many endured, by opening up opportunities for education and social empowerment. In addition to writing many essays and nonfiction volumes on women's issues, Yosano helped establish a girls' arts school, Bunka Gakuin.[14] The school aimed to support and embolden young women who sought to develop their creative spirit in the areas of writing, visual arts, and acting. It was a pioneering effort in the region and attracted both Japanese and Chinese students, some of whom became the next generation of leaders in the art world. I will return to such an artist, Zilan Guan (1903–1986), in the next section.

Yosano traveled to Europe and China, bringing back appreciative impressions of women's newfound freedoms especially after World War I, but she remained a critic of superficial modernity. She saw a danger in the modern fashions many young women were adopting in East Asia without an appreciation for important homegrown traditions. During the last decade of her life, Yosano's public persona shifted toward greater support for Japanese military endeavors in China, which she maintained until her death in 1942.[15] After World War II many literary critics chose not to focus on this troubling part of her life, celebrating instead her early achievements. *Tangled Hair* remains one of the top one hundred books of the twentieth century in Japan.

Many women writers of this period did not self-identify as feminists, and some were even openly critical of feminism. Yet their style, themes, and specific articulation of gender roles greatly influenced others around them who aspired to reshape gender roles and empower women in society. Gertrude Stein did not set out to create a feminist language or novel. Yet her writing challenged readers from the use of grammar to themes and helped usher in a style of automatic or free associative writing that modernist writers and especially feminists found liberating and empowering.

Stein also published some of the earliest titles in what later became the genre of lesbian fiction.[16] *The Little Review*, a well-regarded popular modernist journal published by Margaret Anderson (1886–1973), became one of the outlets for Stein's work, in the company of James Joyce (1882–1941) and Emma Goldman. Anderson, a self-avowed feminist whose perspective openly framed her editorial choices, opened the pages of her journal to writers and artists whose aesthetics and themes challenged gender norms.[17] In the case of Stein, her lesbian themes and collage poetry were thematically and structurally innovative. Her writing appealed to some readers and confounded many others, rendering the writer a cult figure in her lifetime and especially in the later twentieth century, when the queer movement began to identify Stein as a pioneer of queering gender through performance.[18]

Another prominent woman writer openly critical of some forms of feminism while bemoaning the lack of a "room of one's own" was Virginia Woolf (1882–1941).[19] Woolf's writing was rooted in psychological exploration of identity with a specific focus on gender and introduced innovative ways of depicting the modern condition through interior dialogue. *Mrs. Dalloway* (1925) and *To the Lighthouse* (1927) became classics of the modernist novel because of her intense focus on detail and the inner dynamics of the characters, and especially how women in Woolf's novels engage with every aspect of their existence. Through these characters, gender becomes performative as stream-of-consciousness rumination and interior dialogue.

Her novel *Orlando* (1928) went even further in exploring the fluidity of gender identity: in constructing a comedic plot around transgender time travel, Woolf playfully forced readers to consider critically their own assumptions about gender norms, from appearance to social role and economic power. *Orlando* was a call for moving beyond gender polarity toward androgyny, something her contemporaries were not ready for but which found a ready audience by the end of the twentieth century.[20]

The number of prominent women writers around the world grew significantly after World War II, as female education and readership expanded. Some, like the Egyptian Nawal El Saadawi (b. 1931), found in writing an expression for their militant feminist activism. Others, like the South African Nadine Gordimer (1923–2014), wrote about racism in the colonial and postcolonial world and became voices of resistance against apartheid. And a growing number of successful women writers, such as Isabel Allende (b. 1942), found ways to celebrate female identity and pleasure in more escapist ways. Starting in the 1970s, lesbian literature flourished and gained popularity with an increasingly diverse audience, with writers like Rita Mae Brown (b. 1944) as trailblazers.

Trained as a physician, El Saadawi has focused much of her fiction and nonfiction writings on exposing the misogyny of Egyptian society and especially issues of domestic violence and genital mutilation. She built a successful career as a doctor and was able to observe up close the traumatic effects of men's violence against women, especially in rural areas. She used her position in the Ministry of Health to address these egregious abuses, which she identified as out of touch with authentic Islam, and was fired after publishing an unforgiving exposé of these practices, "Women and Sex" (1972).[21] El Saadawi continued her work on behalf of women's welfare in Islamic societies through the UN and eventually established her own feminist magazine, *Confrontation*. Her bold challenge to gender norms in Egyptian society landed El Saadawi in prison and later exile. Through activism, essays, and especially her very popular works of fiction, she has remained one of the most important voices of Islamic feminism in the world.

A trailblazer of her own, Rita Mae Brown came of age in the South during the harsh period of the civil rights movement and was expelled from the University of Florida for her activism against segregation. She made her way to New York City, where she became involved in feminist activism. Brown eventually became disenchanted with the homophobic leadership of the National Organization of Women (NOW) and in the 1970s helped found the "Lavender Menace" as a direct challenge to NOW's distancing from gay rights issues. She went on to publish many novels and write a number of screenplays. Her best-known work is *Ruby-fruit Jungle* (1973), which sold more than seventy thousand copies during its first issue by a small feminist press. The coming-of-age lesbian erotic novel went on to sell more than a million copies.

Overall, women writers became a great deal more appreciated and even celebrated by the end of the twentieth century. Among Nobel Prize-winners, a higher percentage (12.5 percent) of women have won the literature award than in any other category.[22] Between 1901 and 1990, six women won the prize, and eight have won it in the years since then, suggesting an increasing awareness of and interest in women's writing. Yet this type of international recognition doesn't necessarily reflect the boom of women writers from around the world, as the list is overwhelmingly European and white: the Chilean Gabriela Mistral (1889–1957) is the only Latina who has won this prize, and Toni Morrison (b. 1931) is the only black woman.

When the Norwegian Nobel Committee awarded Morrison the Literature Prize in 1993, they cited her novels as "characterized by visionary force and poetic import, giv[ing] life to an essential aspect of American reality."[23] That "essential aspect" was race, and Morrison became the most evocative voice of what slavery and life after emancipation meant for African American women.[24] Up to that point, only two black writers had won the prize, the Nigerian Wole Soyinka (b. 1934) in 1986 and the Trinidadian Derek Walcott (b. 1930) in 1992. Both engaged with questions of race, but their focus was not as squarely on the gendered nature of racism in the raw and overpowering way that Morrison brought these issues to life. Morrison has made it harder to ignore this ugly face of America and has done so with compelling and absorbing craftsmanship.

Though initially women created a room of their own by establishing their own journals and magazines, over the twentieth century they broke through the all-male journalism establishment and began to shape the content of what is published in every type of newspaper, journal, and magazine. The percentage of women in newsrooms and on editorial boards of such publications has changed significantly over the last hundred years, but so has the readership of print media. By the beginning of the twenty-first century women reached a 33 percent presence in the newsroom. But the readership of newspapers continues to drop in most places around the world, suggesting in this case that a greater presence doesn't translate necessarily into greater impact on the population newspapers try to reach.

Furthermore, women are still underrepresented among winners of prestigious awards like the Pulitzer Prize. A few won the prize before 1991, most of them not for journalistic reporting. Since then, they have accounted for around 27 percent of the winners, and their achievements correlate more strongly with privilege (e.g., race, education at an Ivy League school, and elevated economic background) than men's do.[25] The implication is that it is still harder for women to make it to the top of this profession. The consequences for how the news is reported cannot be overstated.

In 2011 Jill Abramson (b. 1954) was appointed the first woman chief executive editor of the *New York Times*. At the time of her appointment, there was a smattering of other female editors-in-chief at first- and second-tier papers in the United States.[26] Overall, around 35 percent of the editors of newspapers in the United States are women, a figure similar to South Africa's and larger than the UK's (16 percent).[27]

Abramson's appointment was hailed as an overdue hire and well-deserved recognition of her journalistic and managerial qualities. Yet her style of running the paper found a growing chorus of criticisms, some expressed in sexist terms, among the primarily male workforce she managed. When she pushed the editors to raise her salary to the level of her predecessor, it was the last straw for the owner.[28] Her tenure lasted three years, and her ousting became a prominent case for how sexism still pervades the newsrooms of the United States, a problem one can also observe around the world.

Around the same time Abramson was fired, a similar fate befell Natalie Nougayrède (b. 1966), who in 2013 became the first woman editor-in-chief at the prestigious French daily *Le Monde*. Her departure came after a number of her staff resigned in protest against changes she was attempting to implement in the paper, judging her style and reforms as too "autarchic" and "rigid."[29] These accusations resembled some of the criticisms leveled against Abramson, suggesting that there is a gendered dimension to the expectations reporters have regarding their managers, expectations that these two women were not interested in entertaining. Nougayrède went on to work for *The Guardian* as a correspondent.

The appointment of women editors-in-chief continues to pop up as news items around the world, from the United States to Saudi Arabia.[30] Yet it is not clear how much this represents real change in the newsroom culture and a shift toward a more diverse set of styles, priorities in terms of content, and overall a different gendered approach to delivering the news.[31] The backlash against Nougayrède and Abramson and the overall decline in women holding top positions is not encouraging.

However, as the media themselves are globally shifting from print to other ways of delivering the news, women as editors, journalists, and readers of news have found other outlets of expressing themselves. In the age of endless proliferation of blogs and other forms of instant uncurated communication over the Internet, it is becoming far more difficult to discern the actual impact of these voices.

IMAGES

The realm of visual arts has dealt most directly with representations of the human form and thus with gender roles, whether in a cave, on a canvas, in the pages of an illustrated manuscript, on the side of a mountain, or on-screen. The power of these images was rendered even more explicit through interdictions imposed by religious authorities. Whether banning images of God or god(s), of the entire human form, or just of the body, Jews, Muslims, and Christians articulated fear of worshipping embodied humanity rather than the sacred. Yet that preoccupation with how our bodies represent beauty and emotion has continued throughout history.

In the twentieth century, this preoccupation veered into new directions, toward the abstract and deconstructive. Technological advances in film and eventually television and the Internet have rendered ubiquitous the presence of bodies. Today, more than ever, we are besieged on a daily basis by various visual representations of gender roles that are the product of and inspiration for artistic visions of who we are as humans. The twentieth century was truly revolutionary in this regard, and though women as artists, curators, and consumers are not singularly responsible for these changes, their role has been central in the process. Women working in media ranging from sculpture to photography and architecture brought spectacular contributions to visual expressions of human creativity, generally speaking, especially to the gendered aspects of these representations.

We can glean the shift in the visibility of women artists by looking at the catalogues of major exhibits at the beginning of the twentieth century and comparing them with exhibits taking place today. Though Paris and Vienna were regarded as leaders in the art world in 1900, it was the Armory Show (1913) in New York that consecrated modernism as a powerful international force in the art world. Women represented fewer than 17 percent of the artists who showed their work at that major exhibit.[32] At that time, the percentage was considered a huge improvement over any previous such show. In the 2017 Whitney Biennial in New York, the curators insisted on having gender parity and produced a show of great diversity and intense political commitment.[33] While art critics commented amply on the quality of the work and especially its political aspects, few focused on the gender parity aspect of the show, considered unremarkable by this point in time.

The 1900s were marked by the beginnings of modernism in the visual arts and the attempt to break down the naturalism and positivism of the nineteenth century. It was an aesthetic and, to some extent, political and social revolt that engaged women in unprecedented ways. As one prominent scholar suggested, modernism encompassed "an amazing variety of visions and ideas that aim[ed] to make men and women the subjects as well as the objects of modernization, to give them the power to change the world that is changing them, to make their way through the maelstrom and make it their own."[34] As artists, collectors, curators, art critics, and objects of the artists' gaze, women helped shape the aesthetic values that came out of this revolt.[35]

Of the various modernist movements that flourished at that time, Dada represented the earliest self-avowed break with the past. The artists of this playful revolt took every assumption about what was "normal," "natural," or "beautiful" in art and turned it on its head. Line and color became tools for breaking down composition and three-dimensional perspective. Ready-made images (photography) became the building blocks for collages that similarly upended expectations about identity. Objects without function were rendered functional, and those with function, nonfunctional. In this group of rebels, women like the German Hannah Höch (1889–1978) and the Swiss Sophie Taeuber-Arp (1889–1943) played a central part. Höch became an early member of the movement in Germany, where she started as a graphic artist and became a photomontage pioneer, together with several other prominent members of the group, such as George Grosz (1893–1959) and Raoul Hausmann (1886–1971), who was also Höch's lover during this period. [36]

Höch's work was marked by a playful and ironic use of printed images and words, which she cut out and rearranged to critique political and social issues of her day. The political overtones of her collages contrasted with the rejection of politics predominant in most other Dada artists' work. Many of them would become more politically engaged in art and life later on, in the late 1920s and '30s, especially with the rise of radical right-wing politics in Germany, Italy, and France. By contrast, in 1919 Höch was already overtly feminist and critical of the German regime when she created her most famous work, *Cut with the Kitchen Knife Dada through the Last Weimar Beer-Belly Cultural Epoch in Germany*. A true original with a strong voice and personal vision, Höch became more influential later in the twentieth century, when her work was "discovered" by feminist art critics and activists, such as the Guerrilla Girls.

Other women artists from this period became better known earlier on, and their impact on the artistic sensibilities of the twentieth century can be seen already in their lifetime. Georgia O'Keeffe (1887–1986) produced a style that came to be viewed as archetypally "feminine." Her lushly colored close-ups of flowers and landscapes fascinated some and repelled others who were intent on reducing her innovations to a Freudian interpretation of repressed sexuality. [37] But O'Keeffe managed to sell her work very successfully, and she became the first woman to have a personal retrospective at the Museum of Modern Art (MoMA) in New York City in the 1940s, less than halfway through her artistic career. By the end of her life, she had become a leading figure and probably the best-known painter of American modernism.

Halfway across the world, modernism was flourishing in the visual arts, and women played an active role in this development. In the late 1920s the Chinese Zilan Guan became one of the students in Yosano's Bunka Gakuin in Tokyo. Guan had been trained as an artist in Shanghai in both traditional Chinese ink–style and Western-style painting. But it was her encounter with the influences brought by Japanese painters from Paris that significantly altered Guan's style. She became a fauvist painter, with a lush palette of bright colors and a preference for oil as a medium, both innovations in relation to the techniques Guan had learned in Shanghai. Her style mixed Western methods with her own preferences for specific themes and compositions. Her work became well known in Shanghai during the 1930s, when modernist aesthetics were celebrated at jazz clubs, through the art deco architecture sprouting all around the city, and through the adoption of modernist styles of dress.[38] The popular magazine *The Young Companion*, significantly more open to featuring modernist female artists than other contemporary Chinese publications, helped make her name, face, and paintings broadly known. Until the communist takeover Guan remained a star of the Shanghai art world. But after 1949 her name was erased from the firmament of great Chinese art and was only reintroduced to a wide public in the late 1990s.[39]

Another realm in which women artists saw early recognition and had an influential presence was photography. As the technology became simpler and more portable, photography became an accessible and relatively inexpensive medium in which women artists were as interested as men were. Women photographers such as the Americans Dorothea Lange (1895–1965) and Lee Miller (1907–1977), and the German Gerda Taro (1910–1937) imprinted their sensibilities in the treatment of every subject matter, from poverty and war to fashion and glamour. Lange became the voice of the dispossessed in her iconic photographs of the Dust Bowl era and later during World War II, when she provided empathetic images of the Japanese internment camps. Her compassionate vision shone through the documentary quality of the framing and the concern for social justice that imbued her thematic focus. Today she is considered one of the most important photojournalists of the twentieth century.

Taro took a similar sensibility into the fields of the Spanish Civil War (1936–1939), where she volunteered because of her antifascist sensibilities. Taro came from a Jewish family living in Austria-Hungary, and in her youth she witnessed the rise of the Nazis. Together with her partner Robert Capa (1913–1954) she produced some of the most gruesome and widely reprinted images of the carnage during that conflict. Her skill was matched by her unfailing passion for bearing intimate witness to human emotions and interactions: she was the first woman photojournalist stationed on the front lines alongside the troops. For that she paid with her life but not before shocking the public with images of the war and helping mobilize greater international attention vis-à-vis the violence engulfing Spain.[40] Taro's work in the front lines and ultimate sacrifice to the cause of exposing the truth of war inspired other women photographers, among them Margaret Bourke-White (1904–1971), who became the first female correspondent during World War II, and Lee Miller. Both of them built successful careers as photojournalists for magazines like *Life* and *Vanity Fair*.

Miller's work has been noted for both its aesthetic qualities and technical innovations. Raised by a photographer father, Miller developed great skill in front of and behind the camera early on. When she moved to Paris in 1929 to become part of the art scene, she was already a veteran of this art form. Man Ray (1890–1976) became her partner in experimenting with new techniques, and together they popularized solarization.[41] Miller spent three torrid years as part of the surrealist movement, appearing in Jean Cocteau (1889–1963) movies and Man Ray's photographs and undertaking her own photographic experiments. She subsequently embarked on a successful career as a photographer and during World War II went to the front to document the Blitz and the horrors of the Nazi concentration camps.

The images captured by Lange, Taro, Miller, and thousands of other women photographers increasingly shaped our visual sensibilities over the twentieth century. Both in their approach as well as the relationship they established with their subjects, women photographers have brought unique and diverse perspectives that enrich and challenge our understanding of human actions and emotions. One young photojournalist featured in a recent exhibit that celebrates the audacity of women photographers working in war-torn environments claimed self-confidently, "We [women] can push boundaries and bend rules a bit more than men can before we're reprimanded. And even then, because they don't take me as seriously as they would a male photographer, we're not kicked out or heavily reprimanded."[42]

Around the beginning of the twentieth century, the Arts and Crafts movement became an important avenue for women to participate in the modernist aesthetic revolution. In the United States, women working at the Tiffany studios, like Clara Driscoll (1861–1944), helped develop the famous and very profitable lamps and stained glass designs with which the company name became synonymous.[43] Though they were central to both the creative process and the crafting of these objects, these women were only "discovered" in 2007, when the New-York Historical Society hosted an exhibit entitled "A New Light on Tiffany."[44]

Women artists interested in interior design found a more welcoming environment in Scotland, which at the dawn of the twentieth century was a virtual laboratory for modernist art, architecture, and many types of craft, from china to furniture. Of this group, Charles Rennie Mackintosh (1868–1928) became the best known, but he was part of a lifelong partnership with his wife, Margaret MacDonald (1864–1933). The couple also collaborated with Margaret's sister, Frances (1873–1921), and her husband, Herbert McNair (1868–1955), starting in their student days at the Glasgow School of Art.[45] Margaret and Frances had worked together on designs early on, and later Margaret collaborated very closely with

Charles, cosigning many of their works that subsequently became known as the "Mackintosh style."[46] Margaret's originality in these collaborations blends with Frances's and Charles's.

In pieces she crafted on her own, from drawings to furniture, Margaret's interest in highly stylized representations of the human form or nature, with geometric patterns interwoven with organic shapes, appears very distinct. Together with Charles, Margaret participated in the famous 1900 Secession Exhibit in Vienna at the invitation of Gustav Klimt (1862–1918). The works she presented there influenced other Viennese artists and designers. Though Klimt never acknowledged this directly, some of Margaret and Frances's techniques and specific visual language later showed up in his work.[47]

For most of the twentieth century, the work of these and scores of other women designers remained submerged. If they were part of a team that included men, the men were recognized. If they were working for a large company, like Tiffany's, their individual contributions were never acknowledged.[48] Subsequently, women designers became better known, especially in the last quarter of the twentieth century. After World War II, a different climate regarding women's participation in the economy and ownership of their ideas made it possible for talented designers to develop businesses out of their artistic gifts. From the rise to fame of the French Coco Chanel (1883–1971) to the ubiquitous American Martha Stewart (b. 1941), women's design has helped shape what people buy and how they aestheticize their everyday existence—through housewares, fashion, or gardens.[49]

It was not just women artists and designers who made an important contribution to shaping visual aesthetics in the twentieth century. Collectors and museum curators played just as important a role. In the United States, the country that continues to have the most important market and museums for twentieth-century art, women were pioneers of these efforts. In the late 1920s three women collectors, Lillie Plummer Bliss (1864–1931), Mary Quinn Sullivan (1877–1939), and Abby Aldrich Rockefeller (1874–1948), set out to create a museum that would feature the best of contemporary trends in American and international art. MoMA opened its doors in 1929 and featured many of the works these women had collected for several decades. It quickly expanded due to the overwhelming public response it elicited.[50]

This was the most spectacular outcome of a larger trend. Women collectors and philanthropists were at the heart of the 1913 Armory Show that brought modernism into public awareness in the United States and helped build impressive private collections. Nineteen out of the twenty-four donors who helped defray the costs of organizing the show were women. Overall, the amount donated by women represents as much as 88 percent of the total funds raised to underwrite the exhibit.[51] Some of those collectors ended up donating their purchases to MoMA.

Other women donated their collections to the Art Institute of Chicago, the Boston Museum of Fine Arts, the Whitney Museum, and the Baltimore Museum of Arts. The Cone sisters (Claribel [1864–1929] and Etta {1870–1949]), who greatly influenced Gertrude Stein by turning her into an art collector, pursued this activity as a lifelong passion. Upon their death they left their entire collection of more than three thousand items to the Baltimore Museum of Arts. Today, its value is estimated at more than $1 billion.[52] Together with Stein's donation to the Baltimore Museum of Arts, the Cone sisters' collection represents the largest and most substantial female-driven effort to bring modern art to the American public.

No other woman collector has gathered as much fame, however, as Peggy Guggenheim (1898–1979), lovingly referred to by friends and critics alike as an "art addict."[53] Her passion and money helped sustain a number of artists' livelihoods (e.g., Constantin Brâncuși [1876–1957] and Marcel Duchamp [1887–1968], whom she also married), as well as establish one of the most important museums of twentieth-century art in Europe, the Peggy Guggenheim Collection in Venice. Guggenheim's glamour and circle of artist friends were featured prominently during her lifetime. With the growing impact of media in shaping tastes, this attention thrust her into the public eye more than any previous woman collector.[54] She became an enormously influential trendsetter for future women art collectors.

There were few places around the world before World War II that showed much interest in women as artists or where women made contributions as collectors as they did in the United States. Mexico is one such important site.[55] There, in the interwar period, the art scene became a vibrant site for aesthetic metissage, a blending of high and popular, traditional and cosmopolitan, all with a significant level of support from the state, through public art projects. The unconventional "open air" painting schools that opened up in Mexico starting in 1913 provided an auspicious environment for aspiring female artists and became an avenue for breaking out of the academic style of painting into a freer visual vocabulary.[56]

Frida Kahlo (1907–1954), along with a number of other women artists (some painters, others weavers, photographers, puppeteers, etc.), became a forceful presence in this world. Though initially better known for her intense relationship with Diego Rivera (1886–1957), who in the late 1920s was becoming a global modernist superstar, Kahlo was at the heart of artistic experimentation in Mexico from the 1920s until her death. She played host to artists and political activists and became an active participant in the activities of these left-wing circles.

More importantly, Kahlo developed an original visual vocabulary that combined her aesthetic and intellectual sensibilities. She honored tradition while standing at a critical distance from it; she embraced magical realism while placing it on a dreamlike plane; she painted from pain and focused on pain and loss as two constants in her life; and she rendered herself a mirror of all her dreams and desires, due to her physical inability to move most of the time.[57] Her modernism was not borrowed from others; it was a product of her experience in the highly auspicious artistic environment present in Mexico.

Kahlo gained some prominence in her lifetime, while she and Rivera lived in the United States for a short period of time and especially after she was offered the opportunity to have a one-woman show first in the United States and then in Paris in 1939.[58] André Breton (1896–1966), the doyen of surrealism, invited Kahlo to show her work in the hope of bringing new life to his movement. He presented her as innocent and described her style of painting as a "spontaneous," while tributary to surrealism. Yet Kahlo never self-identified thus; she simply used Breton as a vehicle for gaining visibility. That validation happened only partially during her lifetime. Kahlo's feminism and metissage began to gain currency internationally only in the 1980s.[59] Through the appropriation of her style, through movies, and through many publications featuring her paintings, she has since become an iconic figure of feminism internationally, from Latin America to Russia.

Since World War II, New York City has remained the undisputed global arts capital for painters, sculptors, and representatives of many other genres, attracting aspiring artists from around the world in the way Paris did before 1940. The art scene in New York had already become friendlier to women artists, with its more open admissions policies for art schools and interest in a greater variety of genres. In the second half of the twentieth century, a growing number of women artists from around the world came to the Big Apple to train, network, and exhibit their work. Some stayed there and diversified the New York art scene. Others went back to Seoul, Accra, Johannesburg, or Rio de Janeiro to open up new avenues for artistic expression for others. Their contributions have remained unevenly appreciated back home, but they are remarkable for their pioneering quality.

The Korean artist Suk-nam Yun (b. 1939) serves as an illustrative example of this rich and diverse development in the visual arts at the end of the twentieth century and especially into the twenty-first century. Born in Manchuria under Japanese occupation, she moved with her family to Seoul after the war and lived the first half of her life as a typical Korean woman: she had limited access to education, had to quit school because of poverty, then got married, and raised children. At forty-four she moved to New York City to study at the Pratt Institute. By 1985 she founded the "October Group," which sought to make visible the work of Korean women artists who at that time were treated with benevolent neglect by the established art world of Korea. New York City represented a welcoming and fertile environment for her experimentation with media and especially with the installations that became one of her most creative outlets.[60]

Yun saw her artistic ambitions and feminism as closely interlinked. Art was a medium for expressing her frustrations with misogyny and especially her desire for bringing greater attention to and aesthetic appreciation of women's lives. The theme of "mother" has been present throughout her evolution as an artist. Her approach has been ambivalent, struggling with questions about strength and lack of appreciation, abuse and invisibility. By the 1990s Yun came to be appreciated both overseas and in South Korea. In 1996 she won the Lee Jung-seop Award, the highest honor conferred upon artists by the government. In 2015 the Seoul Museum of Art hosted a large solo exhibition of her work, a sure sign that her feminist approach had gained appreciation.[61] Still, her works are rarely displayed as part of the museum's permanent collection. Visibility and recognition remain, at best, work in progress for most women artists around the world.

Starting in the 1970s, many more women have helped chart the direction of the art world, from curators of museums to, especially, artists. Cindy Sherman (b. 1954) became a vibrant and original voice, deploying her own body as a merciless ironic mirror that reflects the state of contemporary society. Using photography as a medium and with dramatic stagings of various themes, such as stardom and aging, she has continued to creatively reinvent the meaning of the self-portrait and especially what the female body can represent aesthetically. Her images are disturbing and beguiling at the same time, notable especially for her piercing gaze, which stares directly at the viewer and disallows any kind of voyeurism. By being the "ultimate master of self-morphing," Sherman has influenced generations of artists since her breakout in the late 1970s.[62]

The feminist movement of the 1960s and '70s in North America and Europe also produced its own distinct aesthetic forms that have generated broader art movements. The work of Judy Chicago (b. 1939) celebrated women as both present and silenced in history and has continued to advocate for a feminist aesthetic sensibility through a variety of media, from drawing to stitching. Somewhat didactic in her approach, Chicago has represented female agency and beauty in easily accessible ways. Her Dinner Party is probably the most famous such tribute to women and has been viewed and discussed around the world.[63]

The next generation of feminist artists became more intent on activism than on authorial power to create their own vision. The Guerrilla Girls sought to expose the hypocrisy of the art world by drawing attention to the imbalance between the voyeuristic and deeply sexist aesthetics of the art canon as exposed in the reopening of MoMA in 1984, whose opening exhibit featured fewer than 8 percent women artists. Though primarily focused on critiquing sexism and eventually racism in the twentieth-century art canon, the Guerrilla Girls also generated their own aesthetic and a style of protest that has resonated with future generations of political activists.[64] Their use of posters and billboards, their collages of women's bodies topped with gorilla heads and accompanied by ironic statements, such as "Do women have to be naked to get into the Met. Museum?" were a tribute to earlier feminists like Hannah Höch. These messages and the medium they used also aimed to shake up the reified celebration of consumerism in the 1980s. Subsequent generations of feminist art protesters, like the Russian group Pussy Riot, have taken up many of the Guerrilla Girls' approaches as a model or inspiration.

Despite continuing sexism in the art world, women have had remarkable achievements in recent years. One such moment was the awarding of the Pritzker Prize to the Iraqi-born architect Zaha Hadid (1950–2016), who in 2004 became the first woman to win this most prestigious architecture award. Hadid's work is located throughout the world, in China, Turkey, the United States, and many other countries.[65] Her flowing futuristic style has influenced scores of other architects and has given hope to women in the profession that their creativity might become recognized someday. Yet it remains to be seen to what extent Hadid is an exception or a pioneer in acknowledging women architects. A number of petitions, protests, and controversies over the past two decades related specifically to how the Pritzker Prize has been awarded suggest that this is still very much a disputed issue.[66]

SOUNDS

As music makers, women have long contributed to passing down traditions of singing and performing on a variety of instruments. In the area of formal music training and performance, they have had a more limited role because of gendered obstacles against their equal access to educational and professional opportunities. Even today, the world's most prestigious orchestras and bands are made up overwhelmingly by men, women conductors are a rare sight, and performances featuring the work of women composers are still exceptional events rather than common occurrences.[67] The one exception in classical music are women singers, where their unique vocal range has always ensured an equitable presence in ensembles and as soloists.

An early pioneer among women composers and conductors was the Brazilian Chiquinha Gonzaga (1847–1935). A woman of strong convictions and great talent, Gonzaga was a first in many ways. Although she was married off at sixteen and never received a formal education in music, Gonzaga wanted to dedicate her life to it and left her first husband when he denied her that opportunity. In 1876 she became the first woman to be allowed to play in a "choro" band (she was a great pianist) and made her debut as a conductor in 1885.[68] Along the way she composed around two thousand pieces of music and dozens of plays, many of which have been lost. Her style blended popular traditional music with

European and African influences and helped lay the foundations of what has become the standard repertoire of Brazilian music. Gonzaga's influence extended beyond Brazil. In the early years of the twentieth century she traveled to Europe and collaborated with musicians in Portugal. Her performances helped spread her fame as a talented composer and conductor in other European countries. In addition to her prodigious musical career, Gonzaga was a militant antislavery activist and later became a staunch suffragist. She was also instrumental in passing the first law in Brazil to protect intellectual rights for all future writers and composers.

As jazz grew into a prominent genre of music over the twentieth century, it opened up doors for ambitious women to develop their talents. Billie Holiday (1915–1959) is one of the best-known jazz singers of the twentieth century as well as a talented songwriter. Songs like "Strange Fruit" rendered her one of the most powerful voices to decry the racist violence of the 1930s and 1940s and have since become jazz standards. Her voice evoked myriad emotions and dominated radio and concert halls for decades, yet Holiday passed away penniless, having been abused by managers and the recording industry throughout her career.[69]

A more successful jazz musician was Mary Lou Williams (1910–1981), whose career spanned nearly six decades and is closely interwoven with the history of jazz in the United States.[70] She was a piano prodigy who started touring at twelve, playing with Duke Ellington (1899–1974) and his band when she was thirteen. Over time, Williams began to compose and arrange for various big bands. She became one of the most active jazz musicians and band leaders of the 1930s and 1940s, working with everyone from Art Blakey (1919–1990) to Dizzy Gillespie (1917–1993) and Thelonious Monk (1917–1982).

In the 1950s Williams had a religious awakening and her music began to shift toward the sacred, without losing its jazz roots. She continued to tour but concentrated more on educating and inspiring young audiences and players. By the time she passed away in 1981 she had hundreds of compositions and arrangements to her credit, and more than one hundred records. Her music is a rich stream of the history of jazz.

Over the twentieth century, as a greater variety of musical genres emerged, women musicians used their unique qualities as singers to advance their musical ambitions as instrumentalists, bandleaders, or composers. All-women bands were an early force in making women more visible as musicians and more able to assert creative control over their craft. Yet by the 1960s these bands were largely a thing of the past.[71] Instead, musicians like Miriam Makeba, Nina Simone (1933–2003), Joni Mitchell (b. 1943), and Celia Cruz (1925–2003) began to establish a strong following as the leaders of their bands in the studio and onstage (more on this aspect in the "Performance" section of this chapter).

Miriam Makeba effectively transformed jazz and African music by lending her voice to a style that combined influences from her South African background and the Afro-Caribbean jazz sounds becoming popular in her native Johannesburg in the 1950s. By the 1960s she had become internationally known from Africa to Europe and North America, where she debuted on *The Steve Allen Show* in November 1959, as the first South African musician featured there. The performance earned her an invitation to perform at the famed Village Vanguard jazz club for a four-week engagement, the first African musician to earn this recognition.

Makeba came to influence a host of other musicians all over the world, among them Dizzy Gillespie and Nina Simone. She also inspired scores of other musicians and activists by placing her music in the service of speaking out against apartheid in South Africa and more broadly against the racist legacies of colonialism. She served as a UN ambassador twice, first representing Guinea during her exile from South Africa in the late 1960s and again in 1999 as Ambassador of Goodwill on behalf of the Food and Agriculture Organization. These accomplishments earned her the beloved title of "Mama Africa."[72]

Canadian Joni Mitchell created her own unique blend of music a generation later, when folk music was morphing into pop and other genres. Initially hailed as a talented writer of folk songs with an evanescently beautiful voice, Mitchell became a profound innovator who helped shape rock, pop, and jazz through albums that reimagined every aspect of music making, from melodic line and tempo to gender- and race-bending references in lyrics and the cover art. She brought into the studio some of the most celebrated jazz musicians of her time and led them with visionary aplomb on recordings and in live performances.[73] Mitchell broke new ground in many aspects and has inspired not only other women singer-songwriters, but generations of musicians who aim to move music writing and performance beyond established genres and popular recipes for success.[74] Mitchell is one of a handful of women who have appeared on most of the "top 100" musicians lists of the twentieth century. A recent survey ranking female musicians around the world places her album *Blue* as number one among 150 recordings.[75]

PERFORMANCE

Over the past century, the fluid nature of gender norms was rendered most visible in performance arts such as dance, theater, film, and television. Whether auteurs or performers, women have profoundly influenced how we see and how we embody gender in our everyday existence.

The earliest revolutionaries in this regard were the dancers who rejected the forms of classical ballet. They turned to more natural movement and uses of the body that underscored gender difference without adding artifices to these differences via costume or other elements. Isadora Duncan (1877–1927) was a pioneer of this movement, with her rejection of classic dance techniques and the use of ballet shoes.[76] Around the same time, Josephine Baker (1906–1975) helped introduce an appreciation for African dance on the stages of European concert halls, playing off racial stereotypes through her vibrant unconventional movements and costumes.[77] Cabaret theater, a product of the modernist movement, was heavily influenced by the performance of women as both singers and dancers, none more famous than the powerful and seductive Lola character portrayed by Marlene Dietrich (1901–1992) in the film *Blue Angel*.[78] Subsequently, choreographers like Martha Graham (1894–1991) and Katherine Dunham (1909–2006) created their own schools of dance in the United States. They rose to international prominence as both dancers and as creative spirits who reimagined movement, with women prominently featured as strong and independent.

Successful women choreographers have played an influential role in film. In India, the Bollywood industry came to be dominated in the 1980s by the work of Saroj Khan (b. 1948), who won eight *Filmfare* awards, the equivalent of Oscars in the Indian film industry. Her prominence and independent style became an inspiration for other women choreographers, and the Indian film scene has benefited from their growing participation.[79] In short, women have become prominent in shaping the aesthetics of dance on the stage and the screen, guiding popular taste in this art form into the twenty-first century.

Theater as a medium for performing gender has always had a fluid nature, from the use of masks and other elaborate disguises to all-male-cast performances. The polarization of theatrical performance to fit gender stereotypes rather than playfully subvert them is a rather recent development that solidified in the nineteenth century. It was with the rise of modernism that a serious and more overtly sexualized type of cross-gender acting became popular.[80]

At the beginning of the twentieth century, cabaret clubs became a premier site for this type of renewed theatrical experimentation and playfulness, in cosmopolitan centers like Paris and Shanghai. Cabarets developed initially as speakeasies or liminal spaces between the rich and the working class. They enabled fantasy to become reality for a few hours— passing as rich when poor, as poor when rich, as female when male, as male when female, and on occasion passing as white when nonwhite, and as nonwhite when white. As the urban nouveaux riches of Europe and Asia began to take interest in conspicuous spending and performing modernity, cabaret clubs opened in Manila, Mumbai, Warsaw, and other large urban centers on every continent.

While women were seldom the managers of these places, they were often the main attraction for a largely male customer base, especially outside of Western Europe. In places like Germany and France, there was a greater gender balance among the attendees of cabaret clubs, partly due to different gender norms in relation to going out to any clubs where drinks and sexual innuendos were commonplace. Another important difference was the gender ratio in urban areas of people who lived single and also had the financial means to go out. In Western Europe it was much more balanced than in Eastern Europe and even more so than in Asia.[81]

As a platform for artistic creativity, cabaret became an important site for female empowerment and, on occasion, for contestation of binary gender roles. Plenty of performances catered to voyeuristic sexualized representations of femininity. Yet others pushed the envelope, with the female performer either cross-dressing or acting out satirical takes on gender mores in their societies. These ambiguities made cabaret the exciting type of performance space that attracted those interested in seeing and at times taking part in risqué shows.

Cabaret has morphed over time into a number of performative artistic forms, especially starting in the 1970s. As the gay rights movement grew, interweaving performance and political action, cabaret and dance clubs started to take on many of the elements of those communities. Revue theater retreated toward a less risqué and more "bread and circus" approach. Overall, as people's interest in live entertainment moved toward either pop music concerts or movies, performers in these two genres took on some of the qualities of what had made cabaret popular.

Among the pop superstars who brought the gender-bending aesthetics of cabaret to the concert stage and video screen in the 1980s, none was as prominent as Madonna (b. 1958). With MTV as a new and widely viewed platform for music videos, Madonna became a master of performing gender. Her influence came primarily from the edgy, sexualized style featured in videos and concert performances, an image she cultivated carefully and developed creatively over time, from doll to dominatrix. Generations of future pop stars throughout the world, such as the Americans Taylor Swift (b. 1989) and Beyoncé (b. 1981), the South Korean Lee Hyori (b. 1979), and the Mexican Paulina Rubio (b. 1971), have used similar avenues to develop and maintain their popularity. In a world more and more dominated by visualized versions of musical performances, these styles play well globally, their popularity driven less by innovation in music than by a visual aesthetic that is both sexual and stylish, as well as by danceable rhythms.

The rise of television and subsequently the Internet has also meant a different performance platform for women comedians. If in the 1950s and 1960s the dominant stand-up comedians on-screen and in clubs were men, by the dawn of the twenty-first century female and especially feminist comedians have started to shape satire and our sense of humor.[82] Writers and performers such as Tina Fey (b. 1970) and Samantha Bee (b.

1969) in the United States, Neeti Palta (b. 1982) in India, and Joanna Sio in Hong Kong are using feminist ideas and arguments to critique contemporary gender norms, from politics to sexual predation among their fellow entertainers.[83] This is still a small phenomenon, but it has had a growing impact on what comedy looks like onstage and especially onscreen, both small and large.[84]

Performance art has introduced an approach that focuses less on the entertainment aspects and more on the creative process of enacting or embodying art through gender. Some of the earliest artists of this kind were part of the Dada movement, already discussed in this chapter. The German Emmy Hennings (1885–1948) was one the most creative among such performance artists. Together with Hugo Ball (1886–1927), in 1915 she founded Cabaret Voltaire in Zurich, which became the heart of the Dada movement among all the exiles to Switzerland during World War I.[85] Though little known today, Hennings commanded the stage of Cabaret Voltaire during its heyday with her surreal poetry readings, dances, and singing. She was a charismatic presence onstage, compelling not so much because of classical acting, dancing, or singing talents but because of her ability to act against the norm and expectations of the audience, which rendered her performances compelling.

Early forms of performance art can be seen among other artists, from Japan to Latin America, especially in the form of extended, free-floating one-person theatrical performances. But performance art as an explicit form of visual creativity grew especially in the 1960s. Japanese Yoko Ono (b. 1933) was part of that early avant-garde, initially solo but eventually in partnership with John Lennon (1940–1980). Their "bed-ins" became global media events and drew attention to the cause of activism against the Vietnam War as well as to the artists and their aesthetic vision.[86]

Like Ono, many other women performance artists developed their interest in this form because of their feminist ideas. Carolee Schneemann (b. 1939) moved from painting and film to performance art as a way to express her feminist frustrations and activism more powerfully and authentically and to control the message.[87] Her most famous and influential piece, *Interior Scroll* (1975), featured Schneemann engaging in a number of activities, such as disrobing, reading from a book, and pulling a scroll out of her vagina and reading its contents. The art establishment and feminists alike initially criticized her use of nudity and female sexuality as either narcissistic or playing to patriarchal voyeurism. Yet Schneemann's works have become a canonical example of radical experimentation and an inspiration for generations of feminists and performance artists.[88] One of the best-known feminist performance art events inspired by Schneemann's radical feminism is *The Vagina Monologues*, which developed out of a piece written by Eve Ensler (b. 1953) in 1996. Since its premiere it has been performed thousands of times by an evolving cast of characters and texts in more than four hundred cities and fifty-eight countries.[89] Since the 2010s *The Vagina Monologues* has come under criticism as dismissive of transwomen's experiences and cis-essentialist in defining womanhood. Still, the play continues to be a popular event particularly on college campuses across the United States and in other countries.

Women artists in Korea, Japan, Brazil, and Cuba found great avenues for self-expression in performance art, but none has taken the medium into such experimental long-term explorations of the body as the Serbian native Marina Abramović (b. 1946). Though she has long resisted being identified as a feminist, Abramović made her body the site of artistic experimentation in ways that are both fundamentally gendered and also confront gender norms. In *Rhythm 0*, one of her most famous performances from the 1970s, she sat for six hours and invited the audience to participate in engaging with her still body by using any of seventy-two objects placed on a table, including a flower, perfume, honey, grapes, wine, scissors, nails, a metal bar, and a gun loaded with one bullet. Her body became the canvas on which every individual could enact a ritual or action.

After the performance, Abramović stated, "I felt really violated: they cut up my clothes, stuck rose thorns in my stomach, one person aimed the gun at my head, and another took it away. It created an aggressive atmosphere. After exactly six hours, as planned, I stood up and started walking toward the audience. Everyone ran away, to escape an actual confrontation."[90] Her performances have continuously confronted their audiences as embodied participants in relationships shaped as much by Abramović's intentions as by the audience's interpretations. Whether the thematic focus of these interactions has been war, power relations, love, or longing, by situating her body at the center of the performances, Abramović has been asking us to step into the performance and shape it. By doing so, she has continuously confronted and pushed against gender norms.[91]

As film grew into the most popular form of performative visual art over the twentieth century, it also became the most influential medium through which artists have reimagined gender roles and human interactions more broadly. Its origins were modest, and initially women found it relatively easy to become involved in it as writers, performers, directors, and in other production capacities. The French director Alice Guy-Blaché (1873–1968) was a prominent pioneer in filmmaking, with more than one thousand films to her credit during her career (1896–1920). She cofounded one of the first "all-in-one" film studios, and directed what is considered one of the first narrative films and also the first all-black-cast movie in the United States.

Guy-Blaché paved the way for a generation of other women filmmakers in the 1920s, such as Lois Weber (1879–1939) and Dorothy Arzner (1897–1979). None of these women succeeded in translating her early efforts into a successful career once the film industry moved to Los Angeles. The only exception is Mary Pickford (1892–1979), the cofounder of the very successful studio United Artists. She retired in 1930 as the talkies were on the rise, but she is still considered by some as the most successful woman to work in Hollywood in terms of her power as a producer and appearances in movies.

On the other side of the Atlantic, Leni Riefenstahl (1902–2003) saw her film career soar when she partnered with Adolf Hitler in becoming his main videographer. Unquestionably a talented and sophisticated filmmaker, Riefenstahl is best known for her *Triumph of the Will* (1934), hailed as one of the best-made and most disturbing propaganda/documentary films of all time. Riefenstahl had a remarkably free hand in developing her visual imagery in relation to the Nazi censorship and propaganda machine. Her films are thus as much a product of what was allowed during that time as of her own personal vision, which was unabashedly racist and celebratory of the violence wrought upon European societies by the Nazis.

Since the 1930s women have remained outsiders to the movie studio system that rose first in Hollywood and its counterparts in the UK and France, and subsequently spread throughout the world, into, for instance, India and China. As recently as 2015, a multitude of women in the film industry, such as directors, producers, and screenwriters, commented bitterly about the pervading sexism of this art form.[92] The 2017 scandals that started with women film artists coming forward about the sexual violence they experienced in the film industry have exposed the deep systemic roots of sexism in this art form.

The impact of these artists has been not so much in the pervasiveness of their presence as in the powerful commentaries their films have offered as a distinct, female vision of themes that many more male directors have tackled. The work of African American director Ava DuVernay (b. 1972), especially the movie *Selma* (2014), has been noted with great enthusiasm by feminist critics for its sophisticated and thoughtful engagement with gender issues in dealing with the civil rights movement.[93] But *Selma* remained an outsider at the Academy Awards, and only one woman director thus far has won the coveted directorial Oscar, Kathryn Bigelow (b. 1951), in 2009.[94]

This is not just a US-based phenomenon. At the most prestigious film competition in the world, the Cannes Festival, only one woman director out of ninety recipients has won the highest award, the coveted Palme d'Or, the New Zealander Jane Campion (b. 1954) with *The Piano* in 1993. And only two female directors have won the festival's best director award, the Russian Yuliya Solntseva (1901–1989) with *Chronicle of Flaming Years* in 1961, and the American Sofia Coppola (b. 1971) with *The Beguiled* in 2017. In her speech thanking the jury, Coppola highlighted Jane Campion's influence as "a role model supporting women filmmakers."[95] In doing so, she underscored the continuing need to render visible the contribution of women artists toward enriching this art form in every subsequent generation.

This continuing problem for women artists who wish to work in film as a medium has been addressed partly through the growing influence of television and more recently Internet-based streaming of films through Netflix and other platforms. Older women filmmakers have found new ways to show their work to a wider audience. Younger generations of women producers, writers, and directors have been able to identify audiences whose interest and specifically gendered preferences have provided sufficient financial leverage to turn performance experiments into longer-lasting series. As Internet viewership continues to grow around the world, it is possible that a phenomenon similar to this will take off in other places, such as Ghana, India, Brazil, Turkey, and Japan.

* * *

The twentieth century presents us with a patchwork of contributions and frustrations that women experienced as artists in every genre and part of the world. Though at times successful in a number of media, such as literature, music, and film, women as creators of culture have yet to arrive at a level of parity with men or to garner full appreciation. Too often, women's works are still considered work for women only, even as cultural artifacts made by men pass simply as literature, art, or music, presumably for everyone. A shift brought about especially by feminist cultural critics has been noticeable since the 1970s, toward a more equitable appreciation of the growing diversity and specific sensibilities women artists have brought to the world of culture and entertainment.

Today, highbrow and lowbrow mix in the world of culture significantly more than in the past. The avenues for producing and disseminating one's artistic voice have become incomparably more democratic than they were in 1900. Women have both led the way and benefited from these changes. It is now a great deal easier to find literature, music, and visual and performative art forms that fit with any type of taste. This proliferation has also meant that cultural production and consumption have become much more segmented. Large corporate establishments, whether they are museums, publishing houses, or broadcasting companies, now have the economic means to capture the attention of broad audiences. Women are still at the margins of these establishments, though they have become more present than they once were. It remains to be seen to what extent women, as rising forces in this corporate cultural environment, will bring about greater sensibility in terms of treating gender norms critically and playfully.

NOTES

1. Ping Zhu, *Gender and Subjectivities in Early Twentieth-Century Chinese Literature and Culture* (New York: Palgrave Macmillan, 2015), 138.

2. A notable exception to the gender imbalance noted here can be seen in the "100 Greatest, Gayest albums (of All Time)" generated by *Out Magazine*. The list is fairly gender-balanced and shows gender parity in the top ten titles, accessed August 18, 2017, https://www.out.com/entertainment/music/2012/03/19/100-greatest-gayest-albums-all-time. For examples of more typical rankings, see *Business Insider, Time, Time Out, Rolling Stone, Billboard, Entertainment Weekly, IMDB*, and the American Film Institute.

3. "Turning the Tables," National Public Radio, July 24, 2017, accessed August 18, 2017, http://www.npr.org/2017/07/24/538387823/turning-the-tables-150-greatest-albums-made-by-women. The list doesn't differentiate among women producers, music writers, performers, and bandleaders.

4. Sandra Gilbert and Susan Gubar, *The Madwoman in the Attic: The Woman Writer and the Nineteenth-Century Literary Imagination* (New Haven, CT: Yale University Press, 1979).

5. Ibid.

6. Angelika Psarra and Eleni Fournaraki, "Parren, Callirhoe (born Siganou)," in *A Biographical Dictionary of Women's Movements and Feminisms*, ed. de Haan, Daskalova, and Loutfi, 402–5.

7. Maria Anastasopoulou, "Feminist Discourse and Literary Representation in Turn-of-the-Century Greece: Kallirrhoe Siganou-Parren's 'The Books of Dawn,'" *Journal of Modern Greek Studies* 15, no. 1 (May 1997): 1–28.

8. Ibid.

9. Amy Dooling, *Women's Literary Feminism in Twentieth Century China* (New York: Palgrave Macmillan, 2005); Wang Zheng, *Women in the Chinese Enlightenment: Oral and Textual Histories* (Berkeley: University of California Press, 1999); Yan Haiping, *Chinese Women Writers and the Feminist Imagination, 1905–1948* (London: Routledge, 2006).

10. Dooling, *Women's Literary Feminism*, 23.

11. Ibid.

12. Tanka poetry is part of the haiku family, defined by its short form: five lines, following the pattern 5-7-5-7-7 syllables. A very old tradition, it was revived in the early twentieth century and continues to be popular today.

13. Janine Beichman, *Embracing the Firebird: Yosano Akiko and the Rebirth of the Female Voice in Modern Japanese Poetry* (Honolulu: University of Hawai'i Press, 2002), 259.

14. Laurel Rasplica Rodd, "Yosano Akiko and the Bunka Gakuin: Educating Free Individuals," *Journal of the Association of Teachers of Japanese* 21, no. 1 (1991): 75–89.

15. Steve Rabson, "Yosano Akiko on War: To Give One's Life or Not—A Question of Which War," *Journal of the Association of Teachers of Japanese* 25, no. 1 (1991): 45–74.

16. Lucy Daniel, *Gertrude Stein* (London: Reaktion Books, 2009).

17. Karen Leick, *Gertrude Stein and the Making of an American Celebrity* (London: Routledge, 2009), 91–108.

18. Daniela Miranda, "The Queer Temporality of Gertrude Stein's Continuous Present," *Gender Forum: An Internet Journal for Gender Studies*, no. 54 (2015), accessed December 26, 2017, http://genderforum.org/special-issue-early-career-researchers-iii-issue-54-2015.

19. In *Night and Day* (1919) Woolf presented a critical portrayal of a naïve suffragette and used some of the plot to provide a wider critique of the "fashionable" middle-class aspects of that type of feminism in Great Britain. But, as many scholars have shown, Woolf herself was a feminist and wrote impassioned feminist critiques of British society, especially in *A Room of One's Own* and *Three Guineas* (1938). Sowon S. Park, "Suffrage and Virginia Woolf: 'The Mass behind the Single Voice,'" *Review of English Studies* 56, no. 223 (February 2005): 119–34.

20. See especially Sally Potter's well-received adaptation of the novel for screen in 1992, which featured Tilda Swinton. The British actress confessed she became obsessed with Woolf's novel when she first read it as a young woman. Tilda Swinton, "Tilda Swinton on Virginia Woolf's *Orlando*," January 9, 2012, *Telegraph*, http://www. telegraph.co.uk/culture/books/8995801/Tilda-Swinton-on-Virginia-Woolfs-Orlando. html.

21. Jenna Krajeki, "The Books of Nawal el Saadawi," *New Yorker*, March 7, 2011, http://www.newyorker.com/books/page-turner/the-books-of-nawal-el-saadawi.

22. Fourteen women out of a total of 112 awardees won the literature prize by May 2016. The number of women winners of the peace prize is higher (16), but so is the total number of winners (129).

23. "The Nobel Prize in Literature 1993," Nobel Prize, accessed August 18, 2017, http://www.nobelprize.org/nobel_prizes/literature/laureates/1993.

24. She is in great company here, with Alice Walker (b. 1944), Maya Angelou (1928–2014), Audre Lorde, and many other African American women having become successful authors since the 1980s.

25. Yong Z. Volz and Francis L. F. Lee, "Who Wins the Pulitzer Prize in International Reporting? Cumulative Advantage and Social Stratification in Journalism," *Journalism* 14, no. 5 (July 2013): 587–605.

26. At the beginning of the 2010s they included, among the first tier (i.e., most widely read) papers, the *New York Daily News*, *New York Post*, *Chicago Tribune*, and *USA Today*. By 2014, when Abramson was ousted, there were only two women remaining in these positions of authority. Joe Strupp, "With Jill Abramson's NY Times Ouster, None of the Ten Largest Papers Are Led by Women," *Mediamatters* (blog), March 16, 2014, http://mediamatters.org/blog/2014/05/16/with-jill-abramsons-ny-times-ouster-none-of-the/199349.

27. Julie Posetti, "The Rise (and Fall) of Female Editors," *Mediashift*, September 26, 2014, http://mediashift.org/2014/09/the-rise-and-fall-of-women-editors.

28. Ken Auletta, "Why Jill Abramson Was Fired," *New Yorker*, May 14, 2014, http:// www.newyorker.com/business/currency/why-jill-abramson-was-fired.

29. "Natalie Nougayrède démissionne de son poste de directrice du 'Monde,'"*Le Monde*, May 14, 2014, http://www.lemonde.fr/actualite-medias/article/2014/05/14/natalie-nougayrede-demissionne-de-son-poste-de-directrice-du-monde_4416748_3236.html.

30. Saeed Kamali Dehghan, "Saudi Arabia's First Female Editor of National Newspaper Appointed," *Guardian*, February 17, 2014, http://www.theguardian.com/world/2014/feb/17/saudi-arabia-first-female-editor-national-newspaper; Lydia O'Connor, "*San Francisco Chronicle* Names First Female Editor in Chief," *Huffington Post*, January 13, 2015, http://www.huffingtonpost.com/2015/01/13/sf-chronicle-woman-editor-in-chief_n_6465824.html.

31. The lack of race diversity among top editorial positions at top-tier papers in the United States is as glaring as the gender imbalance. Only 10 percent of these positions are occupied by nonwhites. See American Society of News Editors, "Whites and Minorities by Job Category," accessed August 18, 2017, http://asne.org/content.asp?pl=140&sl=131&contentid=131.

32. "Armory Show 1913 Complete List," Armory Show at 100, accessed August 18, 2017, http://armory.nyhistory.org/armory-show-1913-complete-list/.

33. Nadja Sayej, "Whitney Biennial 2017: Trump's Shadow Looms over Politically Charged Show," *Guardian*, March 17, 2017, https://www.theguardian.com/artanddesign/2017/mar/17/whitney-biennial-2017-trump-politically-charged-show.

34. Marshall Berman, *All That Is Solid Melts into Air: The Experience of Modernity*, 9th ed. (New York: Verso, 2009), 15–16.

35. Rita Felski, *The Gender of Modernity* (Cambridge, MA: Harvard University Press, 1995); Bucur, *Gendering Modernism*.

36. Dawn Ades, Emily Butler, and Daniel F. Herrmann, eds., *Hannah Höch* (Munich: Prestel, 2014).

37. Hunter Drohojowska-Philp, *Full Bloom: The Art and Life of Georgia O'Keeffe* (New York: W. W. Norton 2004).
38. Paul Pickowicz, Kuiyi Shen, and Yingjin Zhang, eds., *Liangyou, Kaleidoscopic Modernity and the Shanghai Global Metropolis, 1926–1945* (Leiden, NL: Koninklijke Brill, 2013).
39. The exhibition "A Century in Crisis: Modernity and Tradition in the Art of Twentieth-Century China" at the Guggenheim Museum in New York in May 1998 featured Guan's most famous work, *Portrait of Miss L.* The exhibit was curated with the support of the Chinese government. See also the accompanying catalogue, Julia F. Andrews and Kuiyi Shen, eds., *A Century in Crisis: Modernity and Tradition in the Art of Twentieth-Century China* (New York: Guggenheim Museum, Distributed by Harry N. Abrams, 1998), 163.
40. Jane Rogoyska, *Gerda Taro: Inventing Robert Capa* (London: Random House, 2013).
41. Reversing the tone on a negative, so that the dark areas appear light and vice versa.
42. The quote belongs to photojournalist Diana Zeyneb Alhindawi. See Jake Wallis Simons, "'Women Push Boundaries and Bend Rules More Than Men': Extraordinary Pictures by Female War Photographers on the World's Deadliest Front Lines," *Daily Mail*, September 22, 2016, http://www.dailymail.co.uk/news/article-3787618/Women-push-boundaries-bend-rules-men-Extraordinary-pictures-female-war-photographers-world-s-deadliest-lines.html.
43. Martin Eidelberg, Nina Gray, and Margaret Hofer, *A New Light on Tiffany: Clara Driscoll and the Tiffany Girls* (New York: New-York Historical Society, 2007).
44. Jeffrey Kastner, "Out of Tiffany's Shadow, a Woman of Light," *New York Times*, February 25, 2007, http://www.nytimes.com/2007/02/25/arts/design/25kast.html; see also "A New Light on Tiffany," New-York Historical Society Museum and Library, accessed August 18, 2017, http://www.nyhistory.org/exhibitions/a-new-light-on-tiffany. A lot of credit for bringing attention to women's contributions to Tiffany goes to historian Louise Mirrer, the president and CEO of the New-York Historical Society.
45. Jude Burkhauser, ed., *Glasgow Girls: Women in Art and Design, 1880–1920* (Glasgow: Canongate, 1990).
46. Ibid.
47. This is an issue around which art historians have tiptoed, given both Klimt's iconic notoriety and the MacDonald sisters' lack thereof. In a recent write-up that accompanied the auctioning at Christie's of one of Margaret MacDonald's pieces from 1902, *The White Rose and the Red Rose*, Roger Billcliffe, one of the foremost experts on the Mackintosh style, came close to acknowledging this influence: "In many ways the use of these gesso panels within the Rose Boudoir bears parallels with the concept of Gustav Klimt's mosaic friezes for the dining room of the Palais Stoclet, created a few years later. The two projects shared close similarities of intention and of theme." See "Margaret MacDonald Mackintosh, The White Rose and the Red Rose, 1902," Christie's, accessed August 18, 2017, http://www.christies.com/lotfinder/lot/margaret-macdonald-mackintosh-the-white-rose-and-5066453-details.aspx. Missing from this description is the fact that MacDonald's work was on display at the Secession exhibit in Vienna in 1900, at which point her style was fully developed, while Klimt did not produce works with similarly stylized human forms ensconced in whimsical geometric patterns until years later. *The Kiss* and the portrait of *Adele Bloch-Bauer*, perhaps his best-known works in this style, were produced in 1907.
48. Furthermore, these companies also discriminated against women by limiting employment to unmarried women. Clara Driscoll was fired by Tiffany Glass after twenty years of working there and being a brilliant manager of the women's studio, simply because she got married. Eidelberg, Gray, and Hofer, *A New Light*.
49. Axel Madsen, *Chanel: A Woman of Her Own* (New York: Macmillan, 1991); Sarah A. Leavitt, *From Catharine Beecher to Martha Stewart: A Cultural History of Domestic Advice* (Chapel Hill: University of North Carolina Press, 2002).

50. Jennifer Pfeifer Shircliff, "Women of the 1913 Armory Show: Their Contributions to the Development of American Modern Art" (PhD diss., University of Louisville, 2014); Charlotte Gere and Marina Vaizey, *Great Women Collectors* (London: Philip Wilson 1999), 170–73.

51. Shircliff, "Women of the 1913 Armory Show," 46.

52. Edward Cone, "Shirtsleeves to Matisses," *Forbes*, October 11, 1999, http://www.forbes.com/forbes/1999/1011/6409098a.html.

53. *Peggy Guggenheim: Art Addict* is a 2015 American documentary film directed by Lisa Immordino Vreeland.

54. Francine Prose, *Peggy Guggenheim: The Shock of the Modern* (New Haven, CT: Yale University Press, 2015).

55. Adrian Locke, *Mexico: A Revolution in Art, 1910–1940* (London: Royal Academy of Arts, 2013).

56. Tatiana Flores, "Strategic Modernists: Women Artists in Post-Revolutionary Mexico," *Woman's Art Journal* 29, no. 2 (2008): 12–22.

57. Kahlo's physical disabilities were connected to contracting polio as a child and not wearing the proper footwear to correct the uneven length of her legs, a massive injury she suffered in youth as a result of a bus accident, and surgery for spina bifida.

58. Alice Gambrell, *Women Intellectuals, Modernism, and Difference: Transatlantic Culture, 1919–1945* (New York: Cambridge University Press, 1997).

59. Elisabeth Malkin, "Frida Kahlo: Feminist, Chicana Heroine," *Ledger*, July 13, 2007, http://www.theledger.com/article/20070713/NEWS/707130335?p=1&tc=pg.

60. Na Young Lee, "Yun Suknam," *Feminist Studies* 32, no. 2 (Summer 2006): 352–64.

61. For a virtual tour of that exhibit, see Suk-nam Yun, 2015 SeMA (Seoul Museum of Art) Green video, accessed August 18, 2017, http://yunsuknam.com/zboard/zboard.php?id=recent_work&page=1&sn1=&divpage=1&sn=off&ss=on&sc=on&select_arrange=headnum&desc=asc&no=125.

62. Phoebe Hoban, "The Cindy Sherman Effect," *Art News*, February 14, 2012, http://www.artnews.com/2012/02/14/the-cindy-sherman-effect.

63. Jane F. Gerhard, *The Dinner Party: Judy Chicago and the Power of Popular Feminism, 1970–2007* (Athens: University of Georgia Press, 2013).

64. Anne Teresa Demo, "The Guerrilla Girls' Comic Politics of Subversion," *Women's Studies in Communication* 23, no. 2 (2000): 133–57.

65. Aaron Betsky, *The Complete Zaha Hadid* (London: Thames and Hudson, 2016).

66. Gareth Cook, "What About Denise?" *New Yorker*, April 15, 2013, accessed August 18, 2017, http://www.newyorker.com/culture/culture-desk/what-about-denise; Robin Pogrebin, "Partner without the Prize," *New York Times*, April 17, 2013, http://www.nytimes.com/2013/04/18/arts/design/bid-for-pritzker-prize-to-acknowledge-denise-scott-brown.html?ref=design.

67. Approximately 30 percent of the musicians playing in the major symphonic orchestras around the world today are women. The proportion has not changed much over the past twenty years. Judith Tick, Margaret Ericson, and Ellen Koskoff, "Women in Music," *Oxford Music Online*, accessed December 26, 2017, https://doi.org/10.1093/gmo/9781561592630.article.52554.

68. Choro is a Brazilian style of music that originated in Rio de Janeiro in the mid-nineteenth century; it is marked by a specific form (AABBACCA) that is said to have both European and African influences.

69. Sherie M. Randolph, *Florynce "Flo" Kennedy: The Life of a Black Feminist Radical* (Chapel Hill: University of North Carolina Press, 2015), 64–67.

70. Linda Dahl, *Morning Glory: A Biography of Mary Lou Williams* (New York: Pantheon, 2012).

71. Ibid.

72. "Miriam Makeba," South African History Online, accessed August 18, 2017, http://www.sahistory.org.za/people/miriam-makeba.

73. They include Herbie Hancock (b. 1940), Jaco Pastorius (1951–1987), Pat Metheny (b. 1954), and Wayne Shorter (b. 1933).

74. The superstar Prince (1958–2016) was a great fan and sought inspiration from her recordings and performances over many years.

75. "Turning the Tables," National Public Radio, July 24, 2017, accessed August 18, 2017, http://www.npr.org/2017/07/24/538387823/turning-the-tables-150-greatest-albums-made-by-women.

76. Ann Daly, *Done into Dance: Isadora Duncan in America* (Middletown, CT: Wesleyan University Press, 2002).

77. Anne Anlin Cheng, *Second Skin: Josephine Baker and the Modern Surface* (Oxford: Oxford University Press, 2011).

78. Christiane Schönfeld, ed., *Practicing Modernity: Female Creativity in the Weimar Republic* (Würzburg: Königshausen & Neumann, 2006).

79. Vikrant Kishore, Amit Sarwal, and Parichay Patra, eds., *Salaam Bollywood: Representations and Interpretations* (London: Routledge, 2016).

80. In 1899, when Sarah Bernhardt (1844–1923) played Hamlet on the French stage, the production was welcomed with nods to her talent but with an equal amount of incredulity and disapproval of the cross-gender performance of the classic Shakespeare role. See "Drama: The Week," *Athenaeum*, no. 3738 (June 17, 1899): 764.

81. Peter Jelavich, *Berlin Cabaret* (Cambridge, MA: Harvard University Press, 1996); James Farrer and Andrew David Field, *Shanghai Nightscapes: A Nocturnal Biography of a Global City* (Chicago: University of Chicago Press, 2015); Beth Holmgren, "Cabaret Liberation," *Cosmopolitan Review: A Transatlantic Review of Things Polish, in English* 5, no. 1 (2013), http://cosmopolitanreview.com/cabaret-liberation.

82. Richard Zoglin, *Comedy at the Edge: How Stand-Up in the 1970s Changed America* (New York: Bloomsbury, 2008).

83. Courtney Iseman, "Meet the Female Comedians Who Are Getting Laughs in Countries Not Known for Their Comedy," *Bust*, April 5, 2016, http://bust.com/entertainment/16051-these-women-are-getting-laughs-in-countries-not-known-for-their-comedy.html.

84. A report on the gender ratio of comedians who performed at Caroline's, one of the premier stand-up clubs in New York City, between 2011 and 2014 revealed that women represented 8 percent of the headliners. Kaitlyn Mitchell, "We Crunched the Numbers on How Much Stagetime Female Comedians Get," *bitchmedia*, February 4, 2015, https://bitchmedia.org/post/we-crunched-the-numbers-on-how-much-stagetime-female-comedians-get.

85. Amanda L. Hockensmith, "Emmy Hennings," in *Dada: Zurich, Berlin, Hannover, Cologne, New York, Paris*, ed. Leah Dickerman (Washington, DC: National Gallery of Art, 2005), 473–74.

86. Claudia Mesch, *Art and Politics: A Small History of Art for Social Change since 1955* (London: I. B. Tauris, 2013).

87. Isabella Smith, "Carolee Schneemann on Feminism, Activism and Ageing," *AnOther*, March 9, 2016, http://www.anothermag.com/art-photography/8462/carolee-schneemann-on-feminism-activism-and-ageing.

88. Robert C. Morgan, "Carolee Schneemann: The Politics of Eroticism," *Art Journal* 56, no. 4 (Winter 1997): 97–100.

89. Kayla S. Canelo, "*The Vagina Monologues*," in *Encyclopedia of Women in Today's World*, ed. Mary Zeiss Stange, Carol K. Oyster, and Jane E. Sloan (Los Angeles: SAGE, 2011), 1:1510.

90. Dobrila de Negri, "Intervista con Marina Abramović," in *Marina Abramović: Performing Body* (Milan: Charta, 1998), 11–22.

91. Cristina Demaria, "The Performative Body of Marina Abramović: Rerelating (in) Time and Space," *European Journal of Women's Studies* 11, no. 3 (2004): 295–307; James Westcott, *When Marina Abramović Dies: A Biography* (Boston: MIT Press, 2010).

92. Maureen Dowd, "The Women of Hollywood Speak Out," *New York Times*, November 20, 2015, http://www.nytimes.com/2015/11/22/magazine/the-women-of-hollywood-speak-out.html.

93. Nijla Mu'min, "'Selma' Is Now," *bitchmedia*, December 23, 2014, https://bitchmedia.org/post/selma-film-review-ava-duvernay-feminist.

94. The film she directed, *The Hurt Locker*, also won Best Picture that year, together with numerous other awards.

95. Manohla Dargis, "'The Square' Wins Top Prize at Cannes; Sofia Coppola Is Best Director," *New York Times*, May 28, 2017, https://www.nytimes.com/2017/05/28/movies/cannes-film-festival-winners-the-square-sofia-coppola.html.

SEVEN

Kinship

Into the Future

When women have more control over the income/resources of the household, the pattern of consumption tends to be more child-focused and oriented to meeting the basic needs, [and] children in female headed households have higher school enrollment and completion rates than children in male headed households.
                                    —C. Mark Blackden and Chitra Bhanu, 1999[1]

Culture has always been shaped by gender norms, both in the sense of artistic performances and production of artifacts, as well as in the anthropological sense of everyday habits and encounters. Thus it is more difficult to identify radical changes that women have produced in this area in the twentieth century. Yet there are many ways in which the kinds of empowerment discussed up to now in the area of politics and especially education and the economy have led to unprecedented shifts in everyday cultural practice over the last fifty years.

   We have entered a new era of kinship relations, which scholars identify as "the second demographic transition." The demographers who first coined this term distinguish it from the first demographic revolution, discussed in chapter 3 ("Population"), in the following way: if the first demographic revolution was about "rationalizing life," the term Max Weber (1864–1920) came up with at the beginning of the twentieth century, the second demographic revolution has been about "individualizing life."[2] At the heart of this transition are shifts in gender norms and in particular women's agency:

   A gender revolution occurred whereby women were no longer subservient to men and husbands, but asserted the right to regulate their fertility. Women's desire for "biological autonomy" was articulated by

181

subsequent quests for the liberalization of induced abortion. Finally, these revolutions fit within the framework of a rejection of authority and an overhaul of the normative structure. Parents, educators, churches, army, and much of the entire state apparatus ended up in the dock. This entire ideational reorientation, if not revolution, occurred during the peak years of economic growth and shaped all aspects of the second demographic transition.[3]

The term "transition" connotes not only change but also uncertainty. We are just beginning to grapple with the impact of these changes, rendering any analysis speculative. Yet historically relevant elements of this transition have become legible. They include the waning of the patriarchal model of gender roles in the family, the dramatic rise of female-headed households, the growing normalization of same-sex families and transgender identities, the decrease in marriage as a choice for cohabitating adults, and the reactions of religious denominations to these trends, which challenge their sociocultural foundations. This final chapter highlights the extent and potential impact of these recent changes, which are closely connected with the twentieth-century shifts discussed up to now.

THE WANING OF THE PATRIARCHAL FAMILY MODEL

Kinship is one of the most fundamental and universal ways in which we associate with each other as human beings. Over the twentieth century we have profoundly altered the meaning of kinship, as well as the value assigned to specific relations, from parenting to marriage. The factors that most directly led to changes in practices have to do primarily with women's entry into the paid workforce, access to education, more equitable civil rights, and access to safe and inexpensive forms of birth control.

In 2007 the Organisation for Economic Co-operation and Development (OECD) published a study that showed the average ratio of married or cohabitating couples in which both adults worked was around 70 percent, with all member states except Turkey and Mexico scoring higher than 50 percent.[4] The change from a single- to a dual-earner norm has taken place over the last half century. What lags behind this achievement is the continuing wage gender gap. This change is notable for the variety of political regimes and cultural differences encompassed by the countries included in the study. There is no single type of political system—democratic, noncapitalist, authoritarian, or theocratic—that aligns singularly with this change. And there are no sociocultural traditions—religious, secular, feminist, patriarchal—absent from this trend. The only "universal" in this equation is women's agency in becoming wage earners.

Furthermore, a large study done in the United States shows that in 2013 women made up 40 percent of the heads of households with children living at home, a spectacular growth from 11 percent in 1960.[5] This statistic includes single mothers who are household heads, now more than 25 percent of the total households in the United States, and mothers whose spouse may or may not be a stay-at-home parent.[6] Nonwhite women, especially African Americans, are disproportionately present in this growing trend. While African American women make up 12.4 percent of all mothers, they represent 27.5 percent of all single mothers.[7] Studies done around the world starting in the 1980s show similar growing numbers of female-headed households in Africa (e.g., Mozambique, 36 percent), Latin America (e.g., 40 percent in Haiti), and Asia (e.g., 17 percent in Bangladesh).[8] In Russia, the significant growth in single mothers as heads of households suggests there is more to these changes than a specific set of policies linked to a type of state or ideology.[9]

What this shift means in terms of our understanding and practice of gender roles in the family is a question that puzzles many scholars and policy makers and has seen feminist observers playing a particularly important role.[10] Some of the reaction has been of discomfort, with words like "alarming" featuring prominently, especially among those who still assume there is a patriarchal "normal" version of the family, with the father as head and the wife and children as the other members of the household.[11] Yet other observers have tried to better understand the causes of this change and especially its sociocultural implications into the future without condemning it on the basis of prevailing norms, especially since this trend seems to be growing in many parts of the world. One scholar has defined this change as a "quiet revolution."[12]

At the very least, these trends signify that what used to be considered "normal" in family relations—a model set up by male scholars, theologians, and politicians more than a century ago—is no longer reflective of how families are formed, how they function, and how individuals relate to each other in kinship groups. Patriarchy as established and rendered hegemonic in the past is waning inside the family. How do we explain this important change?

The first issue to address is this: In heterosexual couples, to what extent are the households headed by women the result of choice on the part of women, choice on the part of male partners, or neither?[13] Historically, women became heads of households most often upon widowhood, which would normally be considered in the "neither" category. Yet women's longevity has been shorter than men's until just a few generations ago, so widows were not a significant proportion of the single-headed households until recently. It is also the case that women's health in old age tends to be poorer than men's, especially in societies where women's bad nutrition is a customary practice.[14] These factors indicate that a widow would outlive her husband more likely through an unnatural incident, a form of violence.[15] The most frequent forms of violence until today have been wars initiated by men against other men, by virtue of their political and social position and as a matter of historical record. That suggests that historically, women's widowhood has come about mostly due to male-dominated political and military power relations and structures—in short, men's choice. This phenomenon continues today, as there are active wars from the Central African Republic to parts of the Middle East (e.g., Syria) and Asia (e.g., Afghanistan), with troops from Western countries actively involved.

In what instances have women become heads of families by making their own choices? And when did that start to occur as a broad transsocietal phenomenon? Over the twentieth century, once women began to gain the individual political and socioeconomic rights they had been denied in the nineteenth century, a shift took place in how women made decisions about marriage. Having access to education with some professional aspirations helped recast the need for women to consider marriage as the only economically and socially acceptable form of security in life. As women in every society around the world began to engage with these opportunities, they tended to want to marry later. In doing so, they prolonged their period of adult life living on their own, as heads of their household of one or as partners in relations that were more open-ended than marriage.[16] For many of these women, educational and economic opportunities would not have come without the knowledge about and access to safe birth control practices. Women now opt for motherhood on the basis of a much more rational choice of self-sustainability as part of a kinship group than ever in the past.

One might refer to that as catching up with choices men had enjoyed for many centuries. Many of these women ended up in stable couples or marriages, but more as partners and eventually as the partners who on occasion became the head of household if economic and professional opportunities tilted that way. There is a growing trend in a number of regions, especially North America and Western Europe, and predominantly among younger generations, to establish such kinship relations based on partnership, sometimes in marriage and sometimes as stable cohabitation. Between 1970 and 2007 marriage rates decreased by an average of around 30 percent in OECD countries, with cohabitation rates increasing in similar proportions.[17]

While a significant percentage of women are heads of households today because they choose to be, a greater number of women live as heads of households out of necessity. In Bangladesh, for instance, abandoned women rank as the highest ratio among categories of single female-headed households: at around 23 percent, with the second highest being widows. A larger percentage (34 percent) of women de facto heads of their households are married, with the husband either unwilling/unable to work or away from the household.[18] Many such households across the world live in dire poverty, suggesting that gender norms in these societies (e.g., preventing girls from getting an education or married women from working) continue to play a deleterious role in terms of meeting these families' basic economic survival needs.[19]

The continuing de facto, if not de jure, unequal rights in cases of divorce generally play out in favor of men leaving their wives impoverished. Divorce laws have changed in most of Europe and North America, but in much of the world there is still gender inequality in terms of women's protection and economic security after divorce.[20] More often than not, these divorces are cases of abandonment, with the husband taking away assets and leaving a wife, with children, unable to take care of herself because she is less likely to work for wages outside the home than the husband and most likely does not own any savings or other assets in her own name.[21]

In some places around the world, including in Asia and in Africa, an abandoned wife is still considered a pariah both in society and the larger kinship group.[22] In Bangladesh, for instance, such women heads of household and their children are frequently shunned by the husband's family and have few familial resources to draw upon. If the law either doesn't protect the abandoned spouse or if it is not enforced, the wife remains impoverished without much choice by virtue of unpunished or even legal biases against her gender. Unfortunately, this problem remains present in many states around the world. Furthermore, it remains a low priority when it comes to police training or even international aid tied to police reform. In 2010 the UN produced a *Handbook for Legislation on Violence against Women*, meant to provide guidance to national governments and including the training of law enforcement personnel.[23] Yet the UN has been embroiled in several high-profile scandals that have exposed an expansive informal network of trafficking in women among its own peacekeeping forces, rendering its advice far less authoritative.[24] In short, international organizations and governments remain complicit in continuing these gender biases.

A welcome development in drawing attention to related problems is the Istanbul Convention on Preventing and Combating Violence against Women and Domestic Violence.[25] At the initiative of feminist leadership in the Council of Europe and open to any state that wants to support it, in 2011 the Istanbul Convention established the first internationally recognized set of principles and best practices associated with the prevention and elimination of violence against women.

An important element of the Convention's provisions is to insist on recognizing this sort of violence as a legitimate basis for seeking asylum overseas. For women stuck in marriages or other familial relations that include physical, psychological, and economic forms of violence, the Convention opens new possibilities for escaping toward safety and starting over again in a more auspicious environment. The recent spurts in migration from Central America to the United States or Canada, and from the Middle East, Africa, and Asia to the EU, include significant numbers of women seeking safety in this fashion.[26] Unfortunately, of the forty-five states that have signed the Convention to date, only twenty-four ratified it in their national legislatures. They include most members of the EU, as well as Georgia, Albania, Turkey, and Serbia. The United States, as the country with still the largest number of refugees, has yet to ratify the Convention. As more states begin to recognize domestic violence as a serious social problem and prioritize it in areas such as training law enforcement and providing access to protective services for victims of domestic violence, more women will likely want to depart from such abusive relationships and start anew as heads of their households.

Other cases of females heading households happen in marriages where the woman becomes the main earner and/or decision-maker, though not necessarily as a form of empowerment through access to new opportunities. In many places in Asia and Africa, women have started to head their households because their husbands are not economically active or because they have left to pursue economic opportunities as migrants. These forms of authority are driven not by women's aspirations but rather by economic desperation on the part of their spouses. Forty-three percent of women heading households in Bangladesh are in this category. A growing percentage of women in parts of Africa as well as the Middle East (especially Syria, Iraq, and Afghanistan) are experiencing this reality.[27] In the postsocialist East European states, a similar dynamic of women becoming the main breadwinner with the husband unemployed was common starting in the 1990s in countries like Romania, Bulgaria, and Bosnia-Herzegovina.[28] Some of these changes have not been permanent, but they brought about a long-term shift in women's behavior and, in some cases, in the thinking of how husbands and wives understand their relationship in the family.[29]

Finally, there are migrants or refugees who leave their families behind and send remittances to El Salvador, Morocco, Afghanistan, and many other countries around the world. With travel being dangerous and expensive, men have attempted to save their families from poverty by seeking risky prospects in Europe and North America.[30] Often they leave behind their wives in charge of the larger kinship group, most likely under another male authority. But sometimes they leave behind households headed by their wives, who come to depend heavily on the remittances while running the household in the absence of their husband.

The lack of security in terms of personal safety and economic benefits, and the overall open-endedness of this sort of migration creates important rifts in these female-headed households, a kind of limbo of both lacking and having to assume authority. With or without remittances, a woman heading such a household has to deal with the financial needs of maintaining the household and raising children. She also often needs to pay back any loans the family would have taken out to enable the husband's journey. In short, these are female-headed households where need and vulnerability rather than empowerment and choice are the main qualities of their experience.

Whether intentionally or not, these trends challenge traditional kinship relations, especially patriarchal norms of gender relations in the family. They have generated entirely new socioeconomic realities in their respective communities as well as new cultural experiences and expectations. Some men and women experience these changes as destabilizing and frightening, while others, especially women, view them as an opening toward new horizons, maybe riskier and less protected but offering the possibilities of a better life. This is even more the case for younger generations. In 2013 a study on attitudes in the United States toward "new values" among voters found that only 44 percent of married white men over 35 still upheld the patriarchal definition of a family, with 39 percent of the rest of the population supporting it. For women, the averages were 31 percent for unmarried women and 24 percent for married women. Another way to think about it is that twice as many men than women who are married believe that men should be the "masters in their own house."[31] A growing number of people in parts of Europe, Latin America, Africa, and Asia accept nonpatriarchal familial relations as a positive value.[32]

The implications of this shift are nothing short of revolutionary in terms of how future generations will develop kinship relations and of how welfare and other types of socioeconomic policies are framed and implemented. The ongoing forms of systemic economic discrimination against women are likely to be challenged more thoroughly when more women become either the sole or main breadwinner in a family. The IMF and World Bank are already starting to draw attention to such issues: if women make less than men for the same work (the regional figures around the world range between 60 and 70 percent of male earnings), then any female-led household is currently predisposed to live in greater poverty than a male-led one, for reasons connected with assumptions about who the primary breadwinner is.[33] By exposing these assumptions and keeping better statistics on these forms of gender discrimination, international bodies like the EU and the IMF are empowering future generations of women to better articulate arguments for ending such behavior as both unjust and unwise.

WOMEN HEADS OF HOUSEHOLDS
AND THE COMMON GOOD

A related finding in female-led households is that they tend to invest more in the education and general well-being of the next generation than households where men are the primary breadwinners.[34] The differences are significant especially in the global South.

A study done in Pakistan in the late twentieth century showed that while 49 percent of female-headed households sent all of their children, including girls, to school, only 40 percent of the male-headed households did.[35] Similar differences can be seen in Ethiopia: a recent study on the socioeconomic determinants of primary-school enrollment found a 4 percent difference between female- and male-headed households in terms of enrolling children in school. The difference is approximately the same for completion rates, with female heads of household showing a 20.5 percent rate of completion of grade 4 compared to 16.7 percent among male heads of household.[36] Overall, scholars doing research on these questions in Latin America, Africa, and South Asia have arrived at the same conclusion: "When women have more control over the income/resources of the household, the pattern of consumption tends to be more child-focused and oriented to meeting the basic needs, [and] children in female headed households have higher school enrollment and completion rates than children in male headed households."[37]

This finding has important implications for our understanding of how men and women continue to have a different interpretation of kinship relations and especially parental responsibility in relation to economic power. Simply put, when given a choice, even a difficult one of placing the needs of children above their own professional or other aspirations, women tend to withhold consumption and care of self to make sure their children have better opportunities than they do. With male heads of households, especially in poorer families, consumption for oneself continues to take precedence over care of others, with deleterious results for their families.[38]

A similar significant difference between men and women regarding their sense of responsibility toward others in the family can be seen in the United States. While only 27 percent of men believe that they "have a personal responsibility to help those worse off than myself," 42 percent of women agree with that statement. This huge difference correlates strongly with the tendency to empathize with someone else, with 40 percent of women versus 29 percent of men self-identifying as strongly empathetic.[39]

These differences are not biological but rather come about through education and personal experience. They are connected to our cultural understanding and performance of gender roles: if women find it so much easier to care and be empathetic across different societies and traditions, it suggests that caring and empathy are important and useful learned assets for addressing social problems, such as lack of access to education and jobs. The key is to develop a more positive and valorizing attitude toward these attributes rather than to simply note and take them for granted. Many individuals already show they understand these important advantages through their increasingly positive attitudes toward nonpatriarchal familial relations. Governments and international organizations interested in development need to follow suit. Investing in women who head households and prioritize the education of the younger generations is a matter of common sense, as they bring a higher return on investment if properly channeled. The IMF and World Bank are starting to pay attention.[40] Alas, most policy makers in states all over the globe, from the United States to Bangladesh, have yet to take these findings to heart.

The other important policy implication of this new trend has to do with economic opportunities for women. The microloans that are now a veritable fashion among international organizations and banks have increasingly targeted women as a safe bet.[41] These programs are a start, but their effectiveness remains debatable, as local contexts (legal, political, economic) tend to differ greatly and need to be taken into consideration in a more nuanced manner than is currently the case in practice. More importantly, the opportunity to become trained in a specific field, access to well-paid jobs, and the availability of childcare seem to be the key to reducing the economic gap between women and men as earners and heads of household.

Once governments and international organizations decide this is an urgent problem that deserves the investment of serious resources in all related areas of public policy, then progress is more likely to happen. The EU and a handful of other countries in Europe, Canada, Australia, and New Zealand are the only political entities to have taken all of these issues seriously into consideration. As they begin to craft and implement gender mainstreaming policies in areas ranging from agriculture and development to research, culture, and climate change, these countries are developing new international standards and leading the way toward greater gender equity. Since 2007, when it began to evaluate its own degree of success toward this goal via eight interrelated measurements, the EU has moved from 51.3 to 52.9 percent, with 100 as the goal.[42] Clearly, we are far from that moment, but with gender equality as a fundamental commitment in the EU, these small increments offer hope that progress is being made.

By contrast, in the *Global Gender Gap Report 2016*, released by the World Bank, the United States ranked forty-fifth in the world, down from twenty-eighth in 2015.[43] All EU countries scored much higher, together with states like Moldova, Nicaragua, and Burundi, suggesting that the US government is not taking the issue of gender inequality seriously. Policy makers here have yet to catch up with cultural changes in terms of gender roles at the familial level. If state institutions and policies are to reflect the societies they represent, these disparities between attitudes and policies need to be addressed with greater attention and investment of resources everywhere in the world.

SAME-SEX FAMILIES

At the beginning of the twentieth century Oscar Wilde did time in hard labor for the crime of being homosexual. Today, same-sex marriage has become legal in twenty-six countries around the world, most of them in Europe and North and South America, with around thirty others, including Italy and Costa Rica, recognizing same-sex unions.[44] In Asia, Taiwan was the first state to legalize same-sex marriage, and Japan is the only other country to legalize civil unions. In Israel and Armenia same-sex marriages performed elsewhere are recognized, though same-sex unions are not yet performed there. Meanwhile, a number of Asian countries still enforce harsh criminal sanctions against the gay population. A similar and even harsher picture describes the situation in the Middle East and Africa. Overall, states that are overwhelmingly or exclusively Muslim have tough antigay regimes.[45]

By contrast with Europe and North America, as well as the colonial territories commanded by European powers, the criminalization of homosexuality in Muslim states is a predominantly twentieth-century phenomenon. In places like Iran, the criminalization of nonheterosexual love came as a form of emulating European "civilization."[46] Similarly, in the Ottoman Empire homosexuality was not considered a matter of criminal law.[47] It was only after the breakup of that empire and the founding of a number of Muslim states that homosexuality came to be a subject of legal concern and criminalization. Penalties for homosexual behavior became harsher over the twentieth century with one important exception: Indonesia. This country with the largest Muslim population in the world has not criminalized homosexuality. At the same time, it doesn't recognize same-sex unions.

We can see increasingly restrictive policies regarding homosexuality over the twentieth century in other Asian states, such as India and China. In both countries there is ample evidence of the acceptance and even celebration of homosexuality over the ages through impressive bodies of art and literature. However, as these countries sought to modernize over the twentieth century, they also rejected these cultural traditions and identified heteronormativity as a core attribute of modernity. In China, it was Mao's puritanical view of the socialist family that drove policies of the Communist Party toward treating homosexuality as a psychological illness and eventually a crime, especially during the Cultural Revolution. China decriminalized homosexuality only in 2001, but further protection of homosexuals against discrimination has yet to take place. It is only in Hong Kong that a limited form of protection of same-sex cohabitating couples was recognized in 2009.[48]

In the second most populous country in the world, India, homosexuality has a very long history that predates colonial rule. Under British rule homosexuality was criminalized in 1860, at the same time as it was in the rest of the empire. After independence in 1947, though many of the civil laws of the British Raj were repealed, the new government upheld the heteronormative view of love and marriage. Activists have sought to change the law since then, with a short-lived victory in 2009 followed by a repeal of the liberalizing law in 2013.[49] It seems the cultural turn toward embracing same-sex couples is a long way from taking place in India.

In Africa, we can observe growing contrasts between progressive gay-rights legislation in South Africa and reactionary legislation in other countries. The postapartheid South African constitution (1994) enacted full civil rights for homosexuals and legalized same-sex marriage years before it became an accepted practice in the United States. Still, these legal protections are sometimes not enough to quell ongoing violence against gays and the violation of their civil rights. In other countries, such as Uganda, evangelical postcolonial churches from especially the United States have played a strong role in fomenting an anti-gay-rights movement.[50] In other African countries, especially where a strong colonial presence impacted kinship relations and institutions, there has been a backlash against homosexuality, depicted sometimes as a legacy of the colonial presence rather than a homegrown reality. In short, there are a multitude of sometimes self-contradictory positions that frustrate solid advances toward greater protection for LGBTQ persons.[51]

Thus, in the area of moving beyond heteronormative views of marriage and the family, important and lasting contrasts developed around the world in the last few decades. While criticisms of same-sex unions continue, we also see a growing acceptance among younger people. In the United States, where backlash against same-sex couples has been strong in the aftermath of legalizing such marriages, we see important generational and gender differences. While only 37 percent of married white men older than thirty-five agree that "society should regard two people of the same sex who live together as being the same as a married couple," 52 percent of the rest of the population (i.e., predominantly female) agree.[52] If this is a sign of changing values, it suggests a gradual shift toward acceptance of same-sex marriage not just as a matter of legal course but more importantly as a cultural-social norm. Within another generation, it is therefore likely that families will become more diverse in terms of what a couple looks like and how they engage with setting up a household and choose to think about reproduction along values that are nonheteronormative.

We do not have sufficient research yet to speak transnationally or globally about the ways in which same-sex families have generated qualitatively different types of kinship relations, especially intergenerationally. There is even less research done on families with transgender spouses. But studies on how such couples compare to heterosexual ones are beginning to provide clues about the meaning of these diversifying tracks in kinship relations. One of the continuing frustrations of women in heterosexual couples is the disproportionate amount of time they spend doing unpaid work at home compared with their male partners or spouses. On the average, in the developing world men spend five hours per day doing paid work and one hour and twenty minutes doing unpaid work. Women spend two hours and forty minutes doing paid work and four hours and thirty minutes doing unpaid work. In the developed world men spend an average of four hours doing paid work and two hours and twenty minutes doing unpaid work, while women spend two hours and twenty-five minutes doing paid work and four hours and twenty minutes doing unpaid work. Overall, women spend between two and three-plus hours of unpaid work per day more than their male spouses. [53]

By contrast, one recent study on time use among same-sex couples in the United States concludes that lesbian families tend to be more egalitarian in terms of the distribution of unpaid household work between the spouses. [54] Another study on trends in Australia concludes that, overall, same-sex couples divide unpaid domestic work more equitably than heterosexual couples. [55] Such data suggest the growing potential for very different models of how the unpaid work of care is done in the family for future generations.

BEYOND MARRIAGE

The rate of marriage among heterosexuals has gone down in the twentieth century, especially in the global North. As women arrived at or close to full equality with men in terms of civil rights, including property, and in politics, their motivations for marriage changed. The role of economic insecurity has gone down, and the benefits of marriage in terms of access to state benefits and specific economic enhancements have become more mixed. When property rights are equal, access to loans and jobs is equal, and taxation and medical insurance do not punish those who live together but are not married, incentives to marry become a matter of personal preference and not economic necessity.

The correlation between love and commitment through marriage has also become weaker. A Pew Research Center study from 2014 focusing on the United States shows the percentage of people married at an all-time low of 51 percent, and a significant 19 percent in a loving relationship without being married. [56] The US percentage of married couples is high by comparison with European and Latin American trends. In Asia and the Middle East they are higher but unevenly so. The rate of cohabitation instead of marriage is high in some parts of Europe (France and Sweden), Latin America (Argentina, Colombia, Peru), as well as Canada, the Philippines, and South Africa. Overall, recent statistics show a global decrease between 1980 and 2010 in the percentage of women married, ages twenty-five to forty-nine. [57] The study includes a culturally, politically, and economically diverse array of countries, such as Ireland, Greece, Jamaica, and Turkey. The only exceptions to this trend of fewer marriages are Vietnam, Indonesia, Thailand, and Costa Rica—again, countries very diverse in their traditions.

In Islamic societies, women and men alike have come to frown upon the traditional common practice of arranged marriages, with women showing a higher degree of rejection.[58] A parallel growth in critical views of polygamy, with women scoring significantly higher than men, suggests that traditional kinship practices in these societies are seeing a major shift, at least in the sense of cultural approval. In Kuwait, 55 percent of women versus 30 percent of men disapprove of polygamy; in Saudi Arabia, the ratio is 72 percent to 38 percent; in Jordan, it is 80 percent to 61 percent; and in Lebanon, 91 percent to 80 percent. The higher degree of disapproval in these last two countries correlates closely with their degree of secularization in law and practice.

Overall, many Islamic societies (e.g., Turkey, Morocco, Senegal) show significant decreases in percentage of women married. However, the most dramatic changes can be seen in the rate of marriage for women ages fifteen to nineteen: in the United Arab Emirates, it has gone down from 57 percent in 1975 to 8 percent in 1995; in Libya, from 40 percent (1973) to 1 percent (2001); in Egypt, 22 percent (1976) to 10 percent (2003); and in Kuwait, 38 percent (1970) to 5 percent (1996).[59] These countries took diverse political and economic paths during the 1970 to 2000 period, so the consistently large decrease needs to be understood as a pattern linked to shifting sociocultural norms. Specifically it is linked to choices made by women to delay marriage for a variety of reasons predominantly connected with education, employment, and more broadly the desire to experience life as a single adult rather than as a married young woman.

FAMILY VALUES

We already know that birth rates went down over the twentieth century, most dramatically since 1960. The highest drop in fertility has been among women in the Middle East, from 6.1 (1980) to 3.5 (1999) children.[60] The highest fertility rate remains in Sub-Saharan Africa. Therefore, in addition to becoming more diverse in the makeup of the couple and kinship responsibilities, families have become smaller. This is what scholars are now calling "the second demographic transition."[61] What do these changes in patterns of forming families bode for how kinship groups function in dealing with the young?

For children growing up in this shifting landscape, learning about the world and gender norms happens more and more in a nonbinary environment, where what used to be defined as traditional gender roles is revealed as a social construct reflected less and less in reality. Scholars have started to look at the impact of these shifts on younger generations and have concluded that some important changes are taking place in the values young people hold in a variety of socioeconomic and political settings.[62] In North America and Europe there has been a decisive shift toward individualism and personal autonomy as important values for both men and women, at the expense of communal alignments and obedience toward established authority.[63] Scholars studying changes in African kinship relations have also noted the erosion of intergenerational solidarity and increasing independence of the young. Since the late 1980s, 75 percent or more of women in Togo stated that they had chosen their spouse on their own, and the percentage is even higher in Gabon (90 percent). A recent qualitative study on marital choices in Burkina Faso concluded that even in rural areas, "the desire to free oneself from the authority of the elders and aspiration toward greater autonomy focuses first and foremost on the free choice of cohabitation."[64] The long-term impact of this change has yet to be sufficiently researched, though a backlash has certainly been seen in some places on the part of religious establishments, political parties, and nongovernmental organizations.

There is also strong evidence that a more egalitarian view of gender roles is gaining support among both men and women across the world, and it is directly related to the kinds of kinship shifts described above. Growing up in societies where nonpatriarchal familial models are becoming frequent has offered new role models to growing numbers of boys and girls in their early years. Educational institutions have started to catch up to this new reality, but the change has been slow particularly due to negative reactions from the political and religious establishments. In the United States, a 2008 proposition in California regarding the legalization of same-sex marriage brought about an avalanche of alarmist warnings that soon children would have to learn about homosexuality in school and turn into nonheterosexuals.[65] Since the legalization of same-sex marriage in the United States such warnings have continued, but it is clear that the younger generation of Americans of every gender and other variables simply do not see any threat in the rise of nonpatriarchal families. They do see the old curricula regarding families and sex education as outdated and in need of reform to reflect current sociocultural realities.[66]

The impact of feminist and, generally, more gender-egalitarian cultural models cannot be overstated here. Whether in music, literature, or especially film and television, the models presented to young learners have shifted to include more positive female characters and a greater diversity of types of gender roles that no longer exalt patriarchy or condemn women's empowerment. In Venezuela, the telenovela *El País de las Mujeres* created strong feminist models that resonated with enormous audiences, and it was subsequently exported for consumption elsewhere in Latin America and overseas.[67] More recently, series like the Ghanaian

An African City, featuring independent, professionally ambitious, and sexually liberated female characters, have become wildly popular across Africa and the Caribbean.[68] Such shows are a type of feminist fantasy rather than social critique of real gender inequality for most African women, but they present appealing cultural models of independence and gender equality.[69] Available for consumption and appropriation to anyone with an Internet connection, these cultural artifacts are normalizing expectations for gender equality into the next generation, especially in Sub-Saharan Africa, the world's region with the highest ratio of young people.[70]

RELIGIOUS INSTITUTIONS: BACKLASH AND ADJUSTMENT

These changes in gender relations and values have also produced backlashes among some communities, especially traditional religious denominations whose very foundations are being challenged by the new reality of nonpatriarchal familial relations. Secularization is not strictly a twentieth-century phenomenon. But the pace of secularization has quickened over the past fifty years and has greatly weakened the social, economic, cultural, and political grip of many religious institutions around the world.[71]

In the face of such challenges, some denominations have tried to catch up to the new sociocultural realities by reevaluating their fundamental institutional setup, the interpretation of religious texts with regard to specific beliefs about the family, marriage, and gender roles, as well as rituals. Many more religious denominations are cautiously considering societal changes in view of their own loss of followers. And there are religious institutions that have redoubled their insistence on a patriarchal understanding of the world, the family, and polarized gender norms in the hope of protecting their core religious dogma. Along the way, changes in religious practice and dogma have been prompted by and fed through criticisms by feminist theologians as well as average followers, especially women whose changing socioeconomic positions have challenged the dogmatic beliefs of their religious affiliation.

The most radical shifts have taken place through the emergence of modern female-centered religions, such as the Goddess-centered movements among the Wicca or contemporary paganism. The movement started in the early twentieth century in Great Britain and grew especially after 1960, with believers around the world. In the United States, there are more than 350,000 such registered believers. Though derided by many, these groups have increased over the past half century and become a mainstream presence in North American and European culture. The beliefs and rituals of these movements vary, but overall they highlight the nonpatriarchal nature of humanity and focus on restoring women's position of authority in terms of spirituality. The social order they advocate and try to adhere to has been identified as "post-patriarchal."[72]

Among well-established religious denominations, several types of Protestant Christianity have been forthcoming in embracing women as leaders and clergy and nonheterosexual marriage as morally acceptable. The Episcopalian and Unitarian Churches, in particular, have been quite liberalizing. Lutherans, Baptists, and Methodists, and some other major religious denominations such as Buddhism have also begun to ordain women as clergy but do not endorse nonheterosexual marriage and families. Reform Judaism allows women to be ordained as rabbis and leaves it up to individual clergy the decision to officiate at same-sex marriages.

The first woman to be ordained as a priest was in the Episcopalian Church in 1944, in Hong Kong, as a matter of expediency (no men were available due to the wartime regime). However, the more systematic acceptance of women as priests started in the 1970s. By the turn of the twenty-first century, the Episcopal Church had ordained women as priests in many countries, among them Rwanda, Uruguay, South Korea, and the United States. Episcopalians were also a pioneering religion to declare in 1976 the equal rights of nonheterosexuals on all matters pertaining to membership and participation in this religious community. In 2003 Gene Robinson (b. 1947) became the first openly gay Episcopal priest to be consecrated as bishop. In 2009 the American Episcopal Church reaffirmed its support for the ordination of gay clergy. Internationally the Episcopal Church has remained tolerant, but not unified, on accepting to officiate at same-sex marriages.

On the more conservative end of reacting to changes in social and cultural definitions of gender identity and roles are Roman Catholicism, the Southern Baptist Convention in the United States, Orthodox Christianity, Mormonism, Islam, and Orthodox Judaism. These religious establishments have reacted to the diminishment of the patriarchal family model by rejecting reform and insisting on a literal reading of the religious texts that place men as the head of the family and the patriarchal family at the center of social harmony.

Starting in Germany in the first decade of the twenty-first century, religious civic groups affiliated with the Catholic Church began to invoke "gender ideology" as the great evil of contemporary society. The most widely disseminated and quoted text of this antigenderist ideology is by a German author of growing international notoriety, Gabriele Kuby (b. 1944).[73] A convert to Catholicism, Kuby had an "awakening" about the threats faced by Western civilization at the hands of gender mainstreaming in the EU, the legalization of same-sex marriage, and anti-discrimination policies that protect LGBTQ populations. In a meandering text that reads more like a confession of one's religious beliefs and frustrations than like a logical argument of someone with credentials as a sociologist, Kuby reserves the harshest criticisms for women: "Gender ideology was made up by radical feminist women, and its implementation has been secured—with unimaginable consequences. Many cultures have perished from moral degeneration. For moral degeneration to be forced on people by the rulers of this world is something new."[74] The fundamental problem for Kuby and proponents of antigenderism is that the patriarchal heteronormative "normal" described at the beginning of this chapter has ceased to be the norm.

A growing chorus of critics of gender ideology in Poland, Hungary, Russia, and other places are fixated on rejecting any definition of gender norms as sociocultural constructions, despite all evidence to the contrary.[75] This has led to calls to end any funding for gender studies, roll back the recognition of same-sex marriage, and introduce religious education in public schools as an antidote. In Poland, criticism of gender as a cultural construct went so far as to delay the ratification of the Istanbul Convention against Domestic Violence for several years, because it defined gender as "the socially constructed roles, behaviors, activities and attributes that a given society considers appropriate for women and men."[76] The ire of the Polish government focused particularly on the word "socially," which implicitly rejects claims that gender roles are founded strictly on biological facts.

These conservative religious denominations have remained limited in their impact on a changing social and cultural landscape, especially in countries where they are not the dominant and state-supported religious institutions. In Germany, for instance, despite opposition by the Catholic Church, Prime Minister Angela Merkel (b. 1954), and the likes of Kuby, in June 2017 the Bundestag voted overwhelmingly to legalize same-sex marriage.

However, in countries where these denominations are the sole religious institution allowed and where the state supports a denomination's position of moral authority through civil law, there has been a growing backlash against women's empowerment and alternative families. In one recent egregious case, in May 2017 the Chechen government was reported to have engaged in torturing gay persons and incarcerating them in camps.[77] At the same time, the Chechen government, with the tacit endorsement of its main patron, Russia, has denied that there are "any such people" in Chechnya.

* * *

Still, even with such criticisms and fundamentalist reactions and admonitions, the choices made by more and more individuals are taking the world's population away from traditional family relations. What our values will be in the future remains to be seen, but a more gender-egalitarian view of kinship roles and a greater diversity in how people understand and perform gender roles is already in the making.

NOTES

1. C. Mark Blackden and Chitra Bhanu, *Gender, Growth, and Poverty Reduction: Special Program of Assistance for Africa, 1998 Status Report on Poverty in Sub-Saharan Africa,* World Bank Technical Paper no. 428 (Washington, DC: World Bank, 1999).
2. Dirk J. van de Kaa, "Is the Second Demographic Transition a Useful Research Concept? Questions and Answers," *Vienna Yearbook of Population Research* 2 (2004): 4–10; discussion of the two terms on page 8.
3. Ron Lesthaeghe, "The Unfolding Story of the Second Demographic Transition," *Population and Development Review* 36, no. 2 (June 2010): 216.
4. I include in this ratio both full- and part-time employment for either or both of the adults. OECD Social Policy Division, "Gender Brief," March 2010, accessed August 18, 2017, http://www.oecd.org/social/family/44720649.pdf, 11.
5. Wendy Wang, Kim Parker, and Paul Taylor, "Breadwinner Moms: Mothers Are the Sole or Primary Provider in Four-in-Ten Households with Children; Public Conflicted about the Growing Trend," Pew Research Center, May 20, 2013, accessed August 18, 2017, http://www.pewsocialtrends.org/files/2013/05/Breadwinner_moms_final.pdf, 22.
6. Not all of these couples are married and/or heterosexual. They are cohabitants, however. Men head only 6 percent of single-parent households.
7. Wang, Parker, and Taylor, "Breadwinner Moms."
8. "Female Headed Households," World Bank, accessed August 18, 2017, http://data.worldbank.org/indicator/SP.HOU.FEMA.ZS.
9. Jennifer Utrata, *Women without Men: Single Mothers and Family Change in the New Russia* (Ithaca, NY: Cornell University Press, 2015).
10. Jennifer Somerville, *Feminism and the Family: Politics and Society in the UK and USA* (Basingstoke, UK: Palgrave, 2000); Germaine Greer, *The Whole Woman* (New York: Anchor Books, 2000); Kate Millett, *Sexual Politics* (1969; repr. New York: Columbia University Press, 2016); Deniz Kandiyoti, "Bargaining with Patriarchy," *Gender and Society* 2, no. 3 (September 1988): 274–90; Zinn, "Feminism and Family Studies for a New Century."
11. Aparna Mathur, Hao Fu, and Peter Hansen, "The Mysterious and Alarming Rise of Single Parenthood in America," *Atlantic*, September 3, 2013, http://www.theatlantic.com/business/archive/2013/09/the-mysterious-and-alarming-rise-of-single-parenthood-in-america/279203.
12. Utrata, *Women without Men*, 12.
13. I focus on same-sex couples in a subsequent section in this chapter.
14. World Health Organization, *Women and Health: Today's Evidence, Tomorrow's Agenda* (Geneva: World Health Organization, 2009).
15. Women's tendency to marry older men is another important factor in generating the potential for their outliving their husbands, but that is not a natural factor either, it is a socially driven preference that is difficult to define globally as neutral. Women and men face different sociocultural constraints against freely choosing a life partner.
16. Adam Isen and Betsey Stevenson, "Women's Education and Family Behavior: Trends in Marriage, Divorce and Fertility," Working Paper 15725, National Bureau of Economic Research, February 2010, accessed August 18, 2017, http://www.nber.org/papers/w15725.pdf.
17. OECD Social Policy Division, "Gender Brief," 7.
18. Tanzima Zohra Habib, "Socio-Psychological Status of Female Heads of Households in Rajshahi City, Bangladesh," *Antrocom* 6, no. 2 (2010): 173–86.
19. Blackden and Bhanu, *Gender, Growth, and Poverty Reduction*.
20. Darla Bardine et al., "International Perspectives on Divorce: Increasing Access for Women," accessed August 18, 2017, http://www.law.georgetown.edu/academics/academic-programs/clinical-programs/our-clinics/community-justice/upload/

international-perspectives-on-divorce-2.pdf. The paper focuses on Canada, the United States, India, and South Africa.

21. Jenny Munro, Patrick B. Patterson, and Lynn McIntyre, "'Your Father Is No More': Insights on Guardianship and Abandonment from Ultrapoor Women Heads of Household in Bangladesh," *Women's Studies International Forum* 53 (November–December 2015): 43–52.

22. Bardine et al., "International Perspectives on Divorce"; Habib, "Socio-Psychological Status."

23. UN Department of Economic and Social Affairs, Division for the Advancement of Women, *Handbook for Legislation on Violence against Women* (New York: United Nations, 2010).

24. "Security Council Condemns 'In the Strongest Terms' All Acts of Sexual Abuse, Exploitation, by U.N. Peacekeeping Personnel," May 31, 2005, http://www.un.org/press/en/2005/sc8400.doc.htm; Neil MacFarquhar, "Peacekeepers' Sex Scandals Linger, On Screen and Off," *New York Times*, September 7, 2011, http://www.nytimes.com/2011/09/08/world/08nations.html.

25. For a full text of the Convention and a list of countries that have signed and ratified it, see "About the Convention," Council of Europe, accessed August 14, 2017, http://www.coe.int/en/web/istanbul-convention/about-the-convention.

26. Anastasia Moloney, "Domestic Violence Pushes Central American Women to Flee for Their Lives," Reuters, May 24, 2017, http://www.reuters.com/article/us-latam-migrants-refugees-idUSKBN18K2FJ; Kristen Chick, "To Fight Domestic Violence among Syrian Refugees, an Outreach to Men," *Christian Science Monitor*, April 26, 2017, https://www.csmonitor.com/World/Middle-East/2017/0426/To-fight-domestic-violence-among-Syrian-refugees-an-outreach-to-men.

27. UN Department of Economic and Social Affairs, *The World's Women 2010: Trends and Statistics* (New York: United Nations, 2010); Sylvia Chant, "Female Household Headship and the Feminisation of Poverty: Facts, Fictions and Forward Strategies," London School of Economics Gender Institute, New Working Paper series, no. 9 (May 2003), accessed August 18, 2017, http://eprints.lse.ac.uk/574/1/femaleHouseholdHeadship.pdf; Mayra Buvinić and Geeta Rao Gupta, "Female-Headed Households and Female-Maintained Families: Are They Worth Targeting to Reduce Poverty in Developing Countries?" *Economic Development and Cultural Change* 45, no. 2 (January 1997): 259–80.

28. Karl Kaser, ed., *Household and Family in the Balkans: Two Decades of Historical Family Research at University of Graz* (Berlin: LIT Verlag, 2012); Kristen Ghodsee, *Muslim Lives in Eastern Europe: Gender, Ethnicity, and the Transformation of Islam in Postsocialist Bulgaria* (Princeton, NJ: Princeton University Press, 2009); Mihaela Miroiu, "State Men, Market Women," *Feminismos: Mujer y participación política* 3 (June 2004): 84–99.

29. Bucur and Miroiu, *Birth of Democratic Citizenship.*

30. Women and children are also part of this exodus. Yet there are disproportionately more men making the journey alone than women doing so, even as female migration is growing. Women are still more likely to travel alone if they are not married and do not have children; otherwise they travel as part of the family.

31. Celinda Lake, Michael Adams, and David Mermin, "New Voters, New Values," *American Prospect*, February 11, 2013, http://prospect.org/article/new-voters-new-values.

32. Rukmalie Jayakody, Arland Thornton, and William Axinn, eds., *International Family Change: Ideational Perspectives* (New York: Routledge, 2008).

33. Haleh Afshar and Stephanie Barrientos, eds., *Women, Globalization and Fragmentation in the Developing World* (Basingstoke, UK: Palgrave, 1999).

34. Amita Chudgar, "Female Headship and Schooling Outcomes in Rural India," *World Development* 39, no. 4 (April 2011): 550–60; Blackden and Bhanu, *Gender, Growth, and Poverty Reduction.*

35. S. Hamid, "A Micro Analysis of Demand-Side Determinants of Schooling in Urban Pakistan," *Pakistan Development Review* 32, no. 4 (1993): 713–23.

36. Eshetu Gurmu and Dula Etana, "Socio-Economic and Demographic Determinants of Children's Primary School Enrollment in Ethiopia," accessed August 18, 2017, http://uaps2011.princeton.edu/papers/110792, 9.

37. Blackden and Bhanu, *Gender, Growth, and Poverty Reduction*, 27.

38. Ibid.

39. Lake, Adams, and Mermin, "New Voters."

40. Christine Lagarde, "The Economic Power of Women's Empowerment, Keynote Speech by Christine Lagarde, Managing Director, International Monetary Fund," International Monetary Fund, September 12, 2014, https://www.imf.org/en/News/Articles/2015/09/28/04/53/sp091214.

41. Bert Preiss and Claudia Brunner, eds., *Democracy in Crisis: The Dynamics of Civil Protest and Civil Resistance* (Berlin: LIT Verlag, 2013).

42. "Gender Equality Index," European Institute for Gender Equality, accessed August 18, 2017, http://eige.europa.eu/gender-statistics/gender-equality-index/2015; the eight measurements are: work, money, knowledge, time spent doing unremunerated work, political power, health, violence, and intersecting inequalities. The last among these categories was new in 2015.

43. "The Global Gender Gap Report 2016," World Economic Forum, accessed August 18, 2017, http://eige.europa.eu/about-eige and http://reports.weforum.org/global-gender-gap-report-2015/rankings.

44. In Mexico, the twenty-sixth among these countries, same-sex marriage is legal in some but not all states.

45. Aengus Carroll, *State-Sponsored Homophobia: A World Survey of Sexual Orientation Laws: Criminalisation, Protection and Recognition* (Geneva: ILGA, 2016).

46. Najmabadi, *Women with Mustaches and Men without Beards*.

47. Stephen O. Murray, "Homosexuality in the Ottoman Empire," *Historical Reflections/Réflexions Historiques* 33, no. 1 (Spring 2007): 101–16.

48. Tabitha Speelman, "Tiptoeing Out of the Closet: The History and Future of LGBT Rights in China," *Atlantic*, August 21, 2013, http://www.theatlantic.com/china/archive/2013/08/tiptoeing-out-of-the-closet-the-history-and-future-of-lgbt-rights-in-china/278869.

49. "Shashi Tharoor: India MP's Bill to Decriminalise Gay Sex Rejected," BBC News, December 18, 2015, http://www.bbc.com/news/world-asia-india-35129361.

50. Nathalie Baptiste et al., "It's Not Just Uganda: Behind the Christian Right's Onslaught in Africa," *Nation*, April 4, 2014, https://www.thenation.com/article/its-not-just-uganda-behind-christian-rights-onslaught-africa.

51. Marc Epprecht, *Heterosexual Africa? The History of an Idea from the Age of Exploration to the Age of AIDS* (Athens: Ohio University Press, 2008).

52. Lake, Adams, and Mermin, "New Voters."

53. UN, *The World's Women 2015: Work*, accessed September 29, 2017, https://unstats.un.org/unsd/gender/chapter4/chapter4.html. The UN statistics do not differentiate between heterosexual and same-sex couples, but implicitly assume heterosexual ones are the norm.

54. Michael E. Martell and Leanne Roncolato, "The Homosexual Lifestyle: Time Use in Same-Sex Households," *Journal of Demographic Economics* 82, no. 4 (December 2016): 365–98.

55. Australian Bureau of Statistics, "Same-Sex Couples," *Australian Social Trends*, July 2013, http://www.abs.gov.au/AUSSTATS/abs@.nsf/Lookup/4102.0Main+Features10July+2013#housework.

56. Gretchen Livingston and Andrea Caumont, "5 Facts on Love and Marriage in America," Pew Research Center, February 13, 2017, accessed August 18, 2017, http://www.pewresearch.org/fact-tank/2014/02/14/5-facts-about-love-and-marriage.

57. "Average Annual Change in Percentage of Women Married," accessed August 18, 2017, https://familyinequality.files.wordpress.com/2013/06/ipums-international-marriage-ols.jpg. Table compiled by Philip N. Cohen.

58. Richard Burkholder, "Love and Marriage within the Islamic World," Gallup, June 18, 2002, http://www.gallup.com/poll/6235/love-marriage-within-islamic-world.aspx.

59. Hoda Rashad, Magued Osman, and Farzaneh Roudi-Fahimi, "Marriage in the Arab World," Population Research Bureau, http://www.prb.org/pdf05/marriageinarabworld_eng.pdf.

60. International Bank for Reconstruction, *Beyond Economic Growth* (Washington, DC: IBR, 2004), https://www.gfdrr.org/sites/gfdrr/files/publication/Beyond%20Economic%20Growth_0.pdf, 20.

61. Ron Lesthaeghe, "The Second Demographic Transition: A Concise Overview of Its Development," *Proceedings of the National Academy of Sciences* 111, no. 51 (2014): 18112–15.

62. Jayakody, Thornton, and Axinn, eds., *International Family Change*; Fred Pampel, "Cohort Change, Diffusion, and Support for Gender Egalitarianism in Cross-National Perspective," *Demographic Research* 25, no. 21 (September 2011): 667–94.

63. Jayakody, Thornton, and Axinn, eds., *International Family Change*, 317–18; Ronald Inglehart and Pippa Norris, *Rising Tide: Gender Equality and Cultural Change around the World* (Cambridge: Cambridge University Press, 2003).

64. Thérèse Locoh and Myriam Mouvagha-Sow, "An Uncertain Future for African Families," in *International Family Change*, ed. Jayakody, Thornton, and Axinn, 73.

65. Jessica Garrison, "A Prop. 8 Fight over Schools," *Los Angeles Times*, October 19, 2008, http://articles.latimes.com/2008/oct/19/local/me-gayschools19.

66. Casey Quinlan, "Can We Adapt Sex Ed for the New LGBT-Inclusive America?" Think Progress, August 3, 2015, http://thinkprogress.org/education/2015/08/03/3686185/can-we-adapt-sex-ed-for-the-new-lgbt-inclusive-america.

67. Carolina Acosta-Alzuru, "'I'm Not a Feminist . . . I Only Defend Women as Human Beings': The Production, Representation, and Consumption of Feminism in a Telenovela," *Critical Studies in Media Communication* 20, no. 3 (2003): 269–94; the telenovela was later shown also in Hungary.

68. Shereen Marisol Meraji, "Sex and 'An African City': A Steamy Ghanaian Show You Don't Want to Miss," *Code Switch. Race and Identity, Remixed*, National Public Radio, March 29, 2016, http://www.npr.org/sections/codeswitch/2016/03/29/471478897/sex-and-an-african-city-a-steamy-ghanaian-show-you-dont-want-to-miss.

69. Elikem Nutifafa Kuenyehia, "Nicole Amarteifio: Sex and the African City—Celebrating Entrepreneurship with Elikem Nutifafa Kuenyehia," *Rising Africa* (blog), May 19, 2016, http://www.risingafrica.org/blog/nicole-amarteifio-sex-and-the-african-city-celebrating-entrepreneurship-with-elikem-nutifafa-kuenyehia.

70. Uri Friedman, "Where the World's Young People Live," *Atlantic*, July 11, 2014, https://www.theatlantic.com/international/archive/2014/07/where-the-worlds-young-people-live/374226.

71. The alarmist discourse about the loss of authority present in the Catholic Church since the Second Vatican Council (1962–1965) presents good evidence about this process and reactions to it among religious institutions.

72. Mary Jo Neitz, "Queering the Dragonfest: Changing Sexualities in a Post-Patriarchal Religion," in *Feminist Narratives and the Sociology of Religion*, ed. Nancy Nason-Clark and Mary Jo Neitz (Lanham, MD: AltaMira Press, 2001), 29–52.

73. Gabriele Kuby, *The Global Sexual Revolution: Destruction of Freedom in the Name of Freedom* (Kettering, OH: Angelico Press, 2015). The book was published originally in German in 2012 and has been translated into several European languages with direct financial support from Catholic organizations and endorsement by the Catholic Church. Pope Francis has publicly endorsed Kuby, denouncing gender ideology (aka feminism) as "demonic." See Edward Pentin, "Gender Ideology's 'Completely Mad Attack' on the Family and Society," *National Catholic Register*, July 10, 2015, http://www.ncregister.com/daily-news/gender-ideologys-completely-mad-attack-on-the-family-and-society.

74. Ibid., loc. 331.

75. Eszter Kováts and Maari Põim, eds., *Gender as Symbolic Glue: The Position and Role of Conservative and Far Right Parties in the Anti-Gender Mobilizations in Europe* (Budapest: Foundation for European Progressive Studies, 2015); Roman Kuhar and David Paternotte, eds., *Anti-Gender Campaigns in Europe: Mobilizing against Equality* (London: Rowman & Littlefield, 2017).

76. Council of Europe, "Convention on Preventing and Combating Violence against Women and Domestic Violence," https://rm.coe.int/CoERMPublicCommonSearchServices/DisplayDCTMContent?documentId=090000168008482e, 3.

77. Nataliya Vasilyeva and Alexander Roslyakov, "Gay Chechens Report Days of Beatings and Electro-Shock Torture at Hands of Russian Government-Backed Thugs," *Independent*, May 2, 2017, http://www.independent.co.uk/news/world/europe/gay-chechens-beating-electro-shock-torture-detain-camps-chechnya-russia-thugs-homophobia-human-a7713391.html.

Epilogue

I started this book in 2015, and today I am grateful for that timing. Since January 2017, living in the United States has been like being trapped in a reality show, each day bringing new shocking developments that make it difficult to think about the present, future, and even the past in the same way as before. More recently, as I write these words at the end of August 2017, the country has witnessed the explosion of radical racist marches that remind me more of Germany in the early 1930s than of the United States I adopted as my country in the 1980s. The spectacle we have been watching is not a strictly male affair, but the leadership and overwhelming majority of the visible participants in these radical right-wing movements are men. Whether they have the active support of their families back home, or whether their mothers and wives are finding out about these activities by watching TV is yet to be discovered.

We have entered a period of uncertainty in politics and economic expectations and of questioning many of the values and institutions that have been the foundations of modernity and postmodernity. In some circles, liberalism, especially of the neo- flavor, has become a dirty word. In others, secularism produces anxiety. Identity politics has become a rhetorical football passed around by opponents. So what sort of significance does a book focusing squarely on women as historical agents and social category have?

The question seems even more pressing today, as the populace has become increasingly polarized in opinions, media outlets they follow, and their perception of academia as either a place where the youth are trained for jobs for the future or as a hotbed of revolutionaries who do nothing but exacerbate tensions between the left and the right. Identity politics has become the subject of extremely polarized opinion-making by prominent public intellectuals, some of them historians and gender scholars.

In November 2016, a week after Donald Trump won the presidential election in the United States, intellectual historian Mark Lilla declared that "the age of identity liberalism must be brought to an end" because "the fixation on diversity in our schools and in the press has produced a generation of liberals and progressives narcissistically unaware of conditions outside their self-defined groups, and indifferent to the task of reaching out to Americans in every walk of life."[1] He traced identity-politics movements back to the Ku Klux Klan but placed emphasis more squarely on the divisive effects of the "personal is political" attitude that emerged in the 1970s among feminists. In an extended version of that article that recently came out as a book, Lilla claimed that a shift took place in the 1980s toward "the political is personal" and turned liberalism and progressive alliances of the previous decades into navel gazing.[2] I beg to differ with this narrative and will say more about that a little later. I support, however, Lilla's call to focus away from only rights and on a more balanced vision of citizenship that draws attention to the duties we bear.

Katherine Franke, a colleague of Lilla's at Columbia and director of the Center for Gender and Sexuality Law, and Susan Cox, a feminist philosopher and activist, have responded to Lilla's critique by denouncing his argument as evidence of the self-righteous white male discourse that produced the need for declaratory identity politics.[3] The "original sin" of identity politics, Franke contends, was not of the Ku Klux Klan but of the founding fathers. When persons of color and women are excluded from having a voice in the founding of a country at the dawn of modernity, what speaks through that document, despite claims to universalism and humanity, is exclusionary identity politics: "We, the white men of this land. . . ." The racist language may not be there in front of us, but it is there in all the qualifications that go with those universalist claims.

Since November 2016 the intensity of polarization and a growing "culture war" about identity politics, as Cox calls it, have gripped many US campuses, from Berkeley to Auburn University. More recently, one of the oldest universities in North America, the University of Virginia in Charlottesville, became the scene of a racist white nationalist rally and counterprotests by a diverse group of ministers, radical anarchists, antifascist activists, students, and other citizens of the city. Lilla was back in the public eye with comments about the causes of this horrific development:

> Why did this fascist march happen now and not, for instance, when we had a black president? The reason is that Donald Trump's president. And he has emboldened these people. Well, how did that happen? It's not just a question of the last election. It's why over two generations we have simply lost a large chunk of the country and liberalism has become a dirty word.[4]

Behind this vague statement about the rise of the alt-right in recent decades lies the argument in Lilla's recent book about identity politics: feminist and antiracist criticisms of liberalism and the "narcissistic" groups they sprouted alienated the mostly white men who make up the alt-right. Implicitly, those individuals and the choices they made to admire Hitler, Andrew Jackson, Robert E. Lee, or Corneliu Zelea Codreanu, the leader of interwar Romanian fascism, are just alienated victims of these developments.[5] It is precisely because of arguments such as Lilla's that it is more important than ever to look past such facile and ill-informed narratives about the twentieth century and where our world is headed today.

The narrative presented in this book focuses on reshaping how we think about the recent past on a global scale as we gaze into the future. Without aiming to be exhaustive in terms of events, people, and major attitudinal shifts since 1900, *The Century of Women* has shown how bringing women fully into the visible sphere of political, economic, social, and cultural activities has fundamentally altered how the world acts and what it looks like today. But the point of looking at women has not been to reify identity politics. On the contrary, the developments and lives depicted here have shown how women sought to extricate themselves from a kind of identity politics already in place—the patriarchal heteronormativity that dominated the world at the end of the nineteenth century.

What women brought to the table in terms of both their critiques of patriarchy and their own contributions to shaping the world is as wildly diverse as the myriad cultural contexts in which these individuals grew up. Alexandra Kollontai saw capitalism and patriarchy as essentially entwined and wished to eliminate marriage and the nuclear family as the only means for liberating women. Christiana Figueres has focused on addressing climate change globally as a means to alleviate the structural inequalities that indigenous women in agricultural areas face disproportionately. Marilyn Waring changed how national statistics are collected as a way to alleviate economic gender inequalities produced by traditional economies. Miriam Makeba carried the torch of anti-apartheid activism through the power of her singing.

Furthermore, though over time many women asserted that sisterhood is universal, that claim has proven difficult to sustain. Racism among some white Western feminists became a barrier against building trust and alliances with women of color. Living in the polarized world of the Cold War reinforced other divisions between the developed and developing worlds. More recently, violent clashes have erupted between some transwomen and ciswomen in their interpretation of what counts as "authentic" womanhood. In short, "identity politics" has not always been a unifying force among feminists, as Rita Mae Brown and Florynce Kennedy found out in the early 1970s.

And yet the multitude of women's voices, which have become more and more present since 1900, built on each other's contributions even when openly critical of one another. They have presented new perspectives and new solutions to the world's problems, from war to poverty. Even nonfeminist or antifeminist activists and thinkers have started to contend with the arguments of feminists to legitimize their actions. Margaret Thatcher defended her harsh view of welfare politics in response to the feminist socioeconomic activism of the 1970s. Gabriele Kuby has built her defense of biological binary essentialism in response to the queer feminist ideas articulated by Judith Butler.

How does this multitude of perspectives and contributions help us better understand the world and gaze into the future? To begin with, it challenges entrenched assumptions about what the actual problems are and what it means to solve them. Environmental degradation cannot be understood just from the perspective of the lab and the boardroom. What tillers of the soil observe around them for decades is as important on the ground, and women today are a majority among agricultural workers, as Margaret Mead and Wangari Maathai have reminded us. How can we understand our biological problems and the medical conditions we face without research on both men and women? Without feminist scientists asking hard questions about science design we would still be unable to fully understand major epidemics in the world, such as AIDS. Without women journalists on the front lines, many current issues would be significantly more two-dimensional and some would never be presented to the public. The problem of sexual violence in society and in the family has risen to international attention in great part because of feminist activists and also because women journalists have insisted on moving away from shaming victims to naming perpetrators.

In the past 120 years women have moved from being primarily observers or objects of policy making and social control to becoming participants in every area of human endeavor. We have not reached full equality, and there has been a backlash against some of the rights and forms of empowerment women fought for during this time. Yet women around the world speak today with voices that need to be taken into account because they have become voters, autonomous taxpayers, and in some places soldiers. As they become voices of social authority, women need to assert the kind of responsibility that comes with the rights gained since 1900. Speaking truth to power is a first important step. Looking beyond one's problems and working with allies to alleviate discrimination and structural inequalities is an ongoing struggle that needs to continue in the face of the current backlash. The possibilities for forging such alliances are limitless. It is up to us to move from competition and confrontation to mutual respect, understanding, and cooperation. The next hundred years can then become *The Century of Partnership*.

NOTES

1. Mark Lilla, "The End of Identity Liberalism," *New York Times*, November, 18, 2016,   https://www.nytimes.com/2016/11/20/opinion/sunday/the-end-of-identity-liberalism.html.

2. Mark Lilla, *The Once and Future Liberal: After Identity Politics* (New York: Harper-Collins Publishers, 2017).

3. Katherine Franke, "Making White Supremacy Respectable. Again," *Los Angeles Review of Books Blog*, November 21, 2016, http://blog.lareviewofbooks.org/essays/making-white-supremacy-respectable; Susan Cox, "Women's Issues Aren't Just 'Identity Politics,'" *Feminist Current*, November 26, 2016, http://www.feministcurrent.com/2016/11/26/womens-issues-arent-just-identity-politics.

4. Mark Lilla, interview by Robert Siegel, *All Things Considered*, National Public Radio, August 15, 2017, http://www.npr.org/2017/08/15/543730312/the-once-and-future-liberal-looks-at-shortfalls-of-american-liberalism.

5. In an impromptu press conference given by Matthew Heimbach, one of the co-organizers of the Charlottesville white nationalist rally on August 12, 2017, after the march, he sported a shirt with a large image of Codreanu. At the very least, his choice signifies admiration for the Romanian fascist, as evidenced also by the sale of similar shirts on Heimbach's white nationalist website. Heimbach focused his statements on criticizing the police for not protecting the alt-right marchers, and his wearing the image of a fascist leader who was killed in the dead of night while in police custody could not have escaped the attention of other alt-right followers. This is the sort of identity politics espoused by the radical right today, not just in the United States but also in places like Hungary, Poland, Romania, and France.

Bibliographic Essay

This study is the accumulation of more than two decades of reading historical and gender studies scholarship. To identify all the sources of inspiration and frustration that have brought me to this book and guided me through its writing would require a much longer discussion than I could possibly provide in this limited space. Many of those sources found their ways into the footnotes of the book, and I will not invoke most of them in the following pages. Yet there is an intellectual trajectory I believe is important to outline by way of explaining what my feminist humanist approach means. I also want to highlight the important work done to advance this type of historiography and to pay tribute to the scholars on whose shoulders I can stand taller and gain a better appreciation for the issues that preoccupy me.

I came of age as a historian at the beginning of the 1990s, when postmodernism had gained a formidable hold on historical research. Much of the work being done at that time was broadly defined as "cultural history" and aimed to deconstruct many of the assumptions and categories of analysis that political, economic, social, and intellectual historians had embraced. Yet my project seeks to move beyond deconstruction, and even beyond rehearsing the arguments and research trajectories that have animated deconstructionism. I am profoundly grateful and fully cognizant of the importance played by the work of Gayatri Spivak, Judith Butler, Joan Scott, Michel Foucault, Donna Haraway, and Jacques Derrida, to name only a handful of the most prominent thinkers among a vast panoply of postmodern knowledge makers.[1] It is only through the space created by their pointed and unyielding questioning of power structures that I could start to imagine a different kind of historical writing, a feminist historical epistemology.

In the past two decades, theoretical calls for rethinking historical writing starting from scratch or, rather, discarding its masculinist epistemologies, have grown into exciting research projects and publications.[2] An early pioneer in this area was Bonnie Smith, who in 1984 was already articulating a powerful argument for why women historians have been important for the discipline in terms of methodologies, themes, and theorizing.[3] Overall, Smith's work as a researcher, mentor, and editor has been seminal to my own approach. In her three-volume edited work, *Women's History in Global Perspective*, and the four-volume *Oxford Encyclopedia of Women in World History*, Smith has brought together and selected historians and themes that greatly advanced our understanding of women's lives in the past.[4] These volumes offer ample evidence for the need to gender historical research, writing, and teaching at every turn and in every aspect of our activities.

Joan Scott's seminal essay in 1986 pushed the questions of women's marginalization in the framing of historical research into more audacious theoretical territory, with a clarion call for placing gender analysis at the center of our intellectual and professional frameworks of historical writing.[5] That has happened in many discrete projects, but not as an overarching successful project in terms of rethinking broad historical narratives. Wendy Brown's equally bold stab at laying bare the masculinist foundations of the contemporary capitalist state, with all of its welfare and citizenship accoutrements, advanced our ability to understand the magnitude of recasting politics in a postmasculinist framework.[6]

A more recent, daring attempt to push us toward better understanding why and how historical analyses continue to be preponderantly masculinist is Mary Spongberg's *Writing Women's History since the Renaissance* (2002). A grand tour through the history of historical writing through gender analysis, the book makes amply clear the connection between the professionalization of historical writing as a masculine endeavor and the marginalization and eventual silencing of women's experiences. The book also wrangles with the complex legacy of feminist challenges to this hegemony, describing with considerable skill the impact of the fragmentation and deconstruction of masculinist historiography since the 1970s at the hands of the many strands of feminist historical gender analysis.

Yet, like other previous feminist critiques mentioned here, the volume stops short of moving beyond that assessment on two crucial, interrelated counts: (1) the impact of women's history on historical knowledge more broadly, and (2) the possibilities for rethinking historical research and writing beyond deconstruction and beyond hegemonic masculinism. The author can't be faulted for not attempting to take her analysis further, especially given the already enormously ambitious scope of the book. But, after reading it, I was left wanting to imagine what its broader implications are for how we write history into the future.

Two other broad surveys have helped me think through the framing and analysis of the themes in my book. The first is Françoise Thébaud's edited volume, *A History of Women*, vol. 5, *Toward a Cultural Identity in the Twentieth Century*.[7] Focusing on Europe and the United States and featuring the work of a number of prominent historians from both sides of the Atlantic, the volume provides a thematic assessment of the most lasting changes since 1900, including political rights, the rise of the welfare state, reproductive policies and nationalism, and cultural shifts in terms of women's representation. Yet the geographic limitations and especially sparse comparative focus on colonial/postcolonial dynamics rendered this book less useful than some of the broader coverage of some of the volumes edited by, for instance, Bonnie Smith.

Sheila Rowbotham's volume, *A Century of Women: The History of Women in Britain and the United States,*[8] provided further inspiration in terms of its title, as well as some of the themes that anchor the comparative narrative of this prominent second-wave feminist scholar. Though buoyant in celebrating women's achievements, her analysis does not shy away from a thorough critique of race and class relations. The approach is chronological, which makes sense for the limited geographic comparative focus of the book. Though I thoroughly enjoyed her thematic foci and the overall tone of this very readable analysis, in framing my own book as a global history, I opted for a thematic rather than chronological division.

When it comes to world or global history surveys or syntheses, the conclusions drawn by a 1996 study have not lost their currency: "Language functions in these textbooks to position women in stereotypical ways or to obfuscate the patriarchal system that accounts for women's demeaning experiences and differential treatment throughout history."[9] While recent world history surveys dedicate more substantial attention to women's issues in relation to nationalism, population control, or feminism, the overall framework of analysis has not changed much in terms of integrating the important new research featured in volumes such as those edited by Bonnie Smith.[10] My book represents both a challenge to this androcentric limited approach and an invitation to consider the intellectual enrichment that gendering history brings to our understanding of the past.

NOTES

1. Gayatri Spivak, "Feminism and Deconstruction, Again: Negotiating with Unacknowledged Masculinism," in *Between Feminism and Psychoanalysis,* ed. Teresa Brennan (New York: Routledge, 1989), 206–23; Foucault, *History of Sexuality;* Jacques Derrida, *Writing and Difference* (Chicago: University of Chicago Press, 1978); Donna Haraway, *Simians, Cyborgs, and Women: The Reinvention of Nature* (London: Free Association Books; New York: Routledge, 1991).

2. Kathleen Canning, *Gender History in Practice: Historical Perspectives on Bodies, Class, and Citizenship* (Ithaca, NY: Cornell University Press, 2006); Leora Auslander and Michelle Zancarini-Fournel, guest editors, "Le genre de la nation," *Clio: Histoire, femmes et sociétés* (Fall 2000); Bonnie Smith and Joanna Regulska, eds., *Women and Gender in Postwar Europe* (New York: Routledge, 2012); Mrinalini Sinha, "Historically Speaking: Gender and Citizenship in Colonial India," in *The Question of Gender,* ed. Judith Butler and Elizabeth Weed (Bloomington: Indiana University Press, 2011), 80–101; Smith, *Gender of History.*

3. Bonnie Smith, "The Contribution of Women to Modern Historiography in Great Britain, France, and the United States, 1750–1940," *American Historical Review* 89, no. 3 (June 1984): 709–32.

    4. Bonnie Smith, ed., *Women's History in Global Perspective*, 3 vols. (Urbana: University of Illinois Press, 2004–2005); Bonnie Smith, ed., *The Oxford Encyclopedia of Women in World History* (Oxford: Oxford University Press, 2008).
    5. Scott, "Gender: A Useful Category."
    6. Brown, "Finding the Man."
    7. Françoise Thébaud, *A History of Women*, vol. 5, *Toward a Cultural Identity in the Twentieth Century* (Cambridge: Belknap, 1994).
    8. Sheila Rowbotham, *A Century of Women: The History of Women in Britain and the United States* (New York: Verso, 2012).
    9. Michelle Commeyras and Donna E. Alvermann, "Reading about Women in World History Textbooks from One Feminist Perspective," *Gender & Education* 8, no. 1 (March 1996): 31–48.
    10. See for instance, William J. Duiker and Jackson J. Spielvogel, *The Essential World History*, vol. II, *Since 1500*, 8th ed. (Independence, MO: Cengage, 2016).

Selected Bibliography

Afshar, Haleh, and Stephanie Barrientos, eds. *Women, Globalization and Fragmentation in the Developing World.* Basingstoke, UK: Palgrave, 1999.

Aguirre, DeAnne, Leila Hoteit, Christine Rupp, and Karim Sabbagh. *Empowering the Third Billion: Women and the World of Work in 2012.* New York: Booz & Company, 2012.

Allman, Jean, Susan Geiger, and Nakanyike Musisi, eds. *Women in African Colonial Histories.* Bloomington: Indiana University Press, 2002.

Alonso, Harriet Hyman. *Peace as a Women's Issue: A History of the U.S. Movement for World Peace and Women's Rights.* Syracuse, NY: Syracuse University Press, 1993.

Anderson, Patricia. *Passion Lost: Public Sex, Private Desire in the Twentieth Century.* Toronto: Thomas Allen Publishers, 2001.

Badran, Margot, ed. *Gender and Islam in Africa: Rights, Sexuality, and Law.* Washington, DC: Woodrow Wilson Center Press; Stanford, CA: Stanford University Press, 2011.

Baker, Jean H. *Women and the U.S. Constitution, 1776–1920.* Washington, DC: American Historical Association, 2008.

Bannerji, Himani, Shahrzad Mojab, and Judith Whitehead, eds. *Of Property and Propriety: The Role of Gender and Class in Imperialism and Nationalism.* Toronto: University of Toronto Press, 2001.

Bashford, Alison, and Philippa Levine, eds. *The Oxford Handbook of the History of Eugenics.* Oxford: Oxford University Press, 2010.

Bauer, Gretchen, and Josephine Dawuni, eds. *Gender and the Judiciary in Africa: From Obscurity to Parity?* New York: Routledge, 2016.

Bauer, Heike, and Matt Cook, eds. *Queer 1950s: Rethinking Sexuality in the Postwar Years.* Basingstoke, UK: Palgrave, 2012.

Bebel, August. *Woman and Socialism.* 1879. Reprint, New York: Socialist Literature, 1910.

Benhabib, Seyla. *The Reluctant Modernism of Hannah Arendt.* Lanham, MD: Rowman & Littlefield, 2003.

Bernhardt, Kathryn. *Women and Property in China, 960–1949.* Stanford, CA: Stanford University Press, 1999.

Blackden, C. Mark, and Chitra Bhanu. *Gender, Growth, and Poverty Reduction: Special Program of Assistance for Africa, 1998 Status Report on Poverty in Sub-Saharan Africa.* World Bank Technical Paper no. 428. Washington, DC: World Bank, 1999.

Bolt, Christine. *The Women's Movements in the United States and Britain from the 1790s to the 1920s.* Amherst: University of Massachusetts Press, 1993.

Boris, Eileen, and Jill Jensen. "The ILO: Women's Networks and the Making of the Women Worker." Alexander Street, 2012, accessed December 24, 2017, http://search.alexanderstreet.com/view/work/bibliographic_entity%7Cbibliographic_details%7C2476919.

Boris, Eileen, and A. Orleck. "Feminism and the Labor Movement: A Century of Collaboration and Conflict." *New Labor Forum* 20 (Winter 2011): 33–41.

Brown, Wendy. "Finding the Man in the State." *Feminist Studies* 18, no. 1 (Spring 1992): 7–34.

Bucur, Maria. *Gendering Modernism: A Historical Reappraisal of the Canon.* London: Bloomsbury Academic, 2017.

Buffington, Robert M., Eithne Luibhéid, and Donna J. Guy, eds. *A Global History of Sexuality: The Modern Era.* Hoboken, NJ: Wiley Blackwell, 2014.

Burkhauser, Jude, ed. *Glasgow Girls: Women in Art and Design, 1880–1920*. Glasgow: Canongate, 1990.

Burton, Antoinette. "'History' Is Now: Feminist Theory and the Production of Historical Feminisms." *Women's History Review* 1, no. 1 (1992): 25–39.

Butler, Judith. *Gender Trouble: Feminism and the Subversion of Identity*. New York: Routledge, 1990.

Butler, Judith, and Elizabeth Weed, eds. *The Question of Gender*. Bloomington: Indiana University Press, 2011.

Cabezas, Amalia L., Ellen Reese, and Marguerite Waller, eds. *Wages of Empire: Neoliberal Policies, Repression, and Women's Poverty*. New York: Routledge, 2016.

Canning, Kathleen. *Gender History in Practice: Historical Perspectives on Bodies, Class, and Citizenship*. Ithaca, NY: Cornell University Press, 2006.

Carroll, Aengus. *State-Sponsored Homophobia: A World Survey of Sexual Orientation Laws: Criminalisation, Protection and Recognition*. Geneva: ILGA, 2016.

Charpenel, Yves, ed. *Rapport mondial sur l'exploitation sexuelle: La prostitution au coeur de crime organisé*. Paris: Economica, 2012.

Chaudhuri, Nupur, and Margaret Strobel, eds. *Western Women and Imperialism: Complicity and Resistance*. Bloomington: Indiana University Press, 1992.

Chaumont, Jean-Michel, Magaly Rodriguez Garcia, and Paul Servais, eds. *Trafficking in Women (1924–1926): The Paul Kinsie Reports for the League of Nations*. 2 vols. Geneva: United Nations Publications, 2017.

Cheng, Anne Anlin. *Second Skin: Josephine Baker and the Modern Surface*. Oxford: Oxford University Press, 2011.

Chodorow, Nancy. *Feminism and Psychoanalytic Theory*. New Haven, CT: Yale University Press, 1989.

Collins, Patricia Hill. *Black Feminist Thought: Knowledge, Consciousness, and the Politics of Empowerment*. New York: Routledge, 2008.

Connelly, Matthew. *Fatal Misconception: The Struggle to Control World Population*. Cambridge: Belknap Press, 2010.

Crenshaw, Kimberlé. "Mapping the Margins: Intersectionality, Identity Politics, and Violence against Women of Color." *Stanford Law Review* 43, no. 6 (July 1991): 1241–99.

Dahl, Linda. *Morning Glory: A Biography of Mary Lou Williams*. New York: Pantheon, 2012.

Daly, Mary. *Gyn/Ecology: The Metaethics of Radical Feminism*. Boston: Beacon Press, 1978.

Davis, Natalie Zemon. "History's Two Bodies." *American Historical Review* 93, no. 1 (February 1988): 1–30.

De Grazia, Victoria, and Ellen Furlough, eds. *The Sex of Things: Gender and Consumption in Historical Perspective*. Berkeley: University of California Press, 1996.

De Haan, Francisca, Krassimira Daskalova, and Anna Loutfi, eds. *A Biographical Dictionary of Women's Movements and Feminisms: Central, Eastern, and South Eastern Europe, 19th and 20th Centuries*. Budapest: Central European University Press, 2006.

Donato, Katharine M., and Donna Gabaccia. *Gender and International Migration: From the Slavery Era to the Global Age*. New York: Russell Sage Foundation, 2015.

Dooling, Amy. *Women's Literary Feminism in Twentieth Century China*. New York: Palgrave Macmillan, 2005.

Eidelberg, Martin, Nina Gray, and Margaret Hofer. *A New Light on Tiffany: Clara Driscoll and the Tiffany Girls*. New York: New-York Historical Society, 2007.

Elborgh-Woytek, Katrin, Monique Newiak, Kalpana Kochhar, Stefania Fabrizio, Kangni Kpodar, Philippe Wingender, Benedict Clements, and Gerd Schwartz. "Women, Work, and the Economy: Macroeconomic Gains from Gender Equity," IMF Discussion Note, September 2013. Accessed August 17, 2017, https://www.imf.org/external/pubs/ft/sdn/2013/sdn1310.pdf.

Eley, Geoff. *Forging Democracy: The History of the Left in Europe, 1850–2000*. Oxford: Oxford University Press, 2002.

Engels, Friedrich. *The Origin of the Family, Private Property and the State*. Chicago: Charles H. Kerr, 1902.

Epprecht, Marc. *Heterosexual Africa? The History of an Idea from the Age of Exploration to the Age of AIDS*. Athens: Ohio University Press, 2008.

Fausto-Sterling, Anne. *Sexing the Body: Gender Politics and the Construction of Sexuality*. New York: Basic Books, 2000.

Felski, Rita. *The Gender of Modernity*. Cambridge, MA: Harvard University Press, 1995.

Fiske, Edward B. *World Atlas of Gender Equality in Education*. Paris: Unesco, 2012.

Flores, Tatiana. "Strategic Modernists: Women Artists in Post-Revolutionary Mexico." *Woman's Art Journal* 29, no. 2 (2008): 12–22.

Folbre, Nancy. *Greed, Lust, and Gender: A History of Economic Ideas*. New York: Oxford University Press, 2009.

Fraser, Nancy. *Fortunes of Feminism: From State-Managed Capitalism to Neoliberal Crisis*. New York: Verso Books, 2013.

Gambrell, Alice. *Women Intellectuals, Modernism, and Difference: Transatlantic Culture, 1919–1945*. New York: Cambridge University Press, 1997.

Gender Working Group, United Nations Commission on Science and Technology for Development, eds. *Missing Links: Gender Equity in Science and Technology for Development*. Ottawa: International Development Research Centre, 1995.

Gere, Charlotte, and Marina Vaizey. *Great Women Collectors*. London: Philip Wilson, 1999.

Gerhard, Jane F. *The Dinner Party: Judy Chicago and the Power of Popular Feminism, 1970-2007*. Athens: University of Georgia Press, 2013.

Gerhard, Ute, Trudie Knijn, and Anja Weckwert, eds. *Working Mothers in Europe: A Comparison of Policies and Practices*. Cheltenham, UK: Edward Elgar, 2005.

Gilmore, Stephanie, ed. *Feminist Coalitions: Historical Perspectives on Second-Wave Feminism in the United States*. Urbana: University of Illinois Press, 2008.

Glendon, Mary Ann. *World Made New: Eleanor Roosevelt and the Universal Declaration of Human Rights*. New York: Random House, 2001.

Glosser, Susan L. *Chinese Visions of Family and State, 1915–1953*. Berkeley: University of California Press , 2014.

Gonzalez, Lélia. *Women Organizing for Change: Confronting Crisis in Latin America*. Rome: Isis International, 1988.

Greer, Germaine. *The Whole Woman*. New York: Anchor Books, 2000.

Hanson, Joyce A. *Mary McLeod Bethune and Black Women's Political Activism*. Columbia: University of Missouri Press, 2003.

Haraway, Donna. *Simians, Cyborgs, and Women: The Reinvention of Nature*. London: Free Association Books; New York: Routledge, 1991.

Harding, Sandra. "Standpoint Theories: Productively Controversial." *Hypatia: A Journal of Feminist Philosophy* 24, no. 4 (2009): 192–200.

Hassim, Shireen. *Women's Organizations and Democracy in South Africa: Contesting Authority*. Madison: University of Wisconsin Press, 2005.

Hewitt, Nancy A. *No Permanent Waves: Recasting Histories of U.S. Feminism*. New Brunswick, NJ: Rutgers University Press, 2010.

Higginbotham, Evelyn Brooks. "African-American Women's History and the Metalanguage of Race." *Signs* 17, no. 2 (Winter 1992): 251–74.

Higonnet, Margaret R., Jane Jenson, Sonya Michel, and Margaret Collins Weitz, eds. *Behind the Lines: Gender and the Two World Wars*. New Haven, CT: Yale University Press, 1989.

Inglehart, Ronald, and Pippa Norris. *Rising Tide: Gender Equality and Cultural Change around the World*. Cambridge: Cambridge University Press, 2003.

Janz, Oliver, and Daniel Schönpflug, eds. *Gender History in a Transnational Perspective: Networks, Biographies, Gender Orders*. New York: Berghahn, 2014.

Jayakody, Rukmalie, Arland Thornton, and William Axinn, eds. *International Family Change: Ideational Perspectives*. New York: Routledge, 2008.

Joannou, Maroula, and June Purvis, eds. *The Women's Suffrage Movement: New Feminist Perspectives.* Manchester: Manchester University Press, 1998.

Jones-Pauly, Christina. *Women under Islam: Gender, Justice and the Politics of Islamic Law.* New York: I. B. Tauris, 2011.

Jütte, Robert. *Contraception: A History.* Cambridge: Polity, 2008.

Kandiyoti, Deniz. "Bargaining with Patriarchy." *Gender and Society* 2, no. 3 (September 1988): 274–90.

Karamessini, Maria, and Jill Rubery, eds. *Women and Austerity: The Economic Crisis and the Future for Gender Equality.* New York: Routledge, 2014.

Kline, Wendy. *Building a Better Race: Gender, Sexuality, and Eugenics from the Turn of the Century to the Baby Boom.* Berkeley: University of California Press, 2005.

Kramarae, Cheris, and Dale Spender, eds. *Routledge International Encyclopedia of Women: Global Women's Issues and Knowledge.* 4 vols. New York: Routledge, 2000.

Kuhar, Roman, and David Paternotte, eds. *Anti-Gender Campaigns in Europe: Mobilizing against Equality.* London: Rowman & Littlefield International, 2017.

Leavitt, Sarah A. *From Catharine Beecher to Martha Stewart: A Cultural History of Domestic Advice.* Chapel Hill: University of North Carolina Press, 2002.

Le Doeuff, Michele. *The Sex of Knowing.* New York: Routledge, 2004.

Lepore, Jill. *The Secret History of Wonder Woman.* New York: Random House, 2014.

Lerner, Gerda. *The Creation of Patriarchy.* Oxford: Oxford University Press, 1987.

Lesthaeghe, Ron. "The Second Demographic Transition: A Concise Overview of Its Development." *Proceedings of the National Academy of Sciences* 111, no. 51 (2014): 18112–15.

———. "The Unfolding Story of the Second Demographic Transition." *Population and Development Review* 36, no. 2 (June 2010): 211–51.

Lewin, Ellen, ed. *Feminist Anthropology: A Reader.* Oxford: Blackwell, 2006.

Lewis, Brian, ed. *British Queer History: New Approaches and Perspectives.* Manchester: Manchester University Press , 2013.

Lichtenstein, Nelson, and Jill M. Jensen, eds. *The ILO from Geneva to the Pacific Rim: West Meets East.* New York: Palgrave and the International Labour Organization, 2016.

Lister, Ruth. *Citizenship: Feminist Perspectives.* New York: Routledge, 1997.

Lutz, Wolfgang, and Qiang Ren. "Determinants of Human Population Growth." *Philosophical Transactions of the Royal Society of London* 357 (2002): 1197–210.

Mann, Michael. *The Sources of Social Power.* 4 vols. New York: Cambridge University Press, 1986–2013.

Mastroianni, Anna C., Ruth Faden, and Daniel Federman, eds. *Women and Health Research: Ethical and Legal Issues of Including Women in Clinical Studies.* 2 vols. Washington, DC: National Academies Press, 1994.

McClaurin, Irma. *Black Feminist Anthropology: Theory, Politics, Praxis, and Poetics.* New Brunswick, NJ: Rutgers University Press, 2001.

McClintock, Anne. *Imperial Leather: Race, Gender, and Sexuality in the Colonial Contest.* New York: Routledge, 1995.

McLelland, Mark. *Queer Japan from the Pacific War to the Internet Age.* Lanham, MD: Rowman & Littlefield, 2005.

Mernissi, Fatema. *The Veil and the Male Elite: A Feminist Interpretation of Women's Rights in Islam.* New York: Basic Books, 1987.

Michel, Sonya, and Rianne Mahon, eds. *Child Care Policy at the Crossroads: Gender and Welfare State Restructuring.* New York: Routledge, 2002.

Micheletti, Michelle, ed. *Political Virtue and Shopping: Individuals, Consumerism, and Collective Action.* Basingstoke, UK: Palgrave Macmillan, 2003.

Millett, Kate. *Sexual Politics.* 1969. Reprint, New York: Columbia University Press, 2016.

Mossuz-Lavau, Janine. "Les femmes et le pouvoir exécutif depuis 1981: La France au regard du monde." *Histoire@Politique* 1, no. 1 (2007). https://doi.org/10.3917/hp.001.0005.

Najmabadi, Afsaneh. *Women with Mustaches and Men without Beards: Gender and Sexual Anxieties of Iranian Modernity*. Berkeley: University of California Press, 2005.
Nason-Clark, Nancy, and Mary Jo Neitz, eds. *Feminist Narratives and the Sociology of Religion*. Lanham, MD: AltaMira Press, 2001.
Ndulo, Muna. "African Customary Law, Customs, and Women's Rights." *Indiana Journal of Global Legal Studies* 18, no. 1 (Winter 2011): 87–120.
Nelson, Cynthia. *Doria Shafik, Egyptian Feminist: A Woman Apart*. Cairo: American University in Cairo Press, 2015.
O'Connor, Karen, ed. *Gender and Women's Leadership: A Reference Handbook*. New York: Sage, 2010.
Offen, Karen, ed. *Globalizing Feminisms, 1789–1945*. New York: Routledge, 2010.
Ogilvie, Marilyn, and Joy Harvey, eds. *The Biographical Dictionary of Women in Science: Pioneering Lives from Ancient Times to the Mid-20th Century*. New York: Routledge, 2000.
Ortner, Sherry. *Making Gender: The Politics and Erotics of Culture*. Boston: Beacon Press Books, 1996.
Oyeronke, Oyewumi. *The Invention of Women: Making African Sense of Western Gender Discourses*. Minneapolis: University of Minnesota Press, 1997.
Pateman, Carol. *The Sexual Contract*. Stanford, CA: Stanford University Press, 1988.
Preiss, Bert, and Claudia Brunner, eds. *Democracy in Crisis: The Dynamics of Civil Protest and Civil Resistance*. Berlin: LIT Verlag, 2013.
Randolph, Sherie M. *Florynce "Flo" Kennedy: The Life of a Black Feminist Radical*. Chapel Hill: University of North Carolina Press, 2015.
Ransby, Barbara. *Ella Baker and the Black Freedom Movement: A Radical Democratic Vision*. Chapel Hill: University of North Carolina Press, 2003.
Rowbotham, Sheila. *A Century of Women: The History of Women in Britain and the United States in the Twentieth Century*. New York: Verso, 2012.
———. *Women in Movement: Feminism and Social Action*. London: Routledge, 1992.
Rubin, Gayle. "The Traffic of Women: Notes on the 'Political Economy' of Sex." In *Toward an Anthropology of Women*, edited by Rayna R. Reiter, 157–210. New York: Monthly Review Press, 1975.
Ruether, Rosemary Radford. *Goddesses and the Divine Feminine: A Western Religious History*. Los Angeles: University of California Press, 2005.
Rupp, Leila. *Worlds of Women: The Making of an International Women's Movement*. Princeton, NJ: Princeton University Press, 1997.
Schandevyl, Eva, ed. *Women in Law and Lawmaking in Nineteenth and Twentieth-Century Europe*. Burlington, VT: Ashgate, 2014.
Schönfeld, Christiane, ed. *Practicing Modernity: Female Creativity in the Weimar Republic*. Würzburg: Königshausen & Neumann, 2006.
Scott, Joan. "Gender: A Useful Category of Historical Analysis," *American Historical Review* 91, no. 5 (December 1986): 1053–75.
Seager, Joni. *The Penguin Atlas of Women in the World*, 4th ed. New York: Penguin, 2008.
Sedgwick , Eve Kosofsky. *Epistemology of the Closet*. Berkeley: University of California Press, 1991.
Sheffield, Suzanne Le-May. *Women and Science: Social Impact and Interaction*. New Brunswick, NJ: Rutgers University Press, 2006.
Sinha, Mrinalini. *Specters of Mother India: The Global Restructuring of an Empire*. Durham, NC: Duke University Press, 2006.
Sjoberg, Laura, ed. *Gender and International Security: Feminist Perspectives*. Abingdon, UK: Routledge, 2010.
Smith, Bonnie. *The Gender of History: Men, Women, and Historical Practice*. Cambridge, MA: Harvard University Press, 1998.
———, ed. *The Oxford Encyclopedia of Women in World History*. 4 vols. Oxford: Oxford University Press, 2008.
———. *Women's History in Global Perspective*. 3 vols. Urbana: University of Illinois Press, 2004–2005.

Solinger, Rickie, and Mie Nakachi, eds. *Reproductive States: Global Perspectives on the Invention and Implementation of Population Policy.* New York: Oxford University Press, 2016.

Somerville, Jennifer. *Feminism and the Family: Politics and Society in the UK and USA.* Basingstoke, UK: Palgrave, 2000.

Spence, Jean, Sarah Aiston, and Maureen M. Meikle, eds. *Women, Education, and Agency, 1600–2000.* New York: Routledge, 2010.

Spivak, Gayatri. "Feminism and Deconstruction, Again: Negotiating with Unacknowledged Masculinism." In *Between Feminism and Psychoanalysis,* edited by Teresa Brennan, 206–23. New York: Routledge, 1989.

Spongberg, Mary. *Writing Women's History since the Renaissance.* Basingstoke, UK: Palgrave, 2002.

Stacey, Judith. *Brave New Families: Stories of Domestic Upheaval in Late-Twentieth-Century America.* Berkeley: University of California Press, 1998.

Stange, Mary Zeiss, Carol K. Oyster, and Jane E. Sloan, eds. *Encyclopedia of Women in Today's World.* 4 vols. Los Angeles: SAGE, 2011.

Stoler, Ann. *Carnal Knowledge and Imperial Power: Race and the Intimate in Colonial Rule.* Berkeley: University of California Press, 2002.

Stryker, Susan, and Jim Van Buskirk. *Gay by the Bay: A History of Queer Culture in the San Francisco Bay Area.* San Francisco: Chronicle Books, 1996.

Tatman, Lucy. *Knowledge That Matters: A Feminist Theological Paradigm and Epistemology.* Cleveland, OH: Pilgrim Press, 2001.

Thébaud, Françoise, ed. *A History of Women.* Vol. V, *Toward a Cultural Identity in the Twentieth Century.* Cambridge: Belknap, 1994.

Thomas, Tracy, and Tracey Boisseau, eds. *Feminist Legal History: Essays on Women and Law.* New York: New York University Press, 2011.

Thompson, Willie. *Postmodernism and History.* Basingstoke, UK: Palgrave Macmillan, 2004.

Tong, Rosemarie, and Tina Fernandes Botts. *Feminist Thought: A More Comprehensive Introduction.* 5th ed. New York: Westview Press, 2017.

Tripp, Aili Mari, Isabel Casimiro, Joy Kwesiga, and Alice Mungwa, eds. *African Women's Movements: Transforming Political Landscapes.* New York: Cambridge University Press, 2009.

Tucker, Judith. *Women, Family, and Gender in Islamic Law.* Cambridge: Cambridge University Press, 2008.

Tyrrell, Ian. *Woman's World/Woman's Empire: The Woman's Christian Temperance Union in International Perspective, 1880–1930.* Chapel Hill: University of North Carolina Press, 1991.

Van der Klein, Marian, Rebecca Jo Plant, Nichole Sanders, and Lori R. Weintrob, eds. *Maternalism Reconsidered: Motherhood, Welfare and Social Policy in the Twentieth Century.* New York: Berghahn, 2012.

Ware, Susan. *Beyond Suffrage: Women in the New Deal.* Cambridge, MA: Harvard University Press, 1987.

Waring, Marilyn. *If Women Counted: A New Feminist Economics.* New York: HarperCollins, 1989.

Watson, Rubie S., and Patricia Buckley Ebrey, eds. *Marriage and Inequality in Chinese Society.* Berkeley: University of California Press, 1991.

Weiss, Gillian, ed. *Trying to Get It Back: Indigenous Women, Education and Culture.* Waterloo, ON: Wilfrid Laurier University Press, 2000.

Wing, Adrien Katherine, ed. *Global Critical Race Feminism: An International Reader.* New York: New York University Press, 2000.

Wood, Elizabeth A. *The Baba and the Comrade. Gender and Politics in Revolutionary Russia.* Bloomington: Indiana University Press, 1997.

Woolf, Daniel. *A Global History of History.* Cambridge: Cambridge University Press, 2011.

World Health Organization. *Women and Health: Today's Evidence, Tomorrow's Agenda.* Geneva: World Health Organization, 2009.

Yamakawa, Kikue. *Women of the Mito Domain: Recollections of Samurai Family Life.* Palo Alto, CA: Stanford University Press, 2002.

Zeisler, Andi. *We Were Feminists Once: From Riot Grrrl to CoverGirl®, the Buying and Selling of a Political Movement.* New York: PublicAffairs, 2017.

Zinn, Maxine Baca. "Feminism and Family Studies for a New Century." *Annals of the American Academy of Political and Social Science* 571, no. 1 (September 2000): 42–56.

Index

abandonment, 184–185
Abbott, Grace, 99
Aborigines, feminist activism
  exclusion of, 19–20. *See also* UN
  Permanent Forum on Indigenous
  Issues
abortion, 48, 50–52, 60, 69
Abramović, Marina, 171
Abramson, Jill, 156, 175n26
abuse, 32, 37–38, 57, 98, 100, 112n101
ACLU. *See* American Civil Liberties
  Union
Addams, Jane, 16, 34, 35
adultery, 57
Advisory Committee on the Traffic in
  Women and Children, 36, 99
affirmative action, 105
African Americans, 19, 25, 26, 87, 121,
  132, 143n36, 155
African dance, 168
African National Congress (ANC), 26
agricultural work, 78, 87, 92, 131, 206
AHA. *See* American Historical
  Association
AIDS, 123, 124, 206
All India Women's Conference, 50
American Association for the
  Advancement of Science, 131
American Civil Liberties Union
  (ACLU), 19
American Episcopal Church, 196
American Historical Association
  (AHA), 118–119
American Medical Association, 49
American Museum of Natural History,
  131
ANC. *See* African National Congress
Anderson, Margaret, 153
Anthony, Susan B., 34

anthropology, knowledge making in,
  131–133, 145n78, 145n82, 146n83,
  146n87
antigenderism, 196–197
apartheid, 26, 167
Arendt, Hannah, 116, 135, 136
Argúas, Margarita, 32–33
Armand, Inessa, 17
Arts and Crafts movement, 160–161,
  176n44, 176n47
Arzner, Dorothy, 171–172
Astrabadi, Bibi Khanoom, 137
Atatürk, Mustafa Kemal, 63–64
Atkinson, Ti-Grace, 28

Bai, Wei, 149, 152
Baker, Ella, 101
Baker, Josephine, 168
bar exam, 31
Barré-Sinoussi, Françoise, 123–124
Bathory, Elizabeth, 40n8
de Beauvoir, Simone, 116, 137–138,
  147n107
Bebel, August, 16
Bee, Samantha, 169–170
Bennett, Mary, 19
Berkshire Conference of Women
  Historians, 120
Bernhardt, Sarah, 178n80
Bethune, Mary McLeod, 25
Beyoncé, 169
Bhanu, Chitra, 181
Bigelow, Kathryn, 172, 179n94
Bill and Melinda Gates Foundation, 94,
  126
biology: biology-as-destiny school, 130;
  eugenics and, 121–122; gender and,
  121–122, 125, 127–128, 130, 138;
  sexology as subdiscipline under,
  122

Dietrich, Marlene, 168
displaced laborers, 131
divorce, 58, 79, 81–82, 185. *See also*
    adultery
domestic abuse, 32
Domestic Worker Bills of Rights, 98
Driscoll, Clara, 160
dual-earner rates, 182, 198n4
DuBois, Ellen, 20
Duchamp, Marcel, 162
Duncan, Isadora, 168
DuVernay, Ava, 172

early-childhood education, 129
ecology, consumption and, 133
economics, 77–78; divorce and, 185;
    education and, 94; equal pay
    struggle, 89; GDP and, 93, 114n125;
    gender gap rankings by country, 91,
    111n63; innovation and leadership
    examples, 104–108; labor unions
    and, 88–89; Mead's scientific work
    applied to, 131–132; migration and,
    95–100; 1900s compared with
    present, 86; in postcolonial regimes,
    85–86; professional training and, 97;
    shift to money economy, 80, 109n16;
    Thibert's reports on women's
    employment and, 88; twenty-first
    century, 86; voting rights and, 85,
    109n36. *See also* consumption;
    property rights, gender inequality
    and; service sector; unpaid labor;
    workforce participation
Edib, Halide, 63–64
editors-in-chief, 156, 175n31
education: access to, global view of, 62;
    birth-rates and, 62, 74n80;
    "civilization" and "patriotism"
    framing of, 64; colonialism and, 63,
    64–65; early-childhood, 129;
    economic power and, 85, 94; female
    household heads investment in,
    187–188, 189; gender and, 62, 66,
    74n83, 94; literacy-fertility
    connection, 61; literature and, 154;
    nationalist tropes and, 63–64;
    oppression through, 65; religion
    and, 62; secularization and, 59;

segregation and, 62; in state socialist
    regimes, 62; successful
    entrepreneurs and, 107;
    transnational efforts towards equal
    access to, 66, 75n98; in Uzbekistan,
    68–69, 75n107; voting rights and, 64.
    See also higher education; illiteracy
Edwards, Robert, 56
Egyptian Feminist Union, 15, 22
Egyptian Representative Council, 15
elderly care, 97
employer abuse, migration and, 98,
    112n101
Engels, Friedrich, 16
Ensler, Eve, 170–171
environmental activism, 28, 30, 102,
    133, 206
Episcopalian Church: first woman
    priest in, 196; gay clergy in, 196
epistemology, 116, 137–140
equal pay struggle, 89
equal rights amendment, 28–29
eugenics, 23–24, 47, 55, 70n10, 121–122

faculty, women, 119, 142n25
family values, second demographic
    transition and, 193–195. *See also*
    kinship relations
Fausto-Sterling, Anne, 130
Federation of South African Women,
    26
female-centered religion, 195–196
female genital mutilation. *See* genital
    cutting
female heads of households. *See* heads
    of households, female
feminism, 28–30, 42n53, 170, 203–205;
    eugenics and, 23; feminist approach,
    5–6; gender equality and, 194–195;
    in Islamic societies, 22–23; politics
    and, 30, 205; racism and, 19–20, 205;
    radical, 28, 170; second-wave, 28–30,
    42n53; transnational networks and,
    36–37. *See also* maternalism;
    nationalism; *specific topics*
feminist epistemology, 137–140,
    147n107
feminist psychology, development of,
    128–129

Organisation for Economic Co-
operation and Development
(OECD), 182
Ortner, Sherry, 131
Oscar award, best director, 172, 179n94

paganism. *See* Wicca
Palme d'Or award, 172
Palta, Neeti, 169–170
parents, stay-at-home, 182, 198n6
Paris Climate Summit. *See* UN Climate
Change Summit in Paris
parliamentary regimes, representation
in, 13, 40n2, 40n4
Parren, Kalliroi, 151
Pateman, Carol, 81
patriarchy: family model decline,
182–187, 198n4, 198n6, 198n15,
199n30; marriage and, 16, 57–58,
72n54; philosophy and, 117, 142n17;
women's knowledge making as
critique of, 116. *See also* property
rights, gender inequality and
performing arts, 167, 168–169, 178n80,
179n94; comedians and, 169–170,
178n84; cross-gender performance,
178n80; dance revolutionaries and,
167–168; film and, 171–173, 179n94;
gender norms in, 167–168;
performance art in, 170–171; pop
superstars and, 169. *See also* cabaret
periodization, military violence focus
of, 2
PhDs, 88, 115, 128, 141, 141n2
philosophy: feminist epistemology,
theology and, 137–140; masculinist
nature of, 117, 142n17; matrilineal
societies and, 115–116, 141n9;
patriarchal hegemony and critiques
in, 116, 117, 142n17; political,
135–136
photojournalists, 159–160, 176n41
Pickford, Mary, 172
piecework, 89
Piketty, Thomas, 86
the Pill, 53, 54, 55, 72n39
Pincus, Gregory, 54
de Pisan, Christine, 137
Planned Parenthood, 49, 50

political participation and activism:
categories of women working
towards, 15; for climate change
mitigation, 102–103; in communist
regimes, 16–19, 41n14;
decolonization leading to, 25–26;
early 1900s struggles for, 15, 24–25;
environmental politics of 1960s
feminists, 30; feminist nationalism
and, 23–24; gender parity and,
13–14, 40n4, 40n6; higher education
and, 67; history gendering and, 117;
ideological orientation of advocates,
16, 41n14; in Latin America, 29–30;
marginalized populations excluded
in, 19; national liberation
movements in Egypt and, 20–23; in
postcolonial regimes, 27;
postsuffrage activism and, 25; post
World War II, 25; racism and
exclusion in, 19–20; second wave
feminism and, 28–29, 42n53;
separatism and, 16. *See also* voting
rights
political philosophers, 135–136
political power, historical research
focus on military and, 2, 3–4
politics: consumer, 101, 103–104;
gender impact on, 39–40; law and,
30, 32, 43n62; parliamentary
representation and, 13, 40n2;
women in legal profession impact
on, 30, 31, 32, 43n62. *See also* identity
politics
polygamy, 193
pop superstars, 169
population, growth and decline, 7, 45,
45–46, 58, 61, 62, 72n58, 74n80
pornography, 46
postmodernism, historical research
and, 209
post-structuralism, 2–3
Power, Eileen, 118, 142n22
power relations, shift in, 5
Prince, 178n74
Pritzker Prize, 165
privilege, agency, marginalization and,
6, 10n8

property rights, gender inequality and, 78–87; colonialism and, 78–79, 82; in communist regimes, 84–85; Islamic societies and, 79–80; marriage and, 83; Napoleonic Code and, 80–82; religion and, 78–79, 83; in rural areas, 83; for urban lower-class women, 83

psychology, knowledge making in, 127–130, 145n70, 145n71

Public Expenditure Committee, 93

Pulitzer Prize, 155

queer studies, 120, 138

race, women historians on colonialism and, 120–121, 143n36

racism: anti-apartheid activism in South Africa, 26; consumer power and, 101; feminist, 19–20, 205; Morrison novels on slavery and, 155, 175n24; Native American education and, 65; in political rights activism, 19–20; in population and birth control decisions, 55; racist marches of 2017, 203; wage earnings and, 87, 110n46. *See also* colonialism; eugenics; identity politics; segregation

Rau, Dhanvanthi Rama, 50

religion and religious institutions: antigenderist ideology and, 196; education and, 62; female-centered, 195–196; female-focused, 139; property rights influenced by, 78–79, 83; response to shifts in kinship relations, 195–197, 201n71, 201n73; Williams music inspired by, 166; women leaders and clergy, 196. *See also* Wicca

reproduction, 46–50, 57–59, 71n21, 71n22

Revue theater, 169

Riefenstahl, Leni, 172

Rivera, Diego, 162

Robinson, Gene, 196

Rock, John, 54

Rockefeller, Abby Aldrich, 161

Roosevelt, Eleanor, 6, 25, 37

Roosevelt, Franklin Delano, 25

Rowbotham, Sheila, 211

Rubio, Paulina, 169

Ruiz, Vicky, 119

El Saadawi, Nawal, 154

same-sex relations, 59, 60–61, 190–192, 200n44; colonialism and, 190–191; legalized marriage and, 191. *See also* homosexuality

Sandberg, Sheryl, 104, 105–106, 114n122

Sanger, Margaret, 25, 45, 47, 48–50

Sartre, Jean-Paul, 137

Schlafly, Phyllis, 28

Schneemann, Carolee, 170–171

School for Social Assistance, 24

science, 124, 144n51; clinical research in, 122–123, 125, 126; gender inequity in field of, 126–127; women researcher percentages, 126–127; women scientists in psychology field, 127–130. *See also* anthropology, knowledge making in; eugenics; medical training schools; natural sciences; sociology

Scott, Joan, 120, 209, 210

second demographic transition: dual-earner rates, 182, 198n4; family values and, 193–195; kinship relations and, 181–182, 187; marriage and cohabitation changes in, 192–193; patriarchal family model and, 182–187, 198n4, 198n6, 198n15, 199n30; policy implications, 189; same-sex relations and, 190–192, 200n44; unpaid labor and, 191–192

second-wave feminism, 28–30, 42n53

secularization, 46–47, 59, 80, 195

secular Western humanism, 6

Sedgwick, Eve Kosofsky, 120

segregation, 62, 101, 154

self psychology, 128

separatism, political activism and, 16

service sector, 77–78; consumer culture and, 100; entertainment category, 99; sex work of women migrants, 99–100, 112n101; women migrants

United Nations (UN), 20; education
focus of, 94; equal pay and, 89;
handbook on violence against
women, 185; impact on gender and
human rights issues, 37–38;
trafficking network scandal in, 185;
US criticized by, 91; war crimes
resolution of, 38
United States (US), 91, 189
Universal Declaration of Human
Rights, 37, 52
unpaid labor (housework and
caretaking), 92–94, 104, 118,
191–192. *See also* work
UN Permanent Forum on Indigenous
Issues, 103
unveiling, in Uzbekistan, 68

violence, 135, 185–186; against gays,
191, 197; sexual, 172, 206; against
women, 59, 183–184, 185–186
visas, 96, 112n84
visual arts, women in, 156–165, 176n41,
177n57; arts-and-crafts movement
in, 160–161, 176n44, 176n47; Dada
movement in, 158; gender roles and,
156–157; major exhibits by, 157, 158,
161, 164; modernism influenced by,
161, 162–163; performance art,
170–171; sexism and, 164–165, 172
voting rights, 7, 15, 20, 25, 166;
economic power and, 85, 109n36;
education activism in countries
without women's, 64; ICW and, 34;
marriage and, 58; migration
impacted by, 96; politics of, 25–30,
34–35, 36; in Romania, 23, 42n37;
Shafik hunger strike and, 22; 2017
status of, 13, 40n3

Waft nationalist movement, 21
wage disparities, 87–88, 89–90; dual-
earner rates and, 182, 198n4; global
economy and, 7–8; PhDs and, 141;
race-based differential in, 87,
110n46; UN focus on, 94
wage labor. *See* workforce
participation
Walentynowicz, Anna, 89

Walker, C. J., 105
war crimes, UN resolution on, 38
Waring, Marilyn, 93–94, 205. *See also*
culture wars
Weber, Max, 181
website, 10
Weinstein, Barbara, 119
Wells, Ida B., 14
White, Luise, 119–120
Whitman, Meg, 104, 105–106, 114n122
Wicca, 195–196
WIDF. *See* Women's International
Democratic Federation
widows, as single heads of households,
183–184
Wilde, Oscar, 59, 73n67
Williams, Mary Lou, 10, 166
WILPF. *See* Women's International
League for Peace and Freedom
Wilson, Woodrow, 35
Winfrey, Oprah, 104, 105, 114n122
Wollstonecraft, Mary, 137
womb envy, 128
women, 6–7, 14, 15, 40n7, 40n8; global
contributions by, 4; wealthiest,
104–108, 114n122. *See also specific
topics*
women historians, 117–121, 142n17,
142n19, 142n22, 142n25, 143n36
women scientists, 127–130
Women's Consultative Committee on
Nationality, 35–36
Women's Health Initiative, 125
Women's International Democratic
Federation (WIDF), 34
Women's International League for
Peace and Freedom (WILPF), 19, 34,
36
Women's Peace Party, 16
Woolf, Virginia, 13, 153–154, 174n19,
175n20
workforce participation, 4, 18, 78,
87–92, 97, 104
working class women, political
participation efforts of, 15
working mothers. *See* caretaking
Working Women's Protective Union,
31
World Bank, 66, 92, 189